BE EVERYTHING AT ONCE

TALES OF A
CARTOONIST
LADY PERSON

DAMI LEE

CHRONICLE BOOKS
SAN FRANCISCO

For my family

Library of Congress Cataloging-in-Publication Data

Names: Lee, Dami, illustrator, author.

Title: Be everything at once : tales of a cartoonist lady person /
    by Dami Lee.
Description: San Francisco : Chronicle Books, [2018]
Identifiers: LCCN 2017061274 | ISBN 9781452167657 (pbk. : alk. paper)
Subjects: LCSH: Lee, Dami. | Cartoonists—United States—Biography—
    Comic books, strips, etc. | Graphic novels.
Classification: LCC PN6727.L3797 Z46 2018 | DDC 741.5/973 [B]—dc23
    LC record available at https://lccn.loc.gov/2017061274

Manufactured in China.

Design by Spencer Vandergrift

Chronicle Books LLC
680 Second Street
San Francisco, CA 94107

www.chroniclebooks.com

10 9 8 7 6 5 4 3 2 1

CONTENTS

INTRO

WORLD'S MOST TIRED

Hello and welcome to my book! Here you will find heartfelt stories of love and loss, like loving tater tots so much you don't know where the tots end and your face begins, and losing your appetite for the actual dinner you had reservations for because you ate too many Tater Tots.

We'll start from the very beginning, with my uplifting story as an immigrant child overcoming adversity by inadvertently making my peers cry. This same language barrier will come back to haunt me when I return to Korea as an adult, and realize I should have saved some space in my brain for remembering how to speak Korean instead of filling it up with all 150 Pokémon names.

Then it'll all come full circle when I make my triumphant return back to the U.S., so I can live my truth as a Cartoonist Lady Person. There's lots of good stuff in here about the joys of being a girl, plus some fun and flirty dating tips (. . . here's a freebie from me to you: stay away from eating any hard-shelled crustaceans on the first date).

Besides all this timeless shellfish advice, you'll find invaluable wisdoms, all based on my real and true experiences. These are the things love learned from being good at some things and being unbelievably horrible at others. But how else would I have found out what I'm okay at and what I should never, ever attempt to do again, unless I tried?

THREE-TIME IMMIGRANT

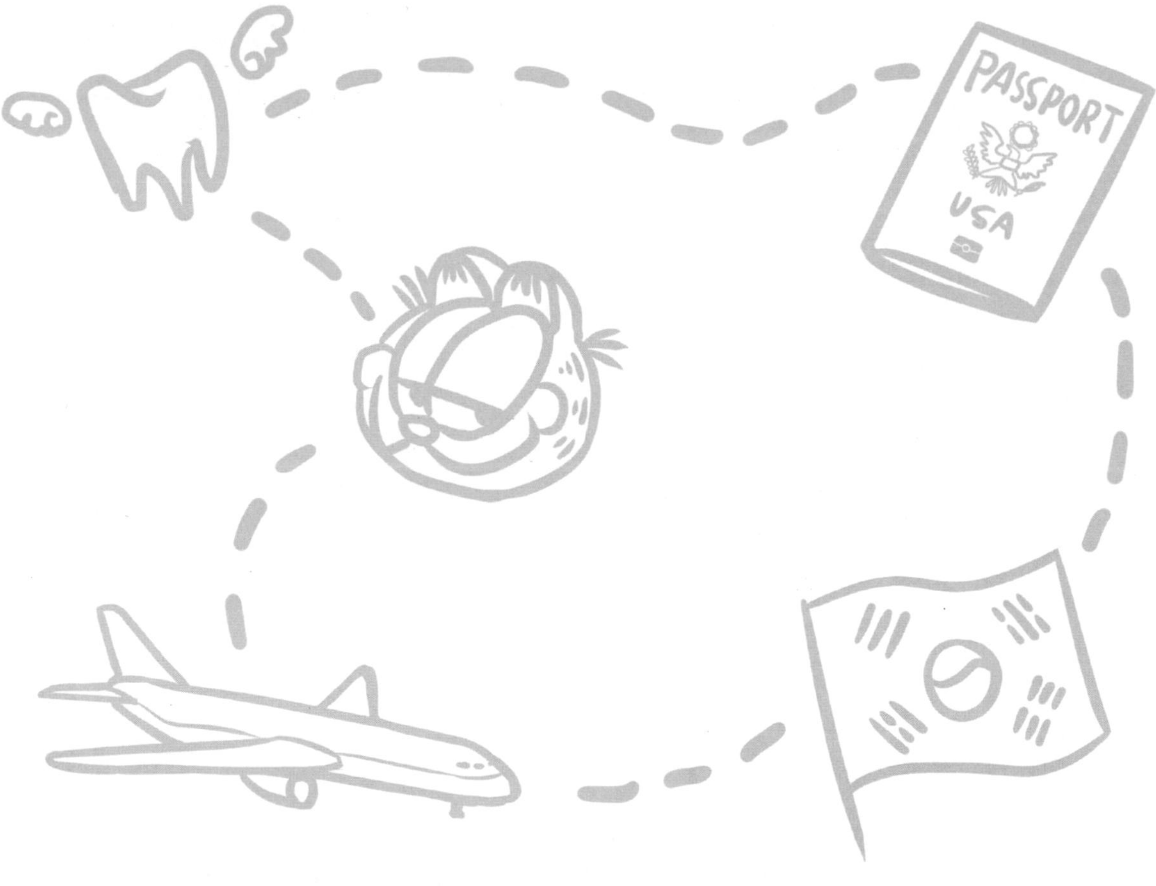
PASSPORT
USA

I've moved to the U.S. three times in my life—twice with my family when I was six and ten, and then alone at 25. Like many things that get better with practice, you get a little bit better at America every time. I was just a small, confused immigrant child that didn't speak English at first, but now look at me! A tall, confused lady with bad posture, who only speaks English when she feels like it.

The first two times we moved when I was a kid were because of my dad's job, which took us from Seoul to Texas, back to Seoul, and then to California. And with my parents' never-ending quest to find a house to turn into a home, it felt like we were moving constantly. I changed schools almost every year and missed part of fourth grade while I was in Korea, which I will forever use as a convenient excuse for not knowing basic U.S. geography.

There were lots of little things that got lost in translation in the beginning, as well as small misunderstandings, but I wouldn't categorize our immigrant experience as a struggle. Instead, I look back on those times fondly as moments when my family was closest. These were the times when we all lived under one roof and watched rented VHS tapes of Korean variety shows. We were just trying to figure things out together, and struggled collectively to understand the weird customs of whichever new world we had just entered.

It's easier to pick up new languages when you're little, but looking back, I can't imagine how much harder it must have been for my older brother, who was 13 when we first moved to America. I also never really stopped to think about the immense sacrifice my parents made, and what a crazy privilege it was to grow up with two cultures. Every day, I'm grateful for the experience—especially the fact that I now possess the ability to shop online from both American and Korean sites.

THE BEGINNING

The first and only time I'd ever been on a business class flight was when my family immigrated to America.

(Courtesy of my dad's company, which was the reason we were moving.)

KOREAN AIR

You can say I acquired a taste for luxury at a very early age.

MR. BEAN, IN-FLIGHT ENTERTAINMENT THAT TRANSCENDS LANGUAGE

WHOA

I enjoyed the business class amenities for six-year olds, such as a coloring book and four entire crayons

OH HELL YEA, GOT ALL THE PRIMARIES

DRAW YOUR NEW LIFE! ☺

AIR CRAYS

ADJUSTING

Everything in America was on a bigger scale than we'd ever known, even where we lived.

AUSTIN ☆

EVERYTHING REALLY IS BIGGER IN TEXAS

The first time we went to Costco was a learning experience for everyone.

COSTCO WHOLESALE

EVERYONE HOLD HANDS SO WE DON'T LOSE EACH OTHER

My mom discovered frozen meals

IT'S AN ENTIRE MEAL! IN A BOX!

HUNGRY FAM!

And I found out it's really rude to gasp loudly at someone's shopping cart.

SO MUCH FOOD!!

SPAM SPAM CHIPS

LEARNING ENGLISH

I could rapidly feel myself shift from thinking in Korean to English. Looking back, I wish I had tried harder not to let it take over completely.

ENGLISH
KOREAN
DOGS

They say the best way to learn a language is through immersion, and boy, did I immerse myself.

TOON
WORD
OREO
NICK

Specifically with TV cartoon binge-fests and literally every Garfield book in the library.

HA HA YOU CRAZY CAT

GARFIELD
GARFIELD
GARFIELD
GARFIELD
GARFIELD
GARFIELD
GARFIELD
GARFIELD
GARFIELD
GARFIELD

Garfield
HIS 28th BOOK

All this pop culture helped me pick up some key phrases to fit in with my peers.

MONDAYS, AM I RIGHT

ADVICE FROM FUTURE ME

My mom used to make me do workbooks and write in a journal so I wouldn't forget my Korean.

CAN'T I JUST DO THIS IN ENGLISH INSTEAD? IT'D BE SO MUCH FASTER!

일기장

WHO ARE YOU?!

I'M YOU FROM THE FUTURE

WHOOSH

JUST DO AS SHE SAYS, TRUST ME

YOU'LL THANK HER FOR IT LATER

THIS IS CALLED THE INTERNET. YOU GET TWO VERSIONS OF IT IF YOU'RE BILINGUAL

23,000 WON

BUY

WHOA!

FUN AMERICAN CUSTOMS

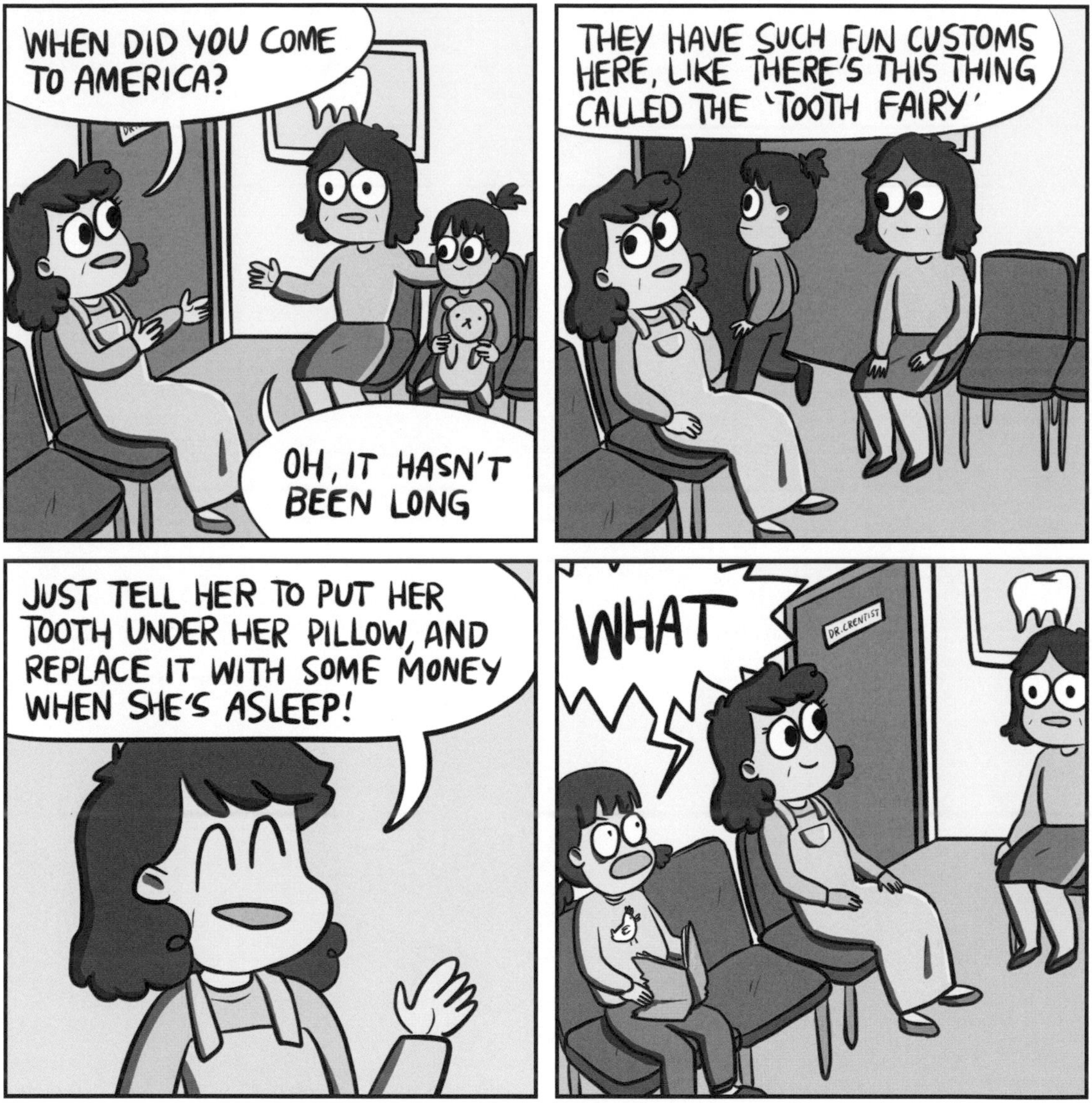
WHEN DID YOU COME TO AMERICA?
OH, IT HASN'T BEEN LONG
THEY HAVE SUCH FUN CUSTOMS HERE, LIKE THERE'S THIS THING CALLED THE 'TOOTH FAIRY'
JUST TELL HER TO PUT HER TOOTH UNDER HER PILLOW, AND REPLACE IT WITH SOME MONEY WHEN SHE'S ASLEEP!
WHAT
DR. CRENTIST

FLIRTING

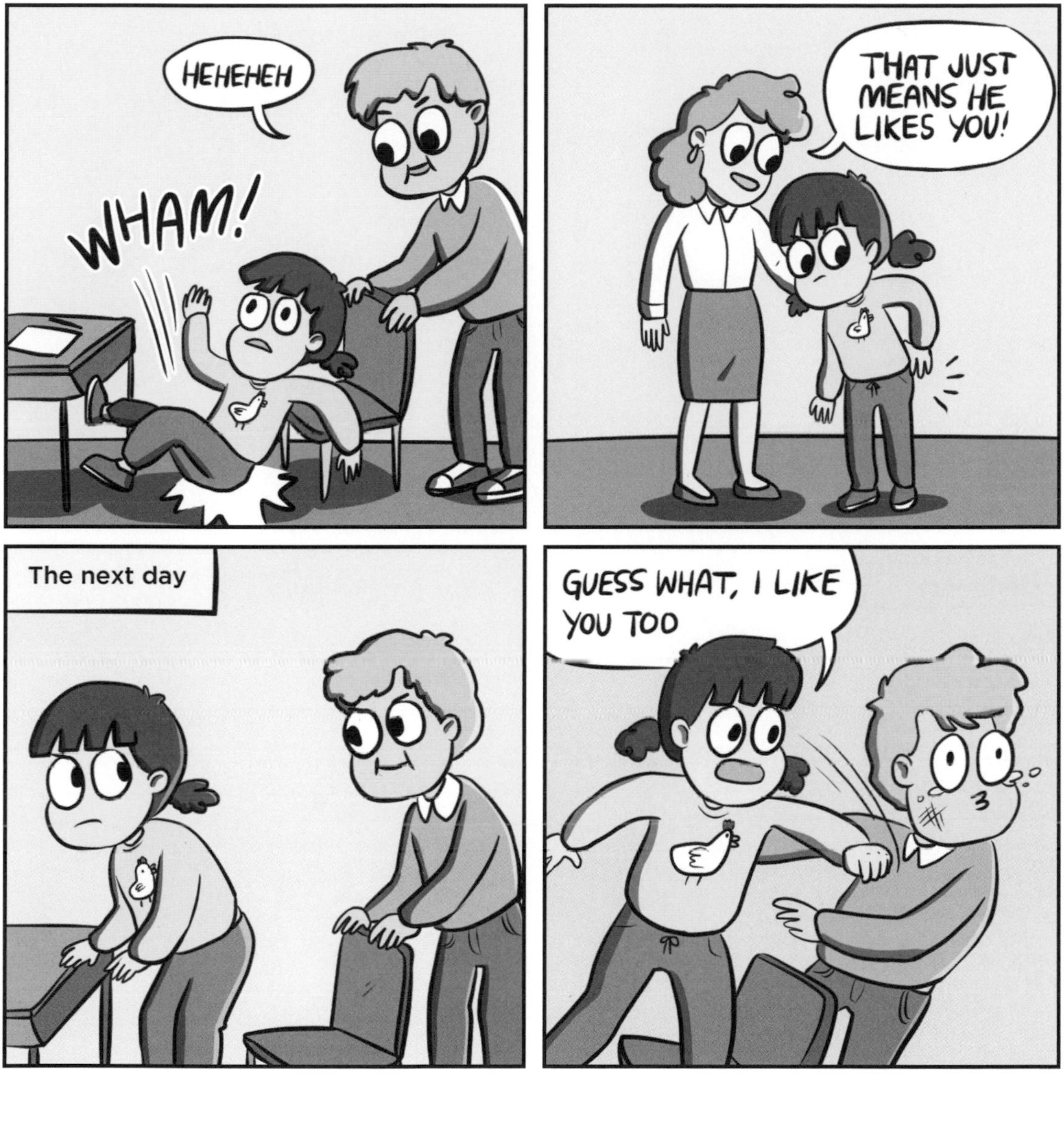
HEHEHEH
WHAM!
THAT JUST MEANS HE LIKES YOU!
The next day
GUESS WHAT, I LIKE YOU TOO

WATCH AND LEARN

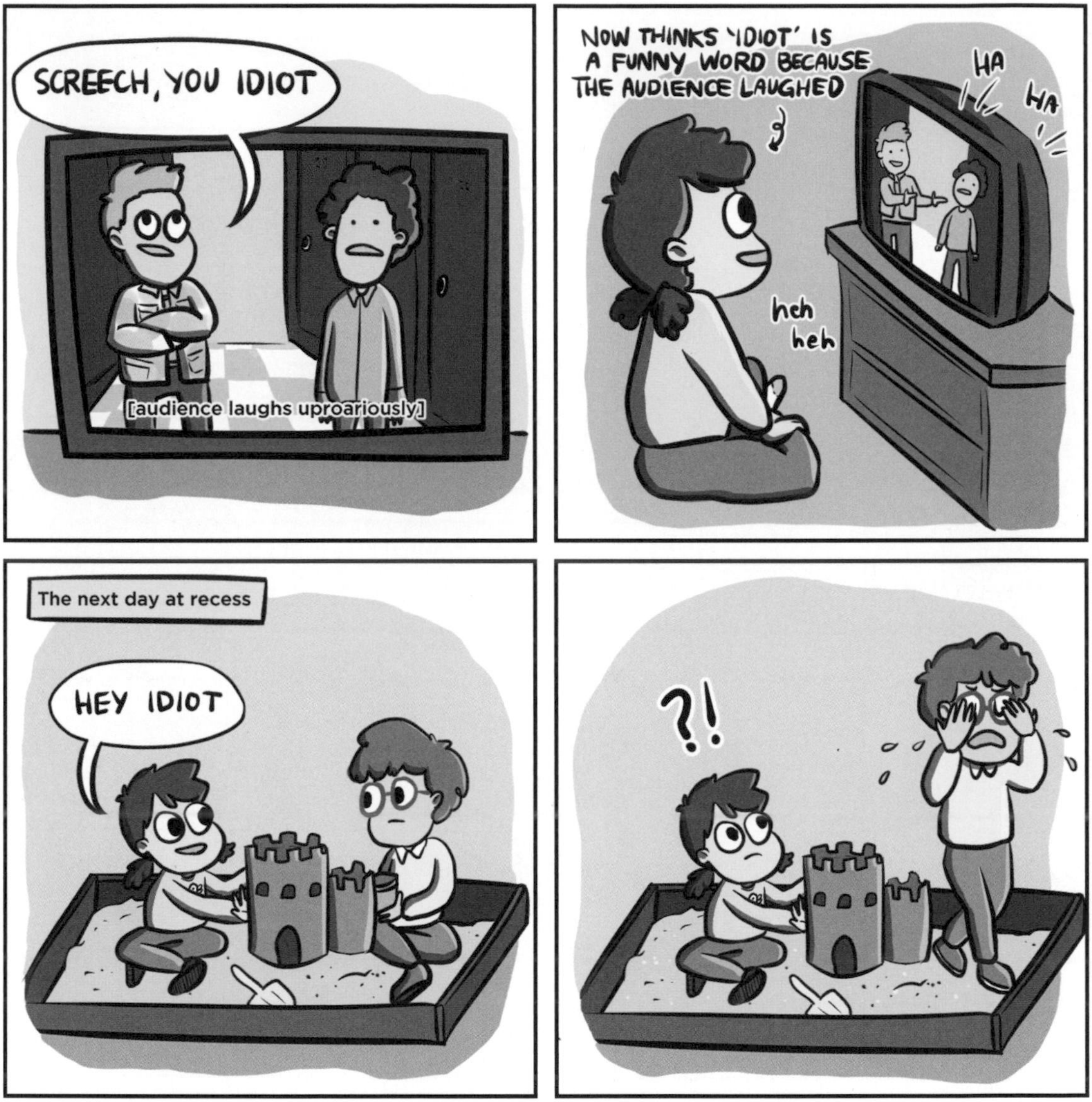
SCREECH, YOU IDIOT
[audience laughs uproariously]
NOW THINKS 'IDIOT' IS A FUNNY WORD BECAUSE THE AUDIENCE LAUGHED
HA
HA
heh heh
The next day at recess
HEY IDIOT
?!

POKÉMON

When I moved back to Korea in third grade for a short stint, I had to brush up on the Korean I'd forgotten.

PLEASE WELCOME YOUR NEW CLASSMATE

ALWAYS THE AWKWARD NEW KID

Poké-mania was in full swing at the time, and I was thrilled to see something familiar in a place that was now foreign to me.

HEY THEY'VE GOT POKEMON HERE TOO!

Strangely enough, reading all the comic books and memorizing their punny names helped me learn Korean.

MAGIKARP: 잉어킹 IN KOREAN, WHICH MEANS KOI KING

And that's why I'm such Pokémon trash today.

FAKEOUT

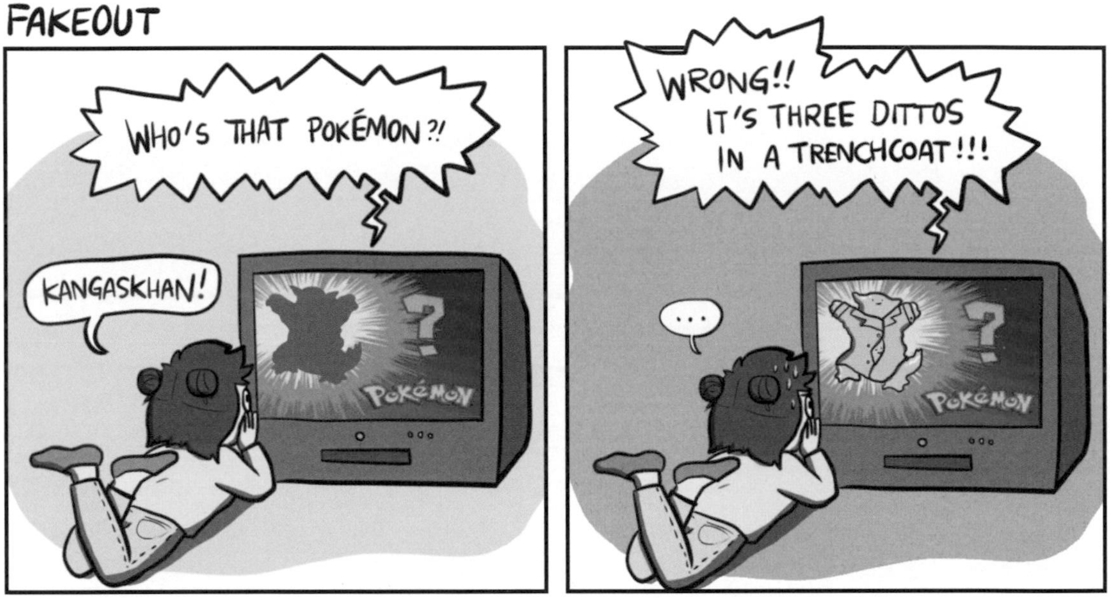
WHO'S THAT POKÉMON?!
KANGASKHAN!
POKéMON
WRONG!! IT'S THREE DITTOS IN A TRENCHCOAT!!!
...
POKéMON

OPPA

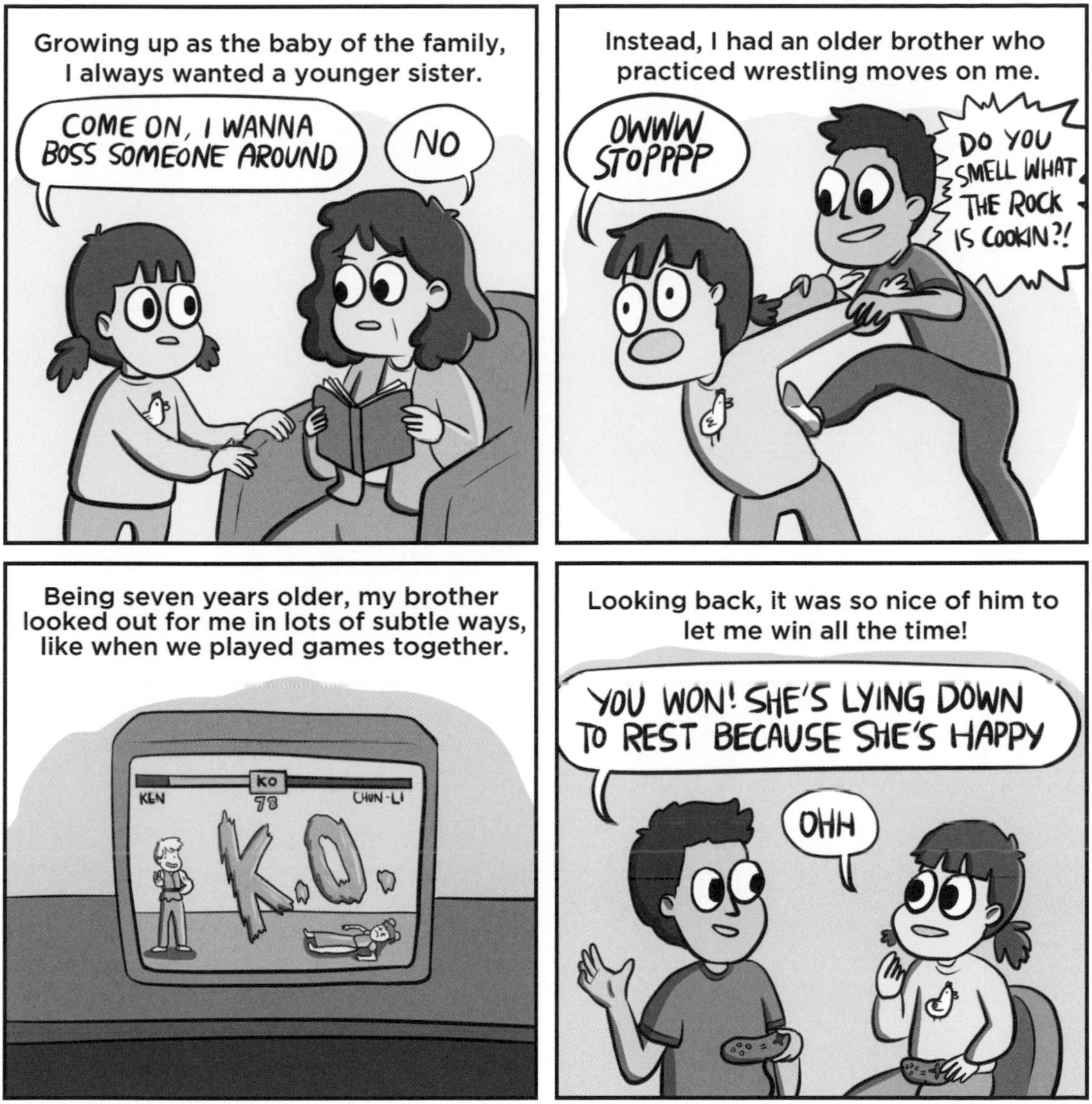
Growing up as the baby of the family, I always wanted a younger sister.
COME ON, I WANNA BOSS SOMEONE AROUND
NO
Instead, I had an older brother who practiced wrestling moves on me.
OWWW STOPPPP
DO YOU SMELL WHAT THE ROCK IS COOKIN?!
Being seven years older, my brother looked out for me in lots of subtle ways, like when we played games together.
KO
KEN
78
CHUN-LI
K.O
Looking back, it was so nice of him to let me win all the time!
YOU WON! SHE'S LYING DOWN TO REST BECAUSE SHE'S HAPPY
OHH

THE DECISION

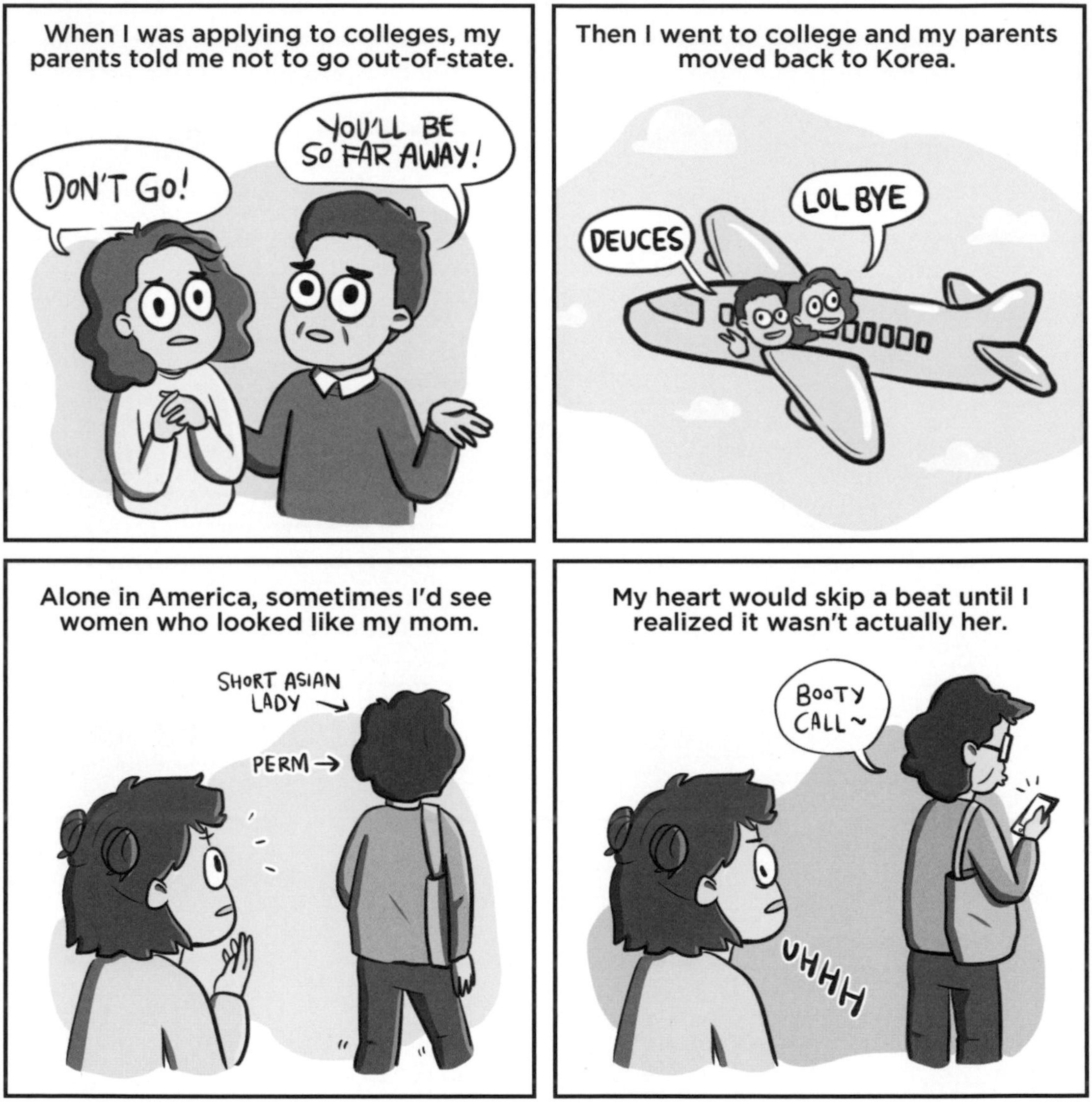
When I was applying to colleges, my parents told me not to go out-of-state.
DON'T GO!
YOU'LL BE SO FAR AWAY!
Then I went to college and my parents moved back to Korea.
DEUCES
LOL BYE
Alone in America, sometimes I'd see women who looked like my mom.
SHORT ASIAN LADY →
PERM →
My heart would skip a beat until I realized it wasn't actually her.
BOOTY CALL~
UHHH

I didn't get to go home and see my parents very often, so I spent breaks with friends and their parents.

DON'T HANG OUT WITH HER ANYMORE

SLUUURRP

My parents wanted me to join them in Korea after college, and I resisted bitterly at first.

I GREW UP HERE! ALL MY FRIENDS ARE HERE!

AND I DO NOT WANT TO SWITCH TO THE METRIC SYSTEM

But I realized they were getting older, and I missed spending time with them.

Dad is sick.

Come home.

So I decided to do it.

You can imagine how confused my brain was when I finally moved back.

M-MOMS?

FLYING

The 14-hour flight from America to South Korea is pretty brutal.

MA
PA
TEDDY
ME

No matter how many times I fly, I never seem to get any better at it.

WHERE IS KINDLE JENNER!!*

*My nickname for my Kindle

Around hour four is when I slowly lose my mind and really start getting restless.

I RELATE TO THIS SO MUCH

WATCHING 'THE MARTIAN,' A MOVIE WHERE MATT DAMON GETS STRANDED ON MARS WITHOUT WIFI

I MISS THE INTERNET

Someday I aspire to be on the level of these ladies, the experienced frequent flyers, the MVPs of the skies.

MOISTURIZING FACE MASK

LOADED UP WITH MOVIES

COMFY NECK PILLOW

RELEARNING KOREAN

At first, my Korean was pretty rusty. I could barely speak on the phone without my voice quivering.

UHH..UH H-HELLO.. I AM... UHH BYE

SWEATING PROFUSELY →

I slowly started to pick up the language, mostly through watching K-dramas and reading webcomics.

SCROLL SCROLL

If you want to learn a new language, I can't recommend anything better than immersing yourself in its culture.

HEHE

And I'm lucky that Korea has so much of it.

KIMCHI SLAP!

SPLAT

YEAH GET HIM

USELESS IN MY MOTHERLAND

APPA

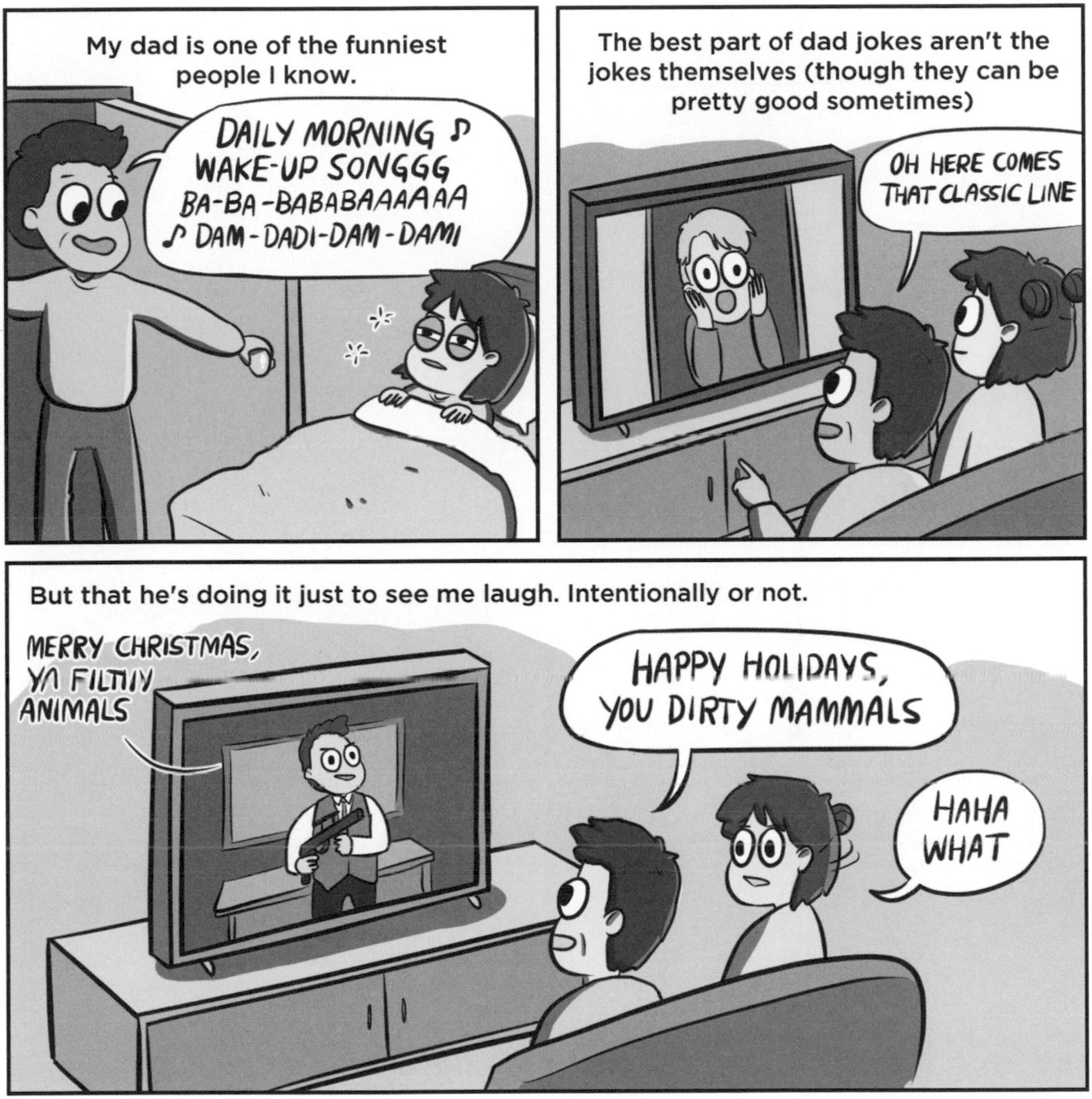
My dad is one of the funniest people I know.
DAILY MORNING ♪ WAKE-UP SONGGG BA-BA-BABABAAAAAA ♪ DAM-DADI-DAM-DAMI
The best part of dad jokes aren't the jokes themselves (though they can be pretty good sometimes)
OH HERE COMES THAT CLASSIC LINE
But that he's doing it just to see me laugh. Intentionally or not.
MERRY CHRISTMAS, YA FILTHY ANIMALS
HAPPY HOLIDAYS, YOU DIRTY MAMMALS
HAHA WHAT

KOREA VS. AMERICA

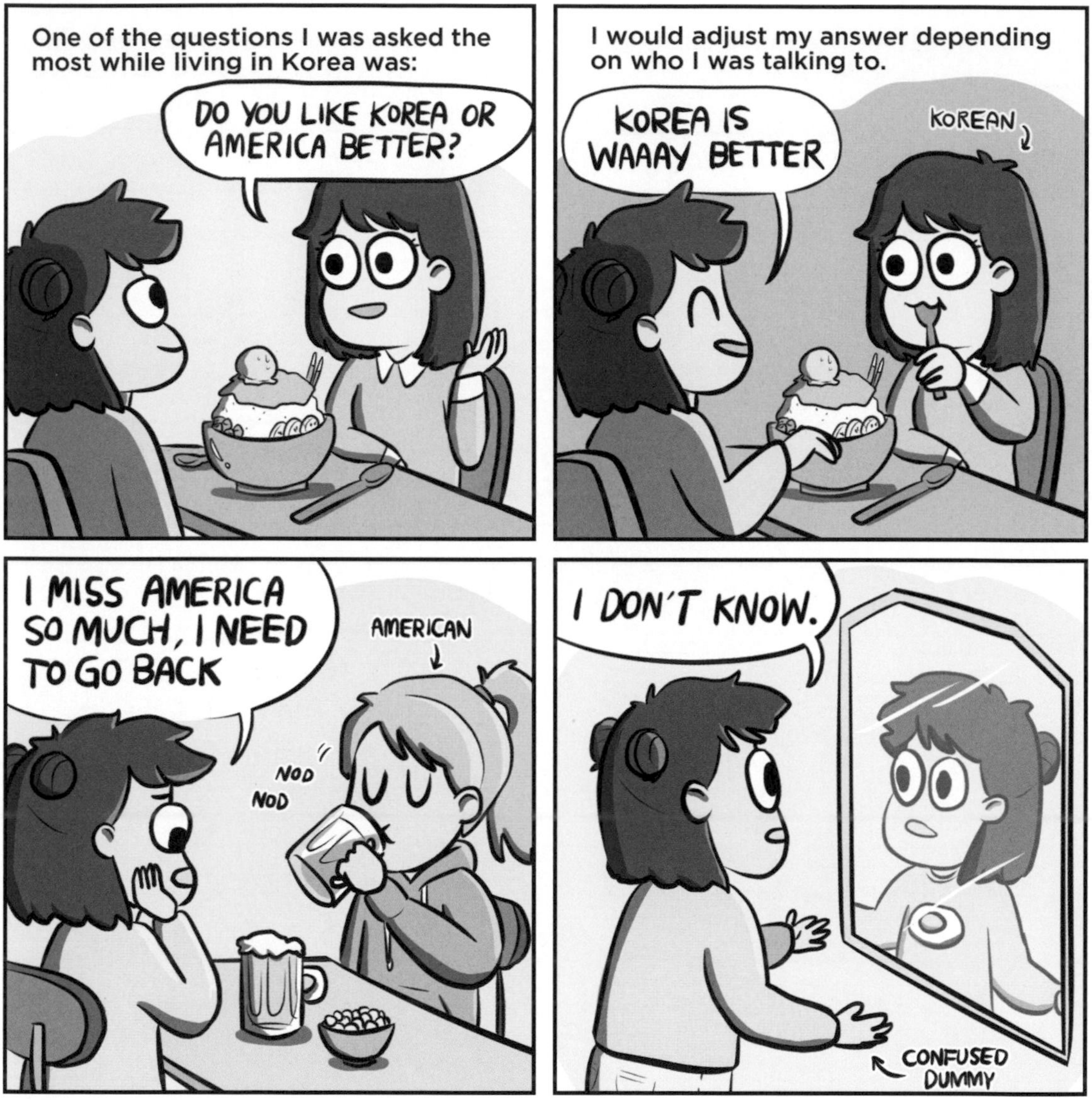
One of the questions I was asked the most while living in Korea was:
DO YOU LIKE KOREA OR AMERICA BETTER?
I would adjust my answer depending on who I was talking to.
KOREA IS WAAAY BETTER
KOREAN
I MISS AMERICA SO MUCH, I NEED TO GO BACK
AMERICAN
NOD NOD
I DON'T KNOW.
CONFUSED DUMMY

GYOPO

A 'Gyopo' is someone who's ethnically Korean, but was raised abroad.

OVERSIZED, EASILY MISTAKEN FOR POLE ON SUBWAY

Spot the Gyopo — Hint: It's me

Life in Korea got easier the more I started to meet people like myself.

THERE ARE DOZENS OF US! DOZENS!!

I even got to be a weekly guest on my friend Rob's radio show at an English-language station.

I'm not sure if anyone was listening, but still, I liked the concept— two weirdos, broadcasting their thoughts into the Seoul night.

TBSefm

SHOPPING IN KOREA

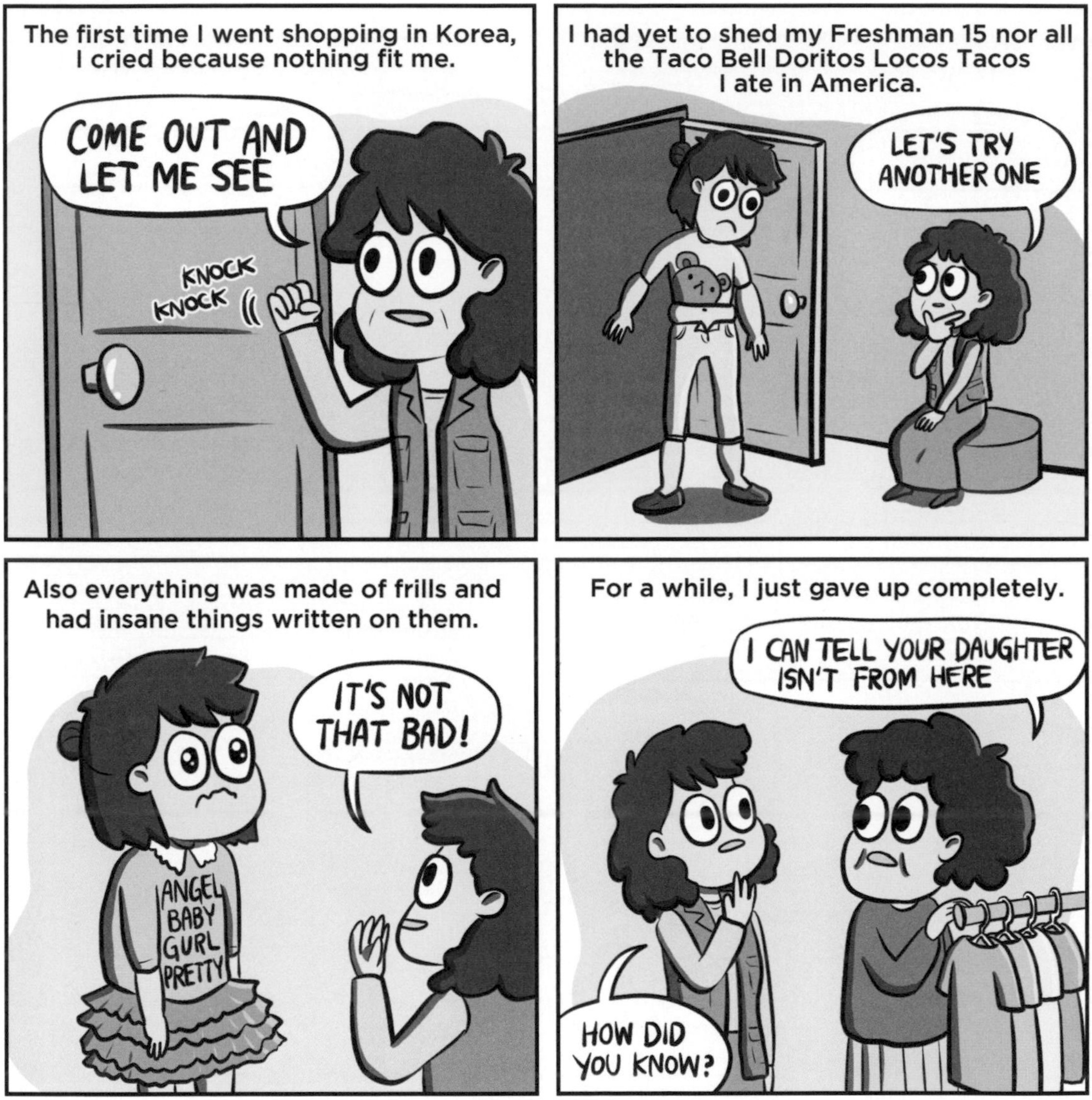
The first time I went shopping in Korea, I cried because nothing fit me.
COME OUT AND LET ME SEE
KNOCK KNOCK
I had yet to shed my Freshman 15 nor all the Taco Bell Doritos Locos Tacos I ate in America.
LET'S TRY ANOTHER ONE
Also everything was made of frills and had insane things written on them.
ANGEL BABY GURL PRETTY
IT'S NOT THAT BAD!
For a while, I just gave up completely.
I CAN TELL YOUR DAUGHTER ISN'T FROM HERE
HOW DID YOU KNOW?

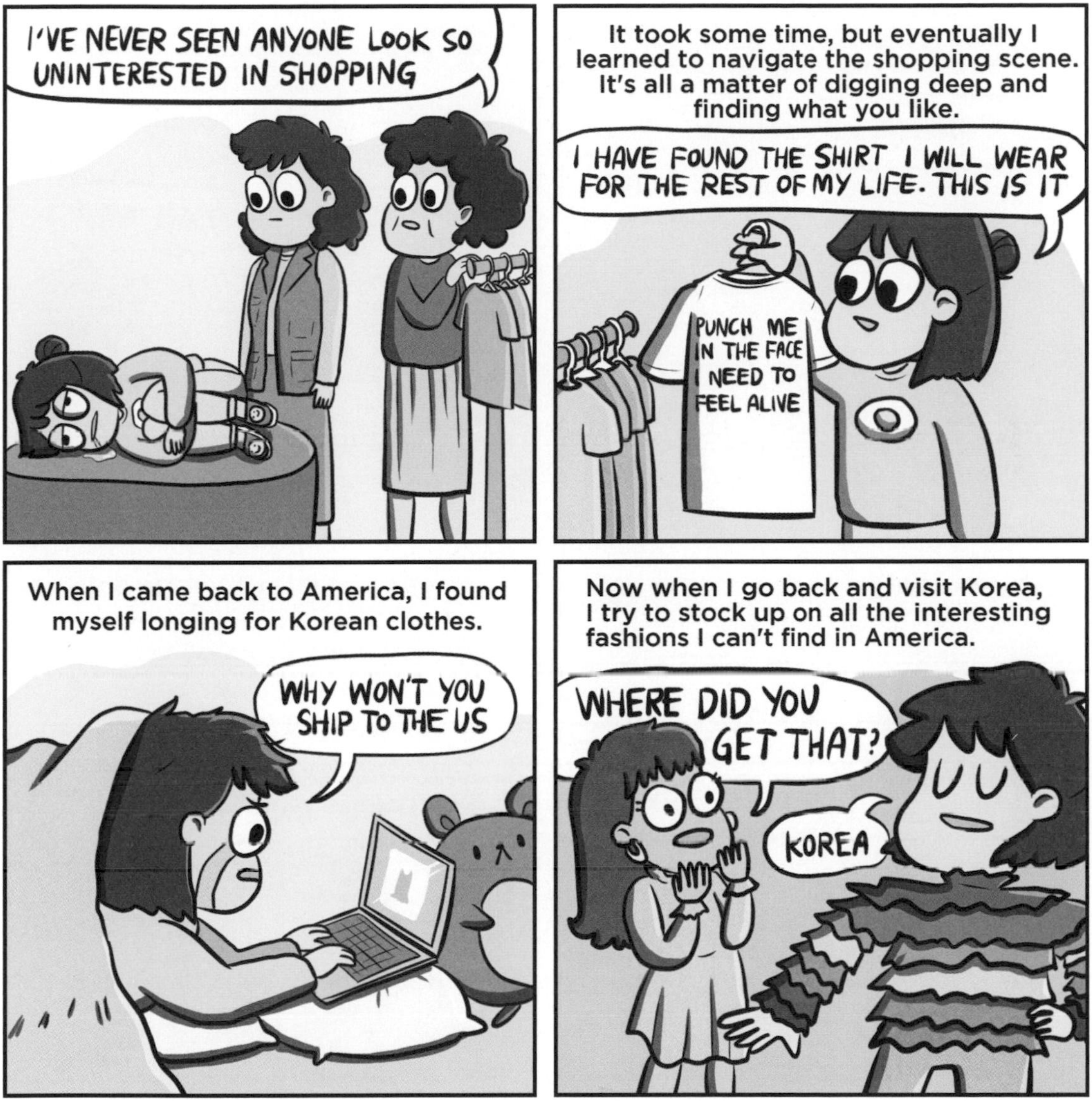
I'VE NEVER SEEN ANYONE LOOK SO UNINTERESTED IN SHOPPING
It took some time, but eventually I learned to navigate the shopping scene. It's all a matter of digging deep and finding what you like.
I HAVE FOUND THE SHIRT I WILL WEAR FOR THE REST OF MY LIFE. THIS IS IT
PUNCH ME IN THE FACE I NEED TO FEEL ALIVE
When I came back to America, I found myself longing for Korean clothes.
WHY WON'T YOU SHIP TO THE US
Now when I go back and visit Korea, I try to stock up on all the interesting fashions I can't find in America.
WHERE DID YOU GET THAT?
KOREA

MINIMALIST LIFESTYLE

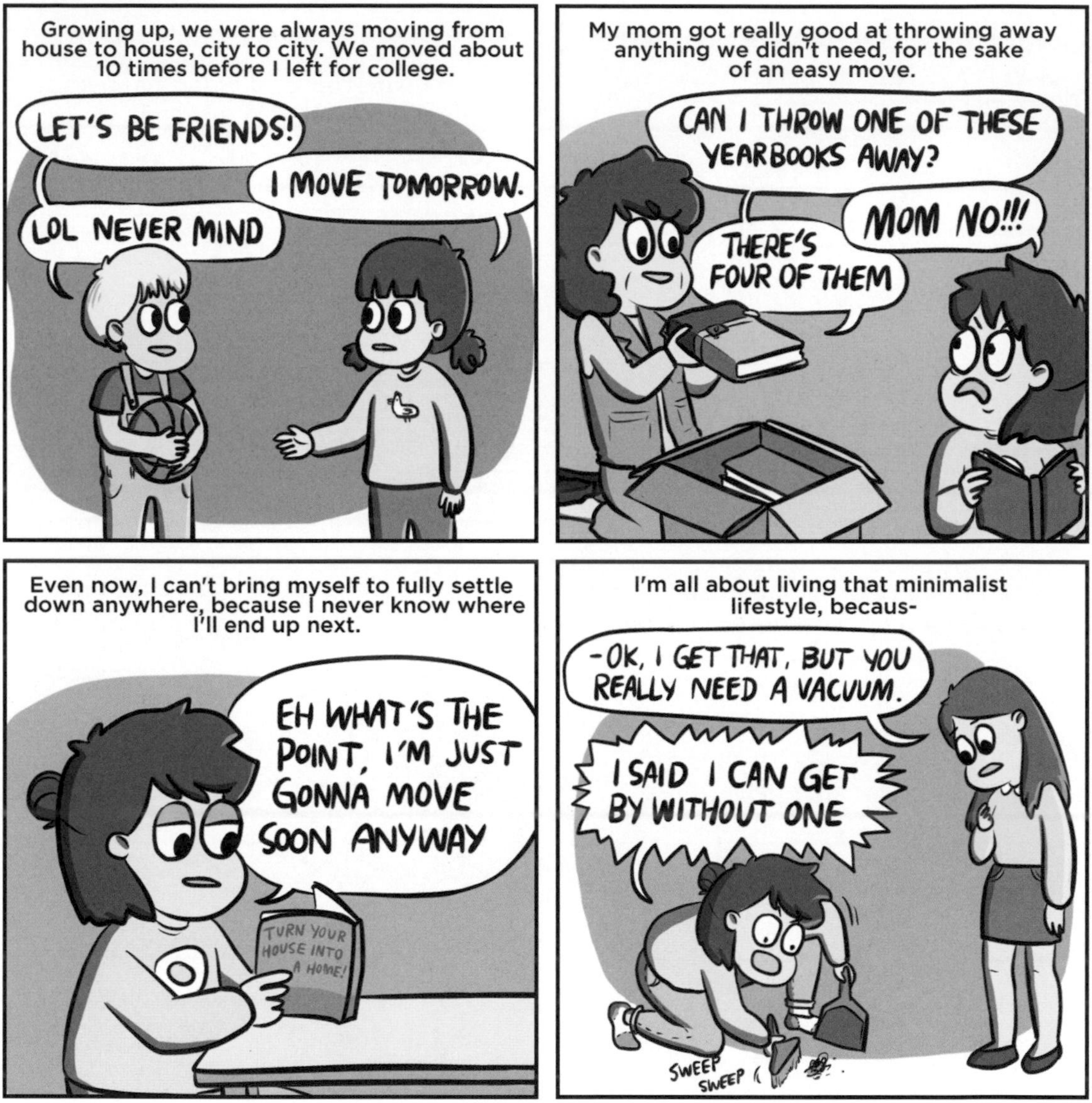
Growing up, we were always moving from house to house, city to city. We moved about 10 times before I left for college.
LET'S BE FRIENDS!
LOL NEVER MIND
I MOVE TOMORROW.
My mom got really good at throwing away anything we didn't need, for the sake of an easy move.
CAN I THROW ONE OF THESE YEARBOOKS AWAY?
THERE'S FOUR OF THEM
MOM NO!!!
Even now, I can't bring myself to fully settle down anywhere, because I never know where I'll end up next.
EH WHAT'S THE POINT, I'M JUST GONNA MOVE SOON ANYWAY
TURN YOUR HOUSE INTO A HOME!
I'm all about living that minimalist lifestyle, becaus-
-OK, I GET THAT, BUT YOU REALLY NEED A VACUUM.
I SAID I CAN GET BY WITHOUT ONE
SWEEP SWEEP

FALSE DICHOTOMY

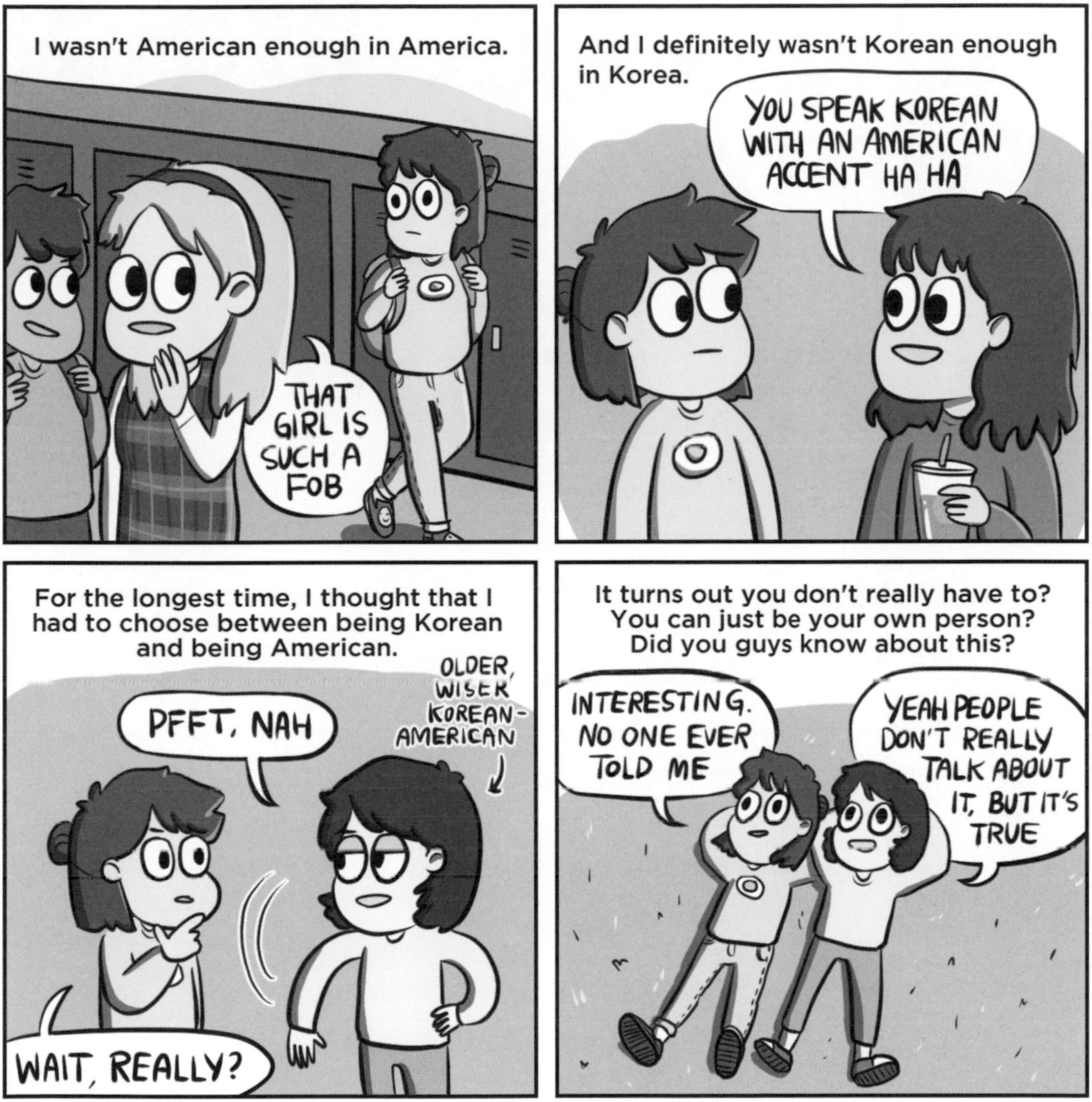
I wasn't American enough in America.
THAT GIRL IS SUCH A FOB
And I definitely wasn't Korean enough in Korea.
YOU SPEAK KOREAN WITH AN AMERICAN ACCENT HA HA
For the longest time, I thought that I had to choose between being Korean and being American.
OLDER, WISER KOREAN-AMERICAN
PFFT, NAH
WAIT, REALLY?
It turns out you don't really have to? You can just be your own person? Did you guys know about this?
INTERESTING. NO ONE EVER TOLD ME
YEAH PEOPLE DON'T REALLY TALK ABOUT IT, BUT IT'S TRUE

HOW I BECAME A CARTOONIST LADY PERSON

The first comic I ever drew happened because I was out of options.

Id always been interested in art, so in college, I ambitiously applied to be a design editor at my school newspaper and was called in to do a layout test. I was in charge of designing our high school yearbook, so I was confident that my skills in punching up pages with made-up quotes like "Marching band is the best thing that ever happened to me!—Rebecca Yue, Grade 10" would translate well into university-level journalism. I was given one hour to look at the front page of the newspaper and recreate it in InDesign.

I knew immediately that I wasn't going to pass, but I still took the entire hour to fail elaborately, and left the office drenched in humiliation sweat.

A couple of months later, I had the reckless nerve to reapply to the paper, this time for an artist position. The assignment was to draw one editorial illustration to accompany an article, and one cartoon. If I can be completely honest here, "illustrator" generally sounds like a way cooler job than "cartoonist." "Illustrator" evokes images of a brilliant artsy-type who just has a natural gift for layering clothes in an effortlessly chic way, whereas a "cartoonist" is someone who you have to pull aside privately to let them know they are wearing their shorts backwards.

Fueled by my fantasy of becoming the former, I tried to focus more on the illustration part of the assignment than the cartooning part, but despite my best efforts, the editors saw me as a backwards-shorts person. This ended up working just fine for me, since I had no art skills or even Photoshop experience, just some weird jokes in my head and ball-point pen. So I accepted my fate, and started drawing my weekly comic strip, which I called *As Per Usual*.

I kept drawing comics for about five years after that, uploading them to the internet to a very devoted audience of four Facebook friends and one guy on Tumblr who probably got lost while searching for a K-pop blog. Cartooning was always just something I'd done as a hobby, yet I couldn't help but daydream about what it would be like as an actual job. And one day, that exact job showed up in the form of an artist fellowship at BuzzFeed.

The job description to make fun memes and comics for the internet seemed to align so perfectly with my experience. It was a little spooky. I almost talked myself out of applying, convinced BuzzFeed would never hire a random person in South Korea for a position in New York. Yet again, blatant audacity made me submit an application, and one week and a shaky Skype call later, I had an offer.

I told my parents the exciting news.

"You want to quit your job to go draw comics in America for three months, and after the fellowship ends, you'll be unemployed? Sounds like a solid plan, go right ahead!!" Just kidding, they absolutely did not say this. They were understandably worried, but I convinced them that this was the right choice for me with a well thought-out, perfectly executed and convincing argument (I cried and tried to look as sad as possible whenever I was in their line of vision). I also boldly told my dad I would "write a book" out of a desperate attempt to look like I knew what I was doing, and he totally bought it.

FIRST DAY ON THE JOB

Looking back, my time at BuzzFeed feels like a fever dream.

I CAN'T BELIEVE I'M ACTUALLY HERE

It had always been my dream job, one my college experience prepared me for.

HEY YOU WANNA GO OUT TO A PARTY?

NO THANKS I GOTTA SCROLL THROUGH TUMBLR FOR 3 HOURS AND CRY

Yes, it was exactly like I imagined it.

THIS IS OUR PRODUCER JEREMY

HE'S CURRENTLY ON VACATION, SO WE'VE REPLACED HIM WITH THIS. WE CALL HIM HORSEDAD.

NEATO!!

SWIVEL

CHILDHOOD DREAMS

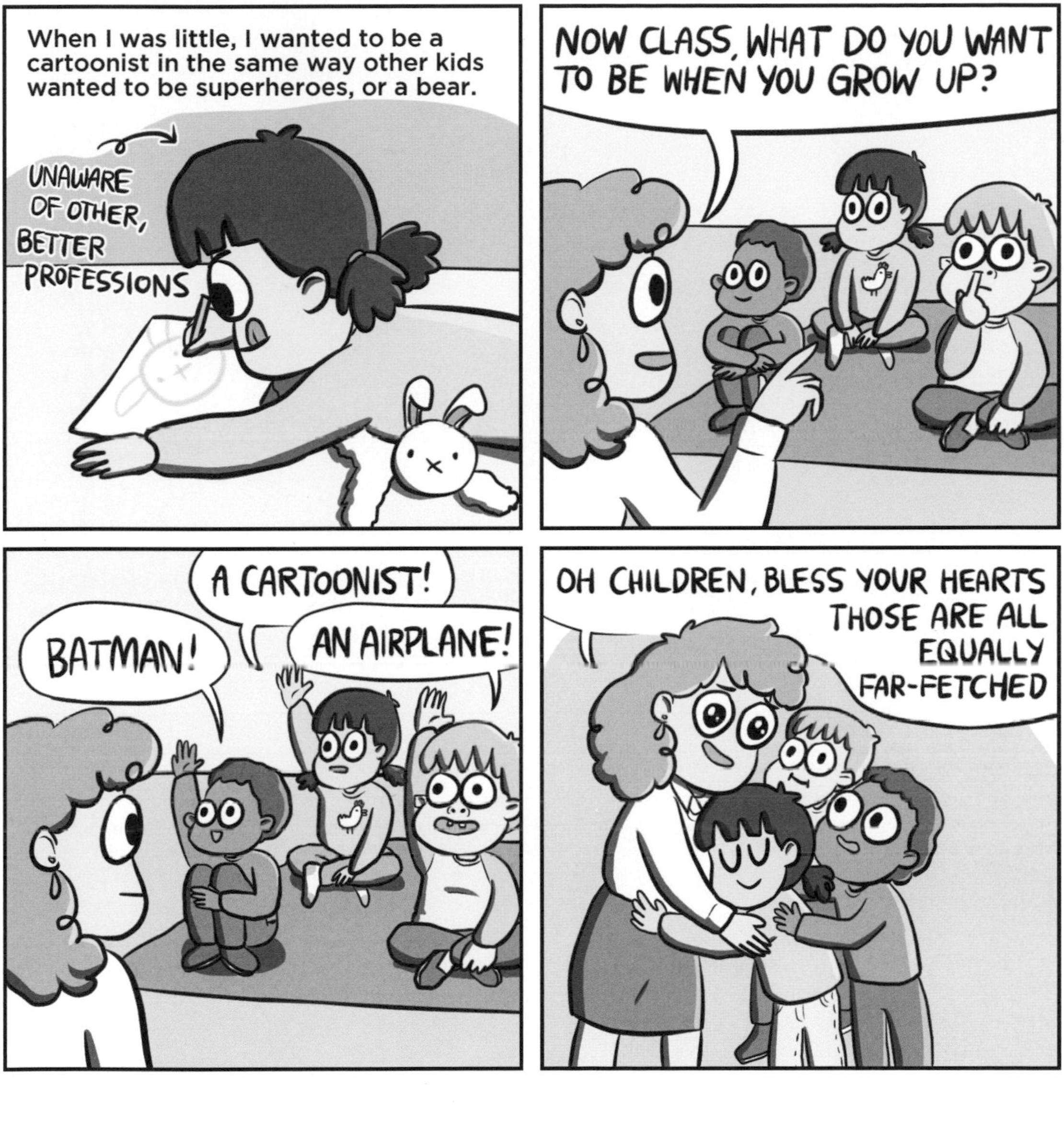

When I was little, I wanted to be a cartoonist in the same way other kids wanted to be superheroes, or a bear.
UNAWARE OF OTHER, BETTER PROFESSIONS
NOW CLASS, WHAT DO YOU WANT TO BE WHEN YOU GROW UP?
BATMAN!
A CARTOONIST!
AN AIRPLANE!
OH CHILDREN, BLESS YOUR HEARTS THOSE ARE ALL EQUALLY FAR-FETCHED

SKETCHY ARTIST

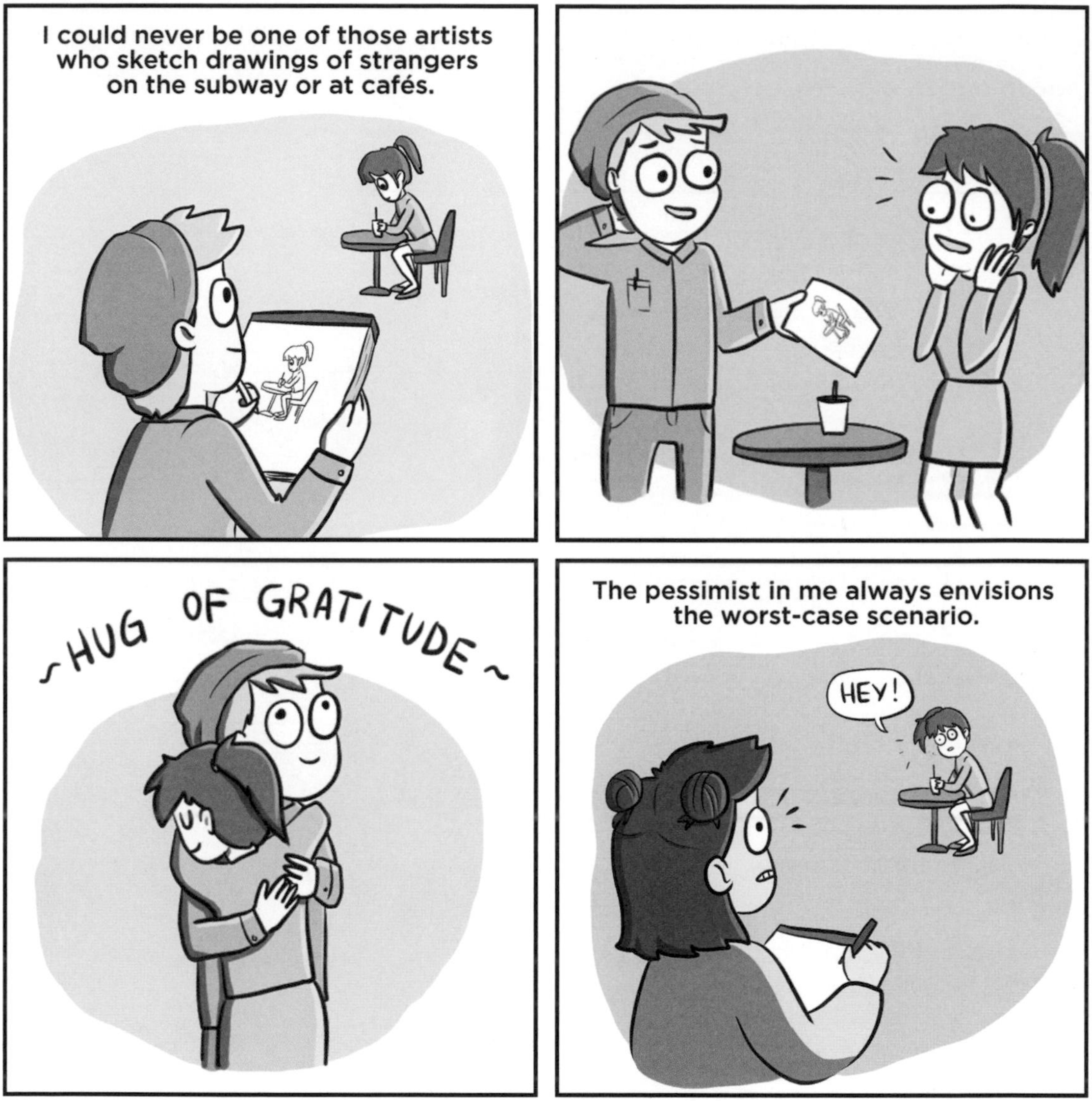

I could never be one of those artists who sketch drawings of strangers on the subway or at cafés.
~HUG OF GRATITUDE~
The pessimist in me always envisions the worst-case scenario.
HEY!

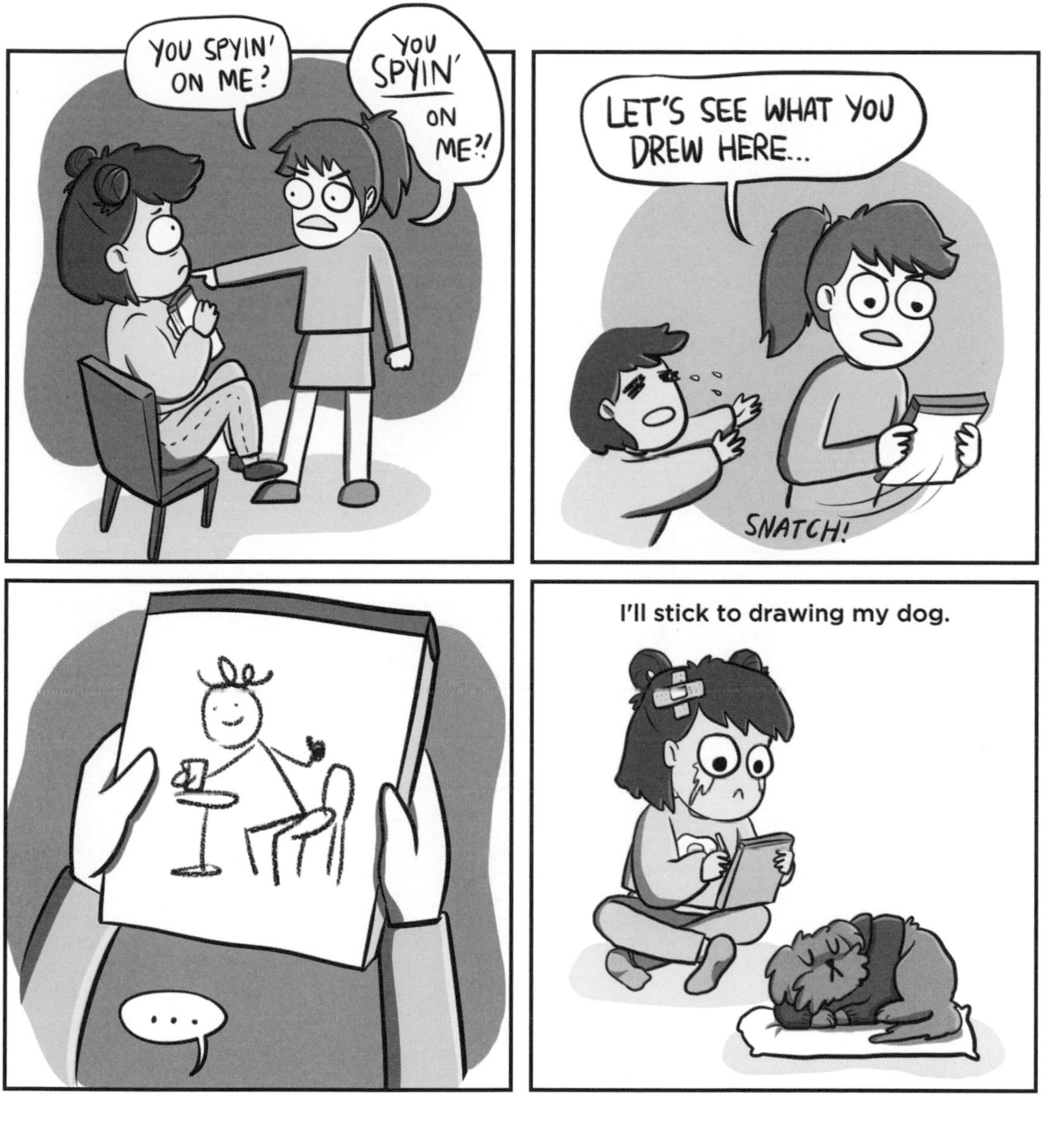
YOU SPYIN' ON ME?
YOU SPYIN' ON ME?!
LET'S SEE WHAT YOU DREW HERE...
SNATCH!
...
I'll stick to drawing my dog.

LISTS

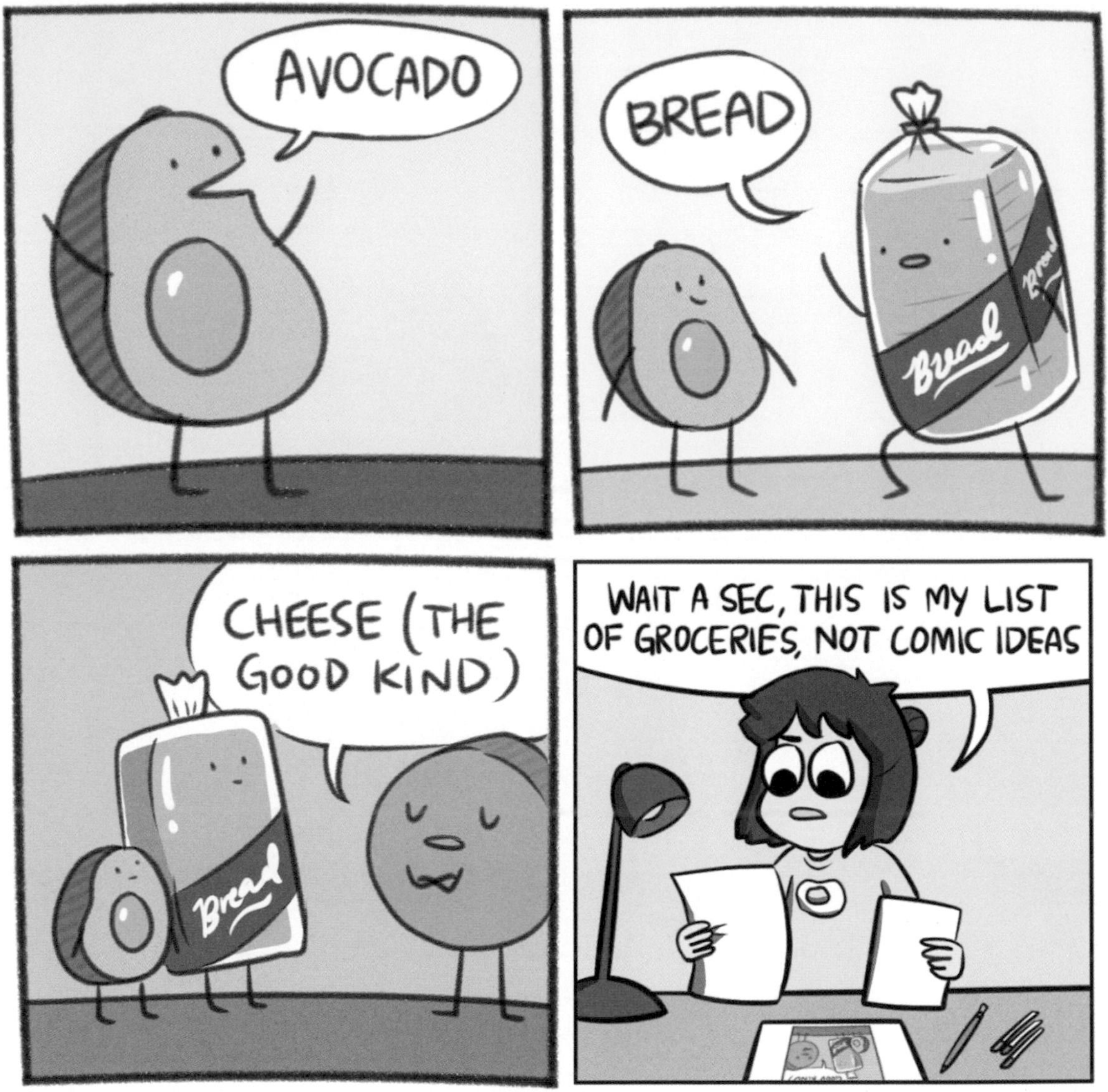
AVOCADO
BREAD
Bread
Bread
CHEESE (THE GOOD KIND)
Bread
WAIT A SEC, THIS IS MY LIST OF GROCERIES, NOT COMIC IDEAS

DRAWING IS HARD

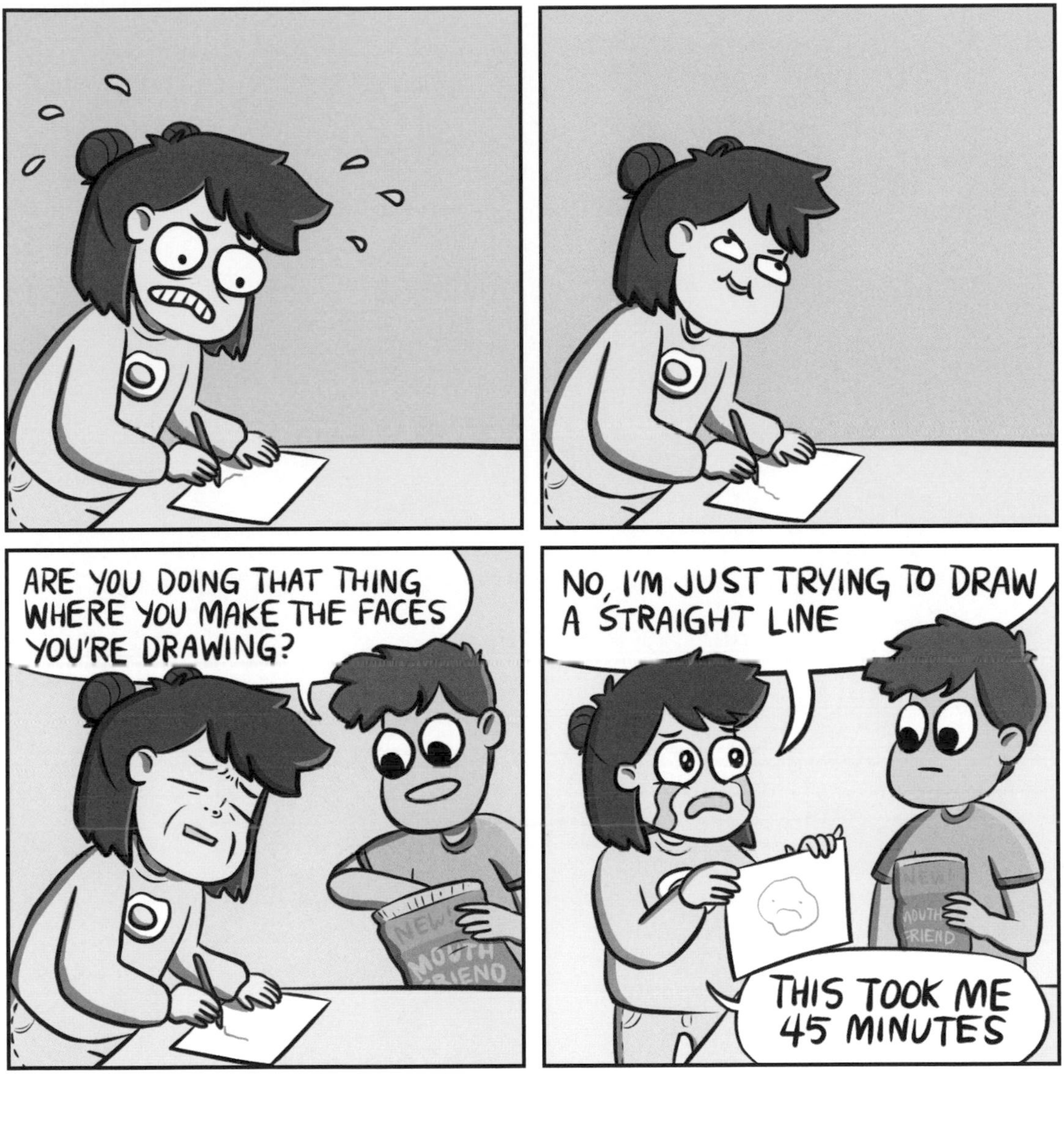
ARE YOU DOING THAT THING WHERE YOU MAKE THE FACES YOU'RE DRAWING?
NEW MOUTH FRIEND
NO, I'M JUST TRYING TO DRAW A STRAIGHT LINE
THIS TOOK ME 45 MINUTES

NOT A GOOD FIT

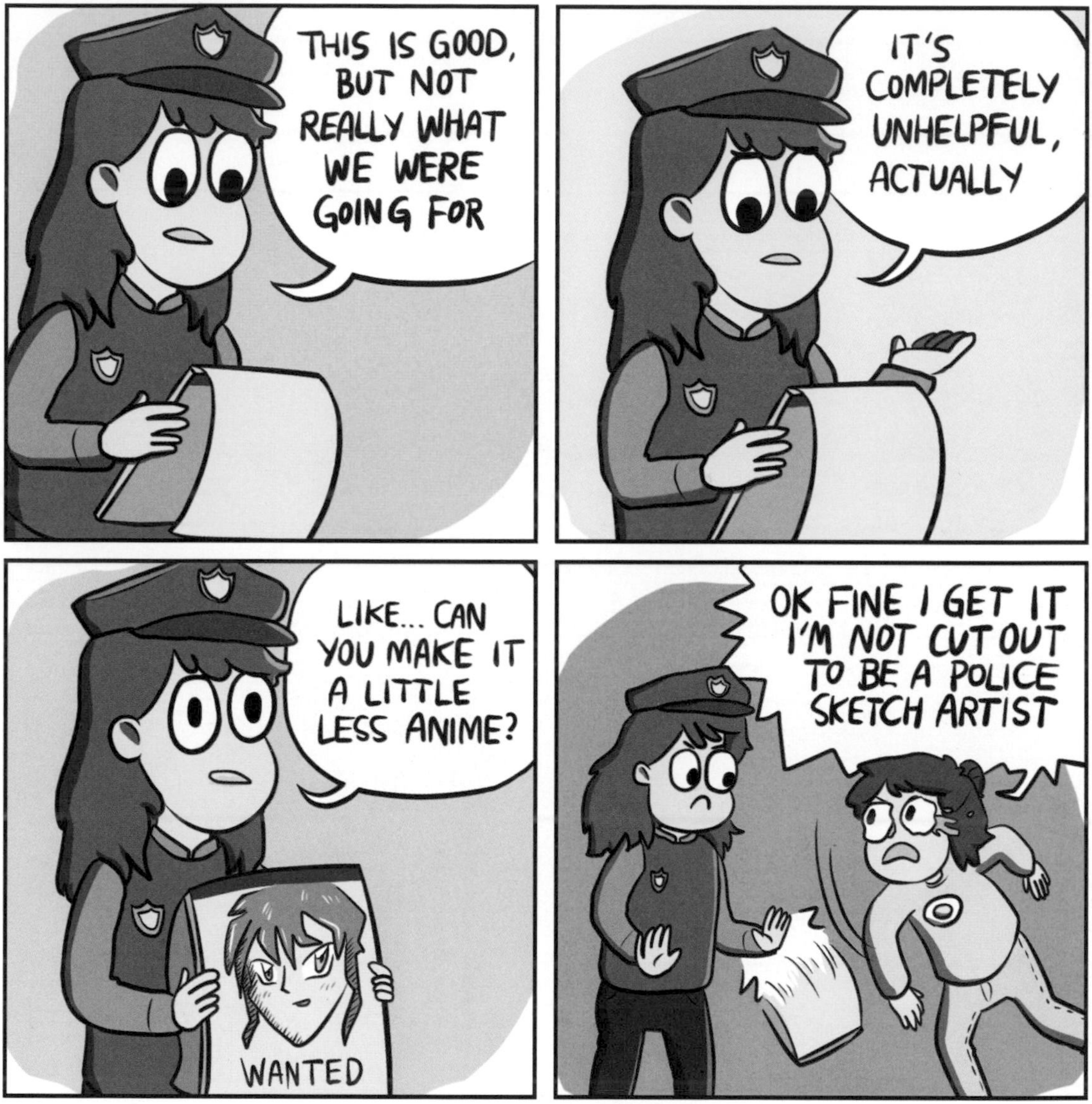
THIS IS GOOD, BUT NOT REALLY WHAT WE WERE GOING FOR
IT'S COMPLETELY UNHELPFUL, ACTUALLY
LIKE... CAN YOU MAKE IT A LITTLE LESS ANIME?
WANTED
OK FINE I GET IT I'M NOT CUT OUT TO BE A POLICE SKETCH ARTIST

BALANCE

It's hard to balance work and play when you have a full-time job and a DEMANDING COMICS CAREER.

WHERE ARE THOSE REPORTS I ASKED FOR!? I NEEDED THEM BY MONDAY!

ACK!!

YES SIR MR.GARFIELD SIR!!

STILL!

I ALWAYS TRY TO LIVE ACCORDING TO MY PERSONAL PHILOSOPHY, WHICH IS TATTOOED ON MY LOWER BACK.

Say Yes 2 *Life!!*

Right now, I want to do everything I possibly can. There's no such thing as balance! But also my body is breaking down and I'm dying please help lol

PLEASE NEVER LET GO OF ME

WORST SUPERHERO

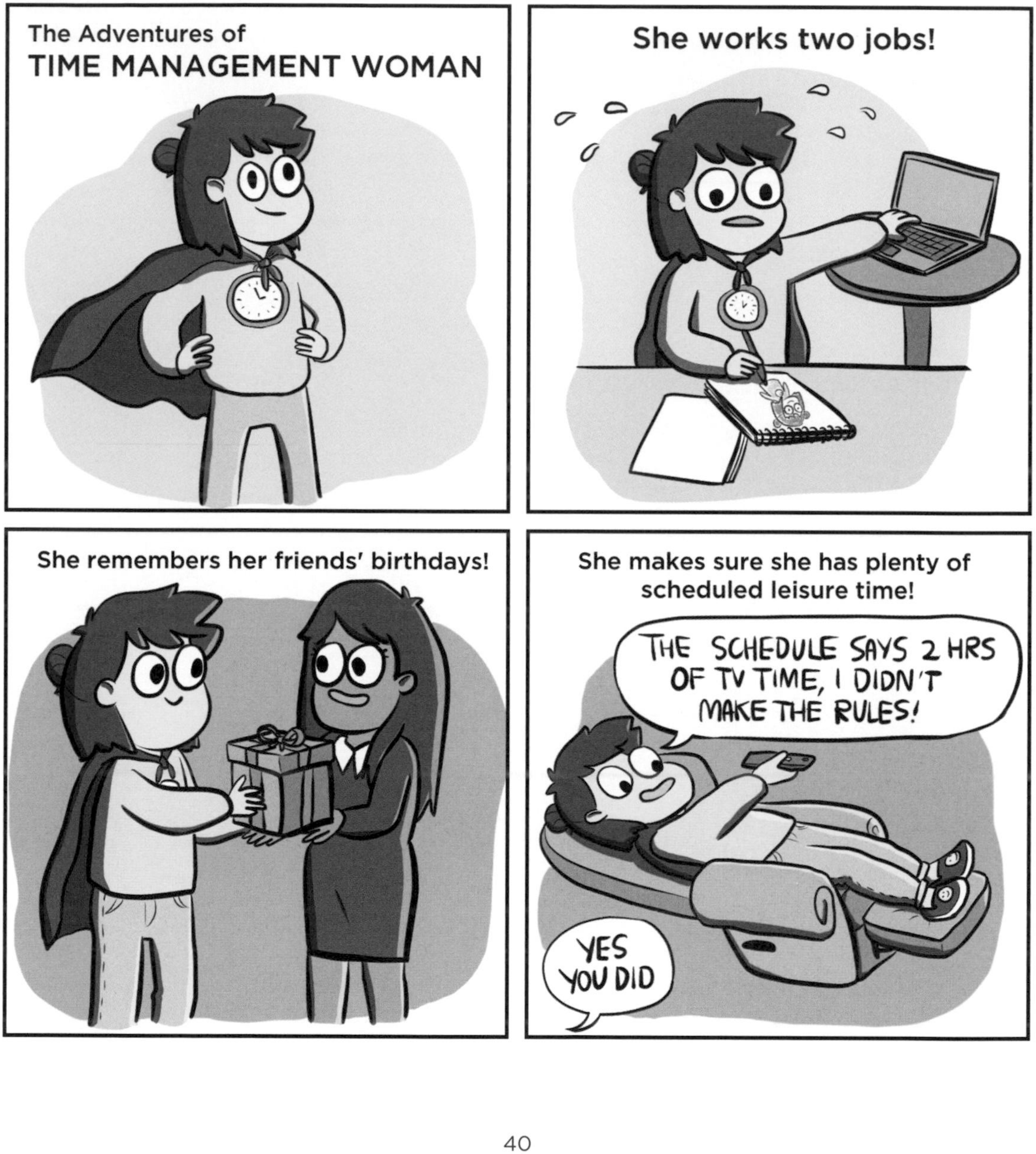

The Adventures of
TIME MANAGEMENT WOMAN
She works two jobs!
She remembers her friends' birthdays!
She makes sure she has plenty of scheduled leisure time!
THE SCHEDULE SAYS 2 HRS OF TV TIME, I DIDN'T MAKE THE RULES!
YES YOU DID

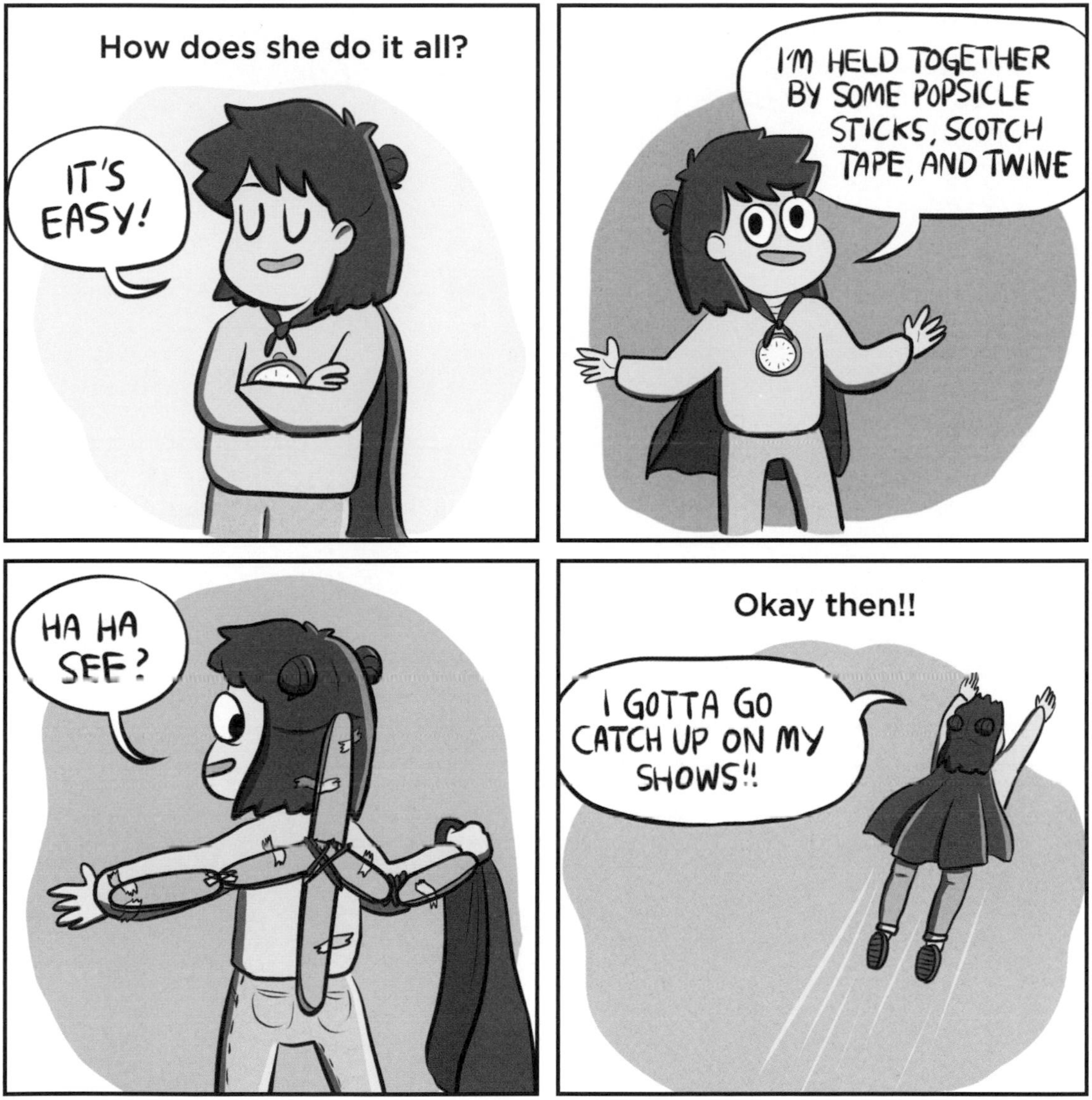
How does she do it all?
IT'S EASY!
I'M HELD TOGETHER BY SOME POPSICLE STICKS, SCOTCH TAPE, AND TWINE
HA HA SEE?
Okay then!!
I GOTTA GO CATCH UP ON MY SHOWS!!

SLEEP DEBT

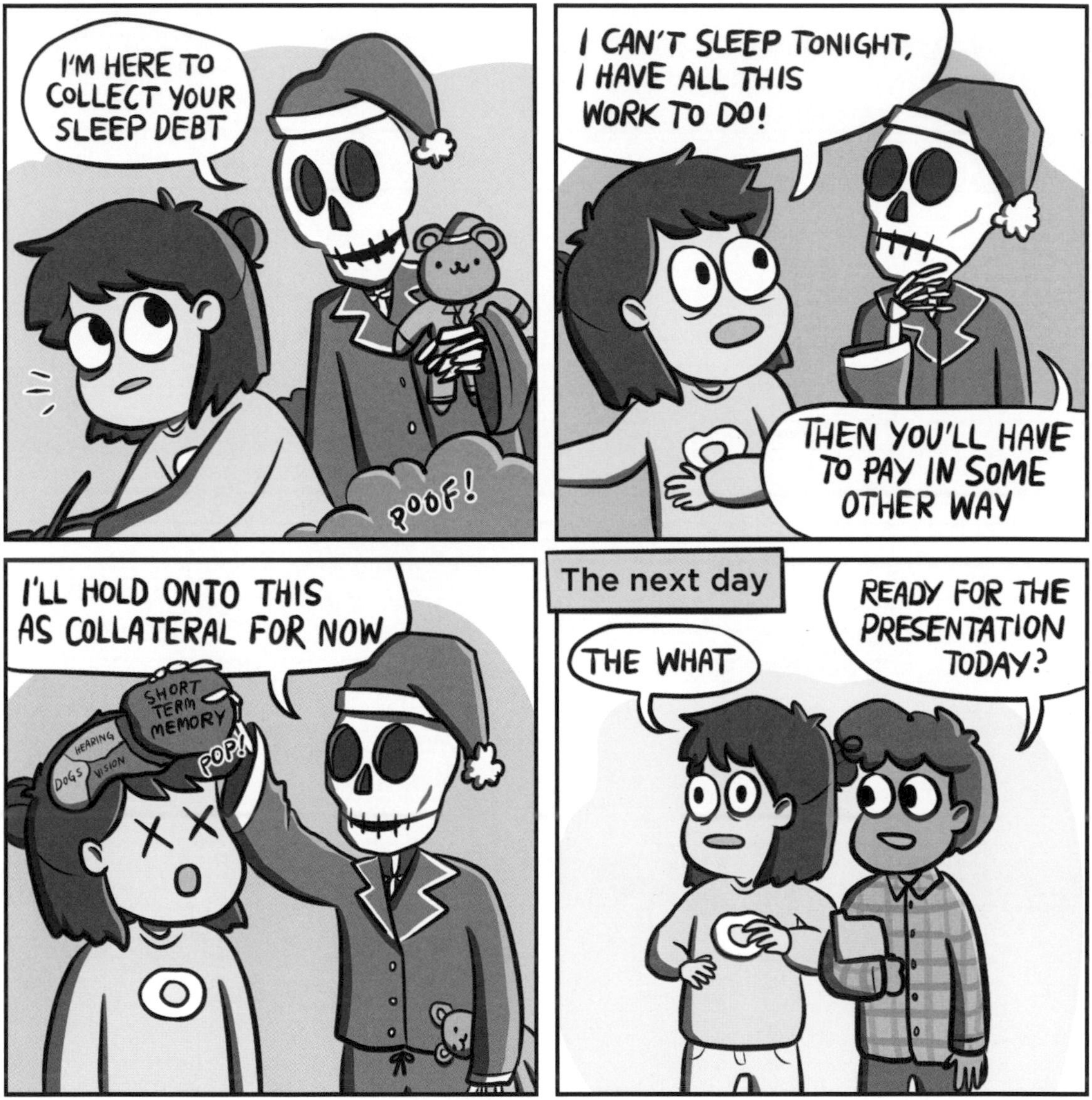

I'M HERE TO COLLECT YOUR SLEEP DEBT
POOF!
I CAN'T SLEEP TONIGHT, I HAVE ALL THIS WORK TO DO!
THEN YOU'LL HAVE TO PAY IN SOME OTHER WAY
I'LL HOLD ONTO THIS AS COLLATERAL FOR NOW
SHORT TERM MEMORY
HEARING
VISION
DOGS
POP!
The next day
READY FOR THE PRESENTATION TODAY?
THE WHAT

NOTEBOOK

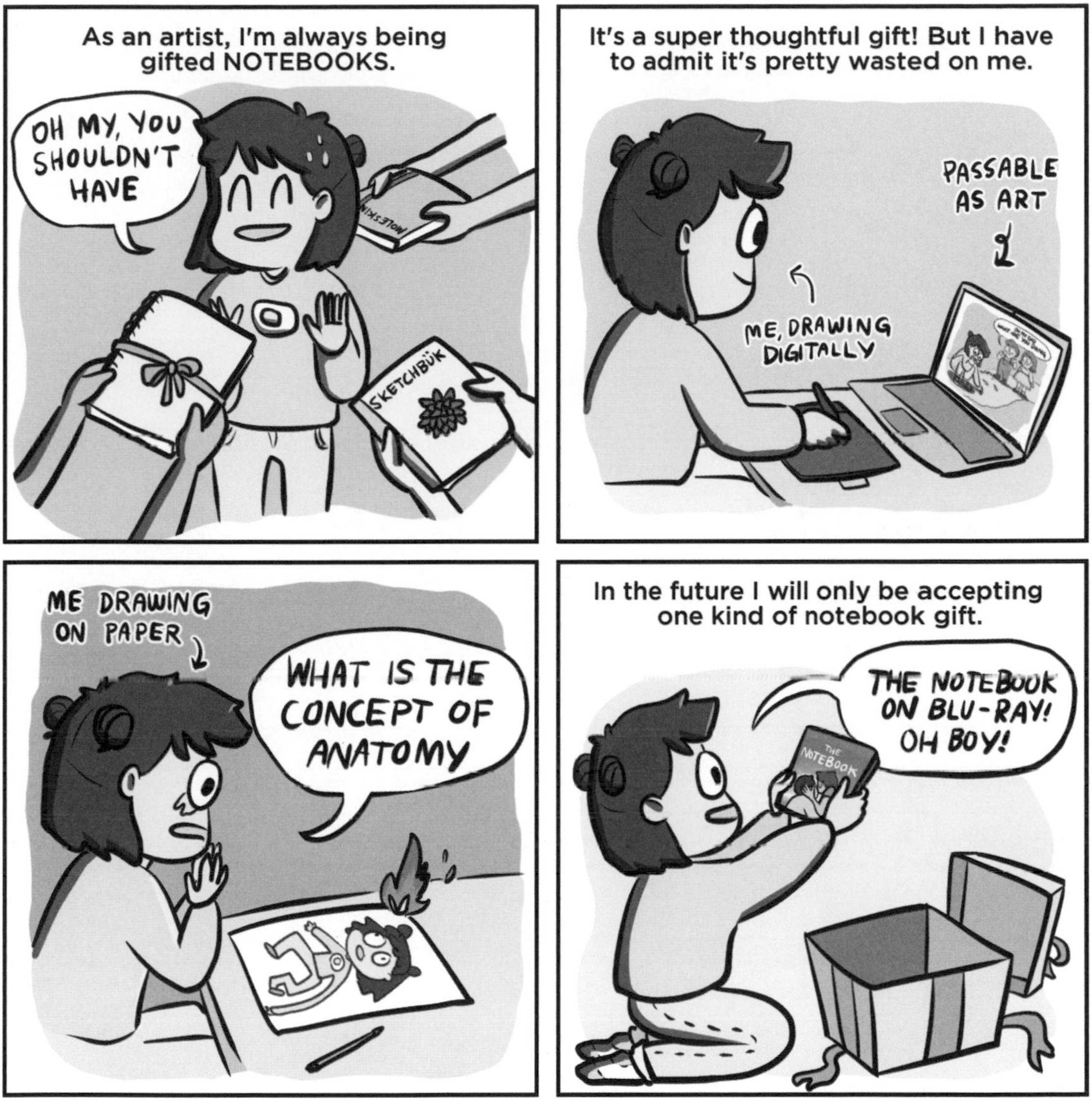
As an artist, I'm always being gifted NOTEBOOKS.
OH MY, YOU SHOULDN'T HAVE
MOLESKIN
SKETCHBÜK
It's a super thoughtful gift! But I have to admit it's pretty wasted on me.
PASSABLE AS ART
ME, DRAWING DIGITALLY
ME DRAWING ON PAPER
WHAT IS THE CONCEPT OF ANATOMY
In the future I will only be accepting one kind of notebook gift.
THE NOTEBOOK ON BLU-RAY! OH BOY!
THE NOTEBOOK

HOW TO GAIN RECOGNITION FOR YOUR WORK

SHEDDING

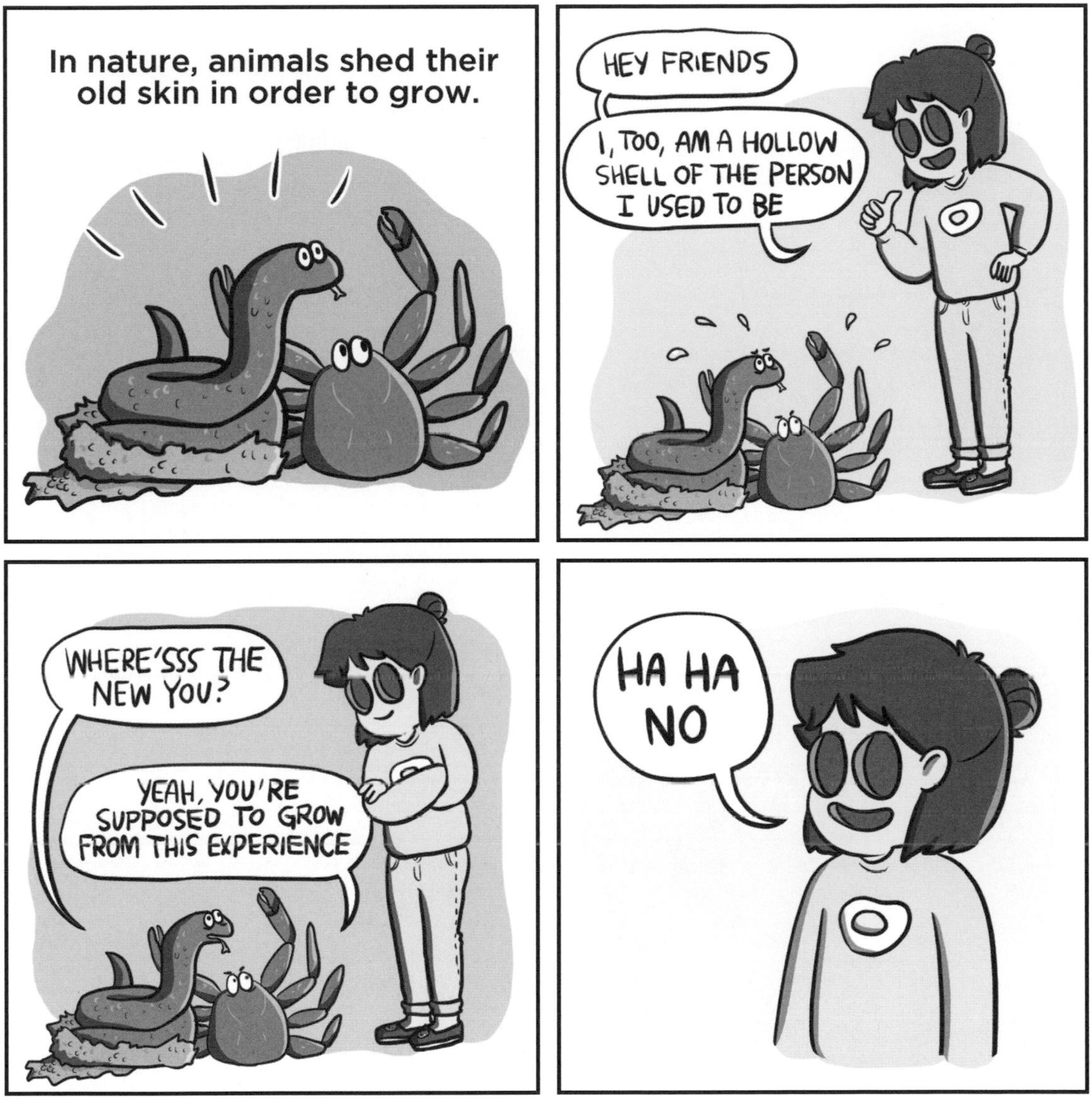

In nature, animals shed their old skin in order to grow.
HEY FRIENDS
I, TOO, AM A HOLLOW SHELL OF THE PERSON I USED TO BE
WHERE'SSS THE NEW YOU?
YEAH, YOU'RE SUPPOSED TO GROW FROM THIS EXPERIENCE
HA HA NO

INVESTED

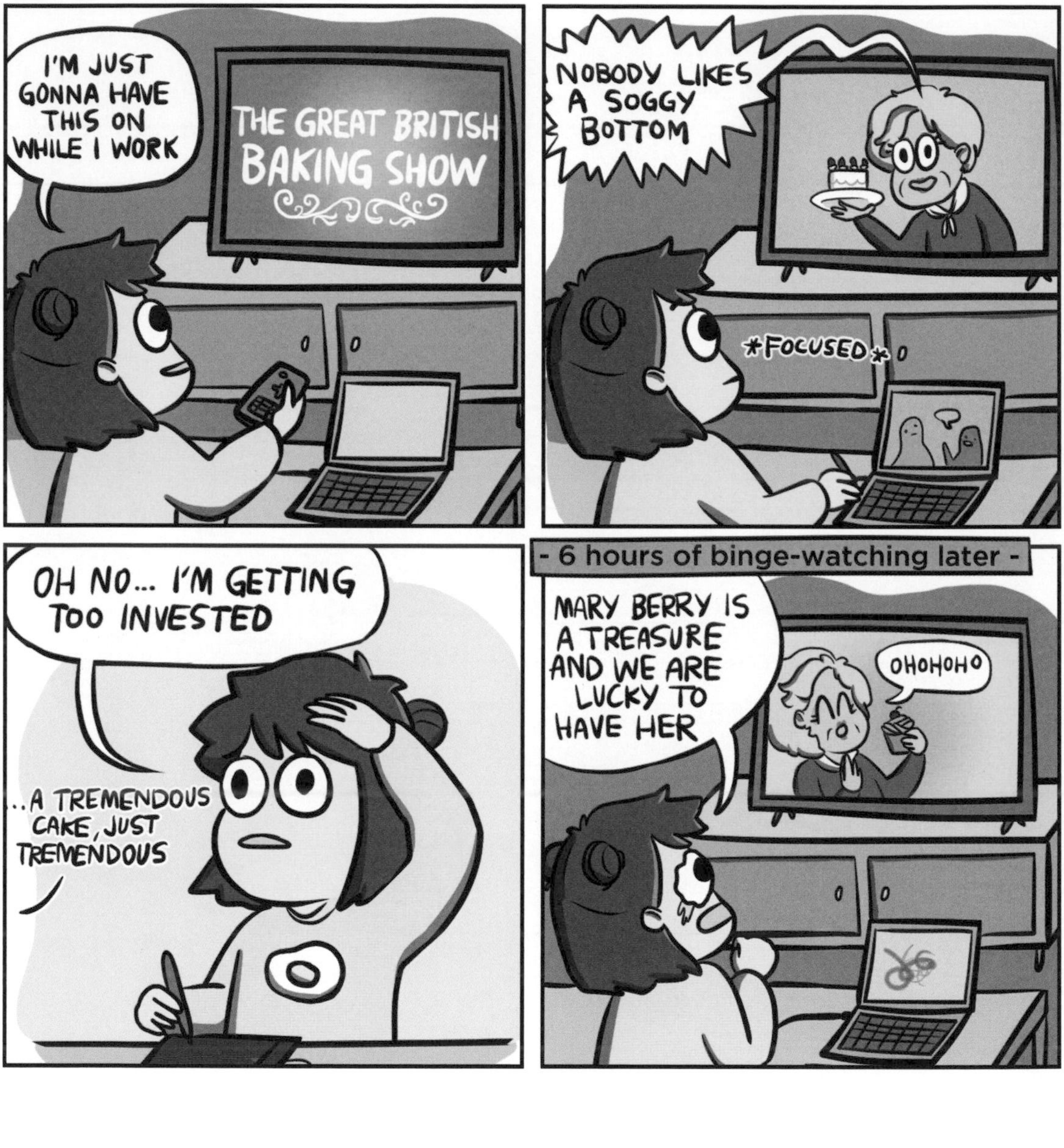
I'M JUST GONNA HAVE THIS ON WHILE I WORK
THE GREAT BRITISH BAKING SHOW
NOBODY LIKES A SOGGY BOTTOM
FOCUSED
OH NO... I'M GETTING TOO INVESTED
...A TREMENDOUS CAKE, JUST TREMENDOUS
- 6 hours of binge-watching later -
MARY BERRY IS A TREASURE AND WE ARE LUCKY TO HAVE HER
OHOHOHO

THE CREATIVE PROCESS

8AM

9AM

10AM

11AM

12PM

1PM

2PM

3PM

4PM

5PM

6PM

7PM

8PM

9PM

10PM

11PM

12AM

1AM

LITERALLY ME

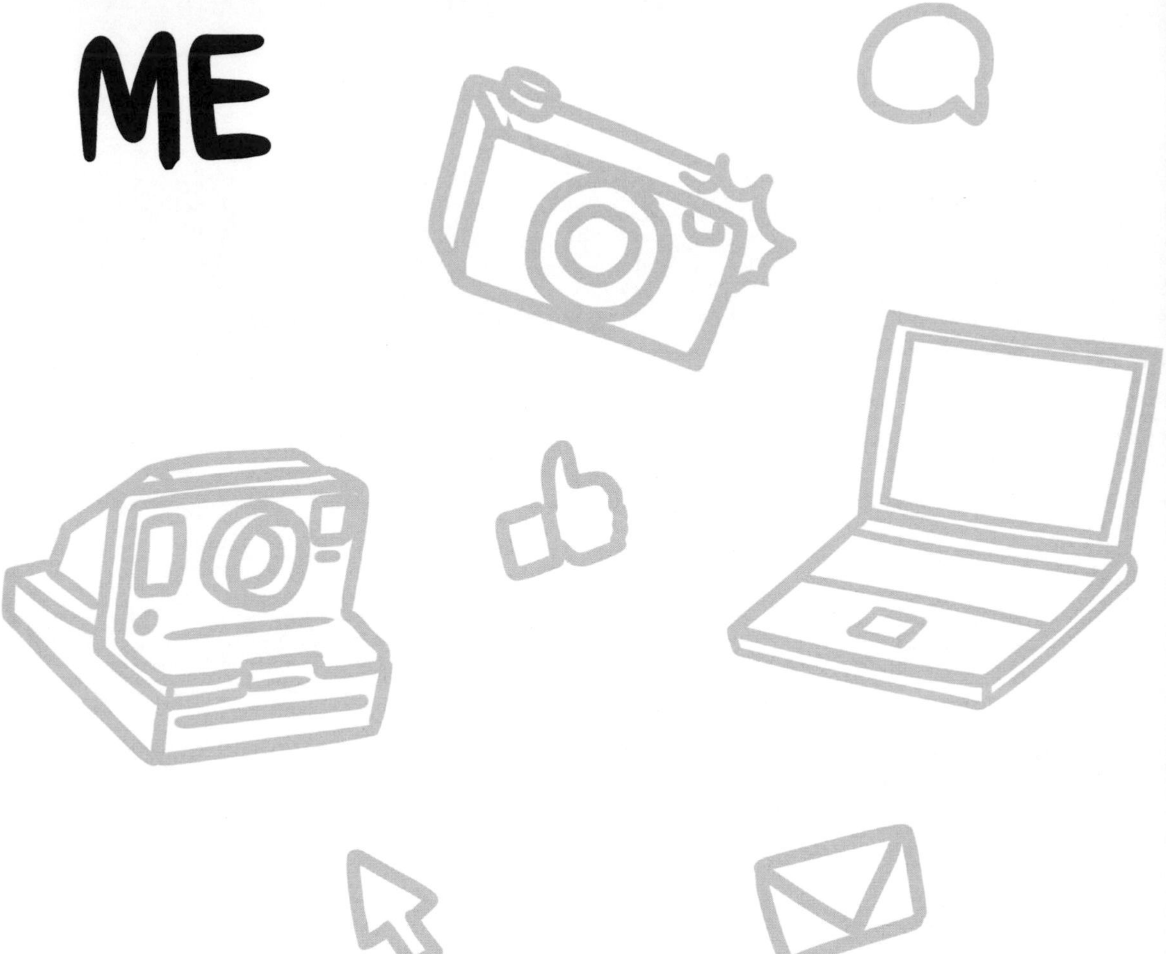

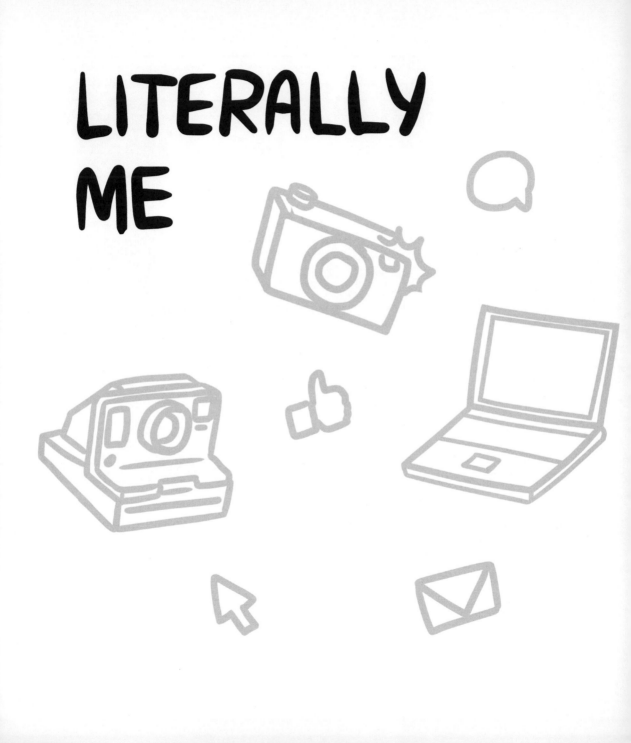

My relationship with technology is fraught and subject to the whims of whatever is happening on the internet that day. In TV sitcom terms, it's a sexy "will-they-won't-they" kind of tension. If some random jerk comments, "Why is this on my feed? This is stupid" on my comic? Blocked and reported. This relationship arc is going nowhere! A sweet, uplifting message from a young reader? I love the internet, let's get married!

As much as I like to dramatically claim that I'm "quitting the internet to become a shepherd," drawing a webcomic still has its merits. There's always someone out there in this vast world who will respond to the most obscure things that I think no one will be able to connect to. Sometimes, people relate more to my drawings than I do. Once, someone sent me a picture of a tattoo they got, which was inspired by one of my drawings—a man with four eels for a head. I can't say that image has any personal meaning for me, but I'm genuinely thrilled that it does for someone else.

One of the internet's greatest strengths is how it can remind you that you're never the only person to experience anything. I once drew a comic about wearing a traditional hanbok as a costume for my first Halloween, and was surprised to learn that other immigrants did this as well with their respective cultures' clothing.

So for the most part, the internet is good and I have enjoyed being on it. But if things ever get too overwhelming, I still follow a handful of farmers on Twitter to remind myself that a shepherd's life isn't too far out of reach.

EVERYDAY ON THE INTERNET

INTROSPECTION

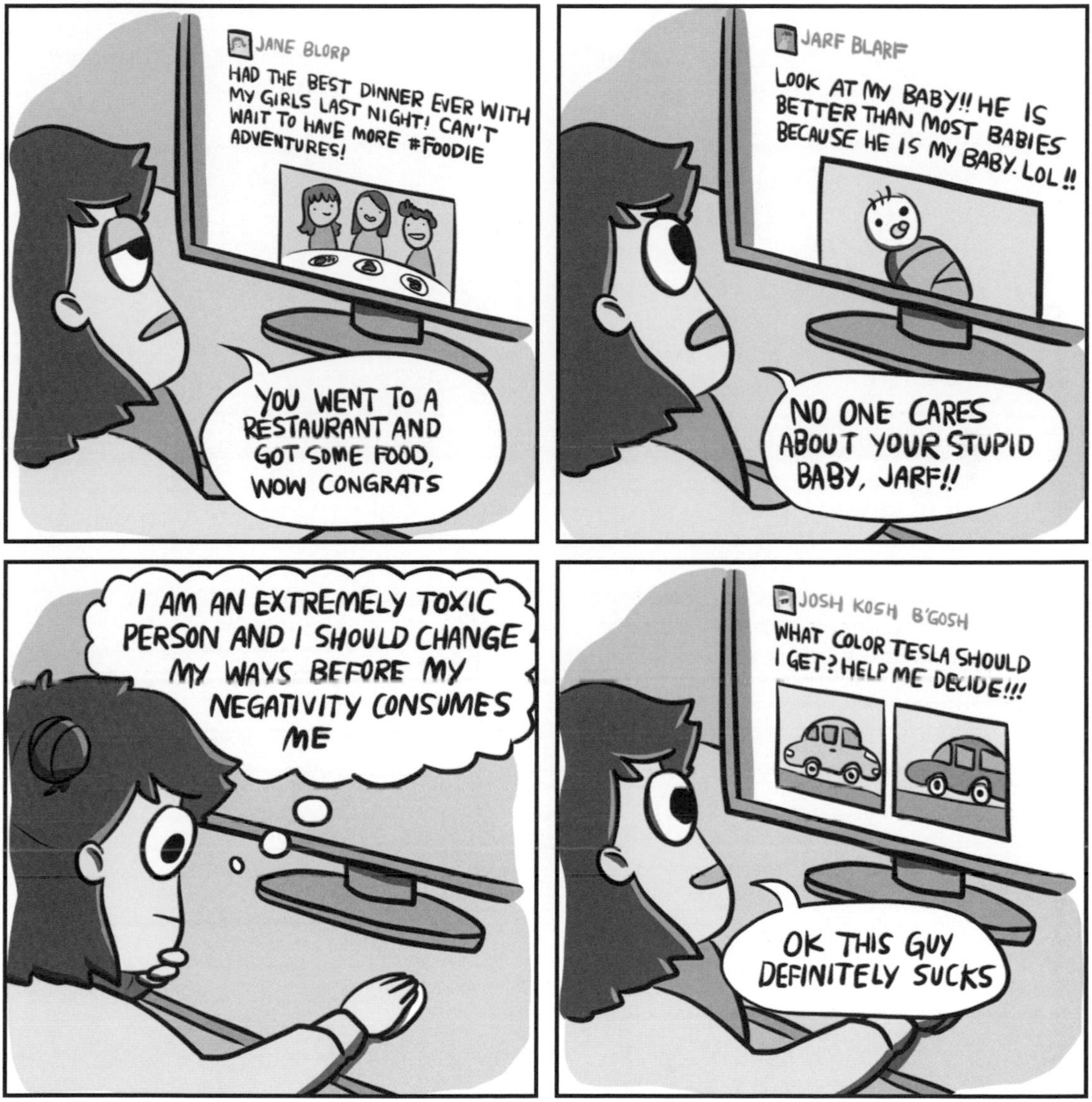
JANE BLORP
HAD THE BEST DINNER EVER WITH MY GIRLS LAST NIGHT! CAN'T WAIT TO HAVE MORE ADVENTURES! #FOODIE
YOU WENT TO A RESTAURANT AND GOT SOME FOOD, WOW CONGRATS
JARF BLARF
LOOK AT MY BABY!! HE IS BETTER THAN MOST BABIES BECAUSE HE IS MY BABY. LOL!!
NO ONE CARES ABOUT YOUR STUPID BABY, JARF!!
I AM AN EXTREMELY TOXIC PERSON AND I SHOULD CHANGE MY WAYS BEFORE MY NEGATIVITY CONSUMES ME
JOSH KOSH B'GOSH
WHAT COLOR TESLA SHOULD I GET? HELP ME DECIDE!!!
OK THIS GUY DEFINITELY SUCKS

HAUL VIDEOS

If I had a YouTube channel, I would only do Korean grocery store hauls.

HEY GUYS! TODAY, LIKE ALL DAYS, I'M GONNA SHOW YOU WHAT I GOT FROM H-MART!

H MART

The series would start off with a lot of promise...

LOOK AT ALL THIS STUFF!!

...but quickly devolve as I realize that constantly buying large quantities of groceries is unsustainable.

TODAY I JUST HAVE THIS, UM, CARTON OF SOY MILK

It would be deeply unsatisfying to viewers.

OH HERE'S AN OLD, DRIED-UP SHRIMP CHIP I FOUND UNDER THE TABLE, DOES THIS COUNT?

COMMENTS

R RyanBananas
i didn't think I could be so let down so much by a youtube video, but i was

T Teriyaki_Bob
i'm depressed now

ALWAYS ANSWER YOUR PHONE

ONLINE SHOPPING

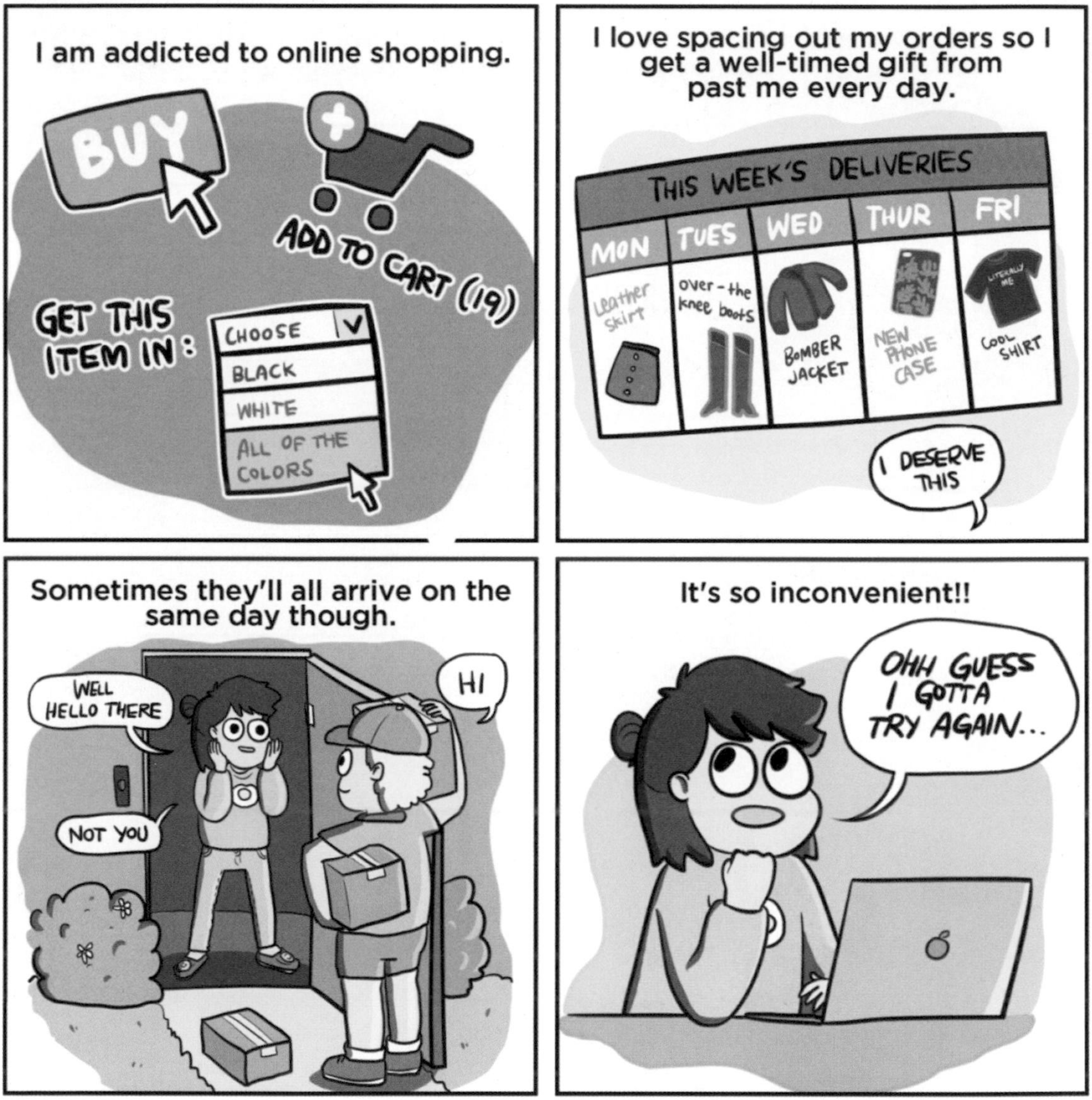
I am addicted to online shopping.
BUY
ADD TO CART (19)
GET THIS ITEM IN:
CHOOSE
BLACK
WHITE
ALL OF THE COLORS
I love spacing out my orders so I get a well-timed gift from past me every day.
THIS WEEK'S DELIVERIES
MON
TUES
WED
THUR
FRI
Leather Skirt
over-the knee boots
BOMBER JACKET
NEW PHONE CASE
COOL SHIRT
I DESERVE THIS
Sometimes they'll all arrive on the same day though.
WELL HELLO THERE
HI
NOT YOU
It's so inconvenient!!
OHH GUESS I GOTTA TRY AGAIN...

UNREALISTIC EXPECTATIONS

FLÜRB, THE SOCIAL NETWORK I INVENTED TO NOT DO ANY WORK

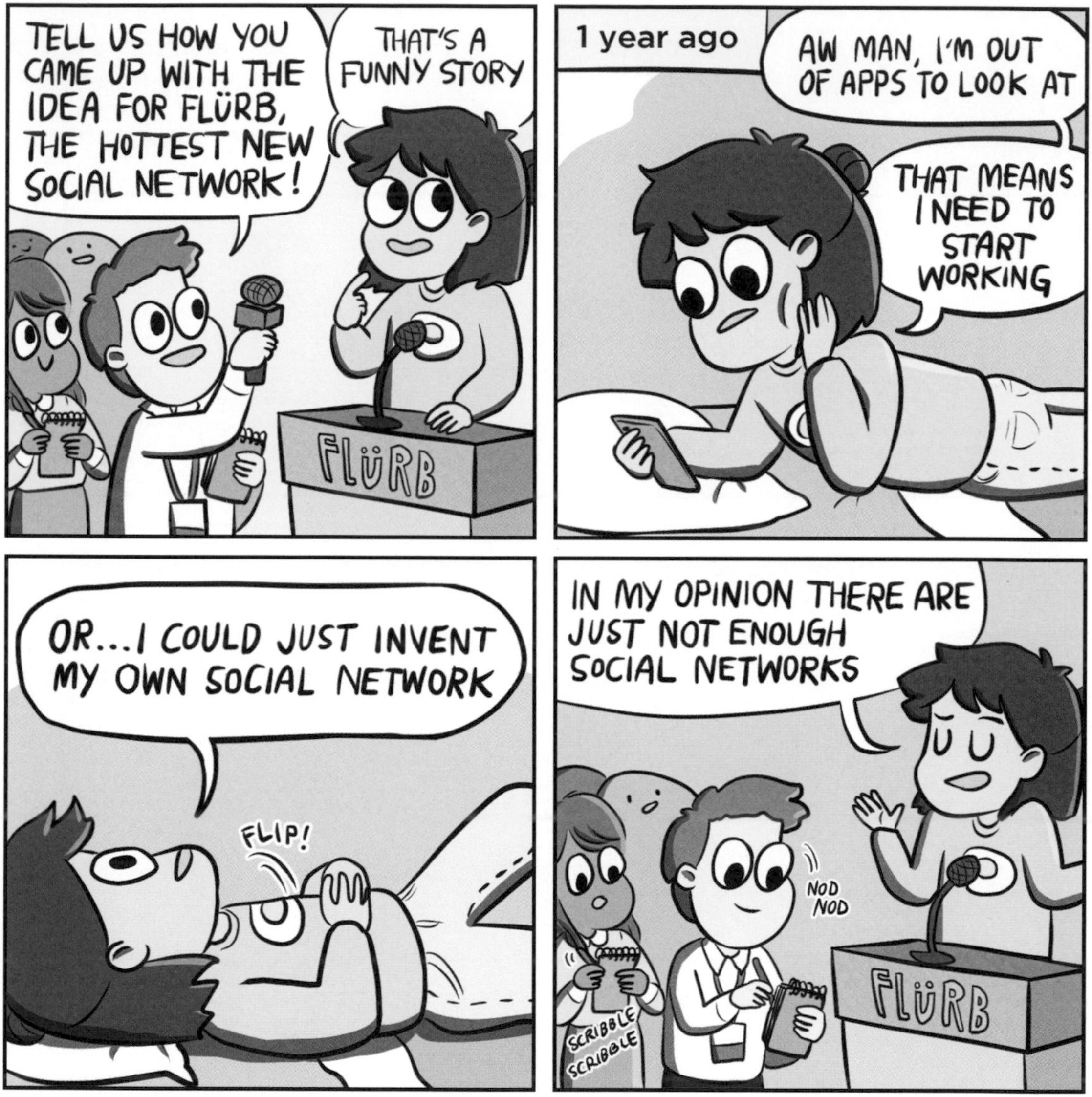

TELL US HOW YOU CAME UP WITH THE IDEA FOR FLÜRB, THE HOTTEST NEW SOCIAL NETWORK!
THAT'S A FUNNY STORY
FLÜRB
1 year ago
AW MAN, I'M OUT OF APPS TO LOOK AT
THAT MEANS I NEED TO START WORKING
OR...I COULD JUST INVENT MY OWN SOCIAL NETWORK
FLIP!
IN MY OPINION THERE ARE JUST NOT ENOUGH SOCIAL NETWORKS
NOD NOD
SCRIBBLE SCRIBBLE
FLÜRB

GOOD SHIBES

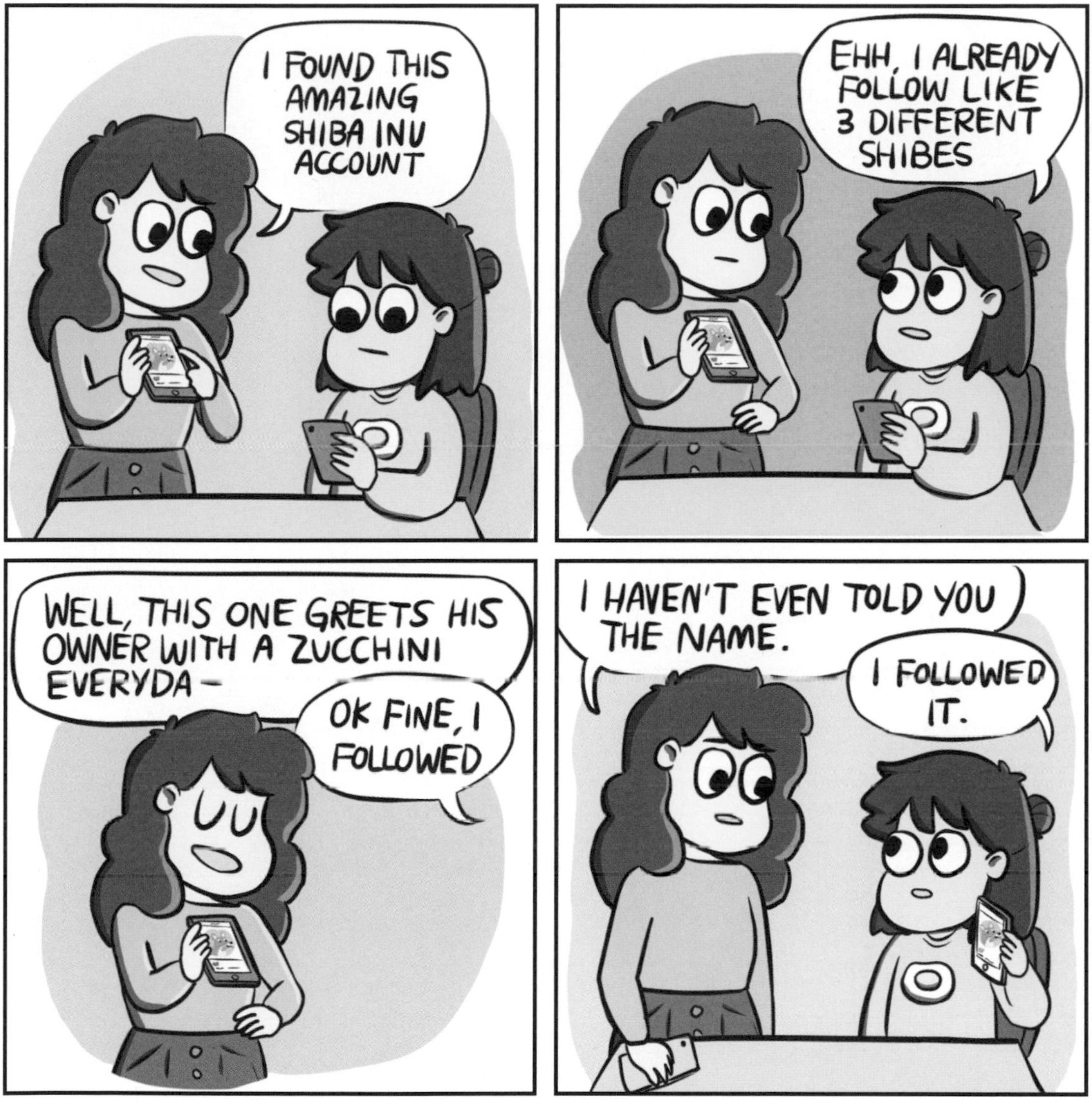
I FOUND THIS AMAZING SHIBA INU ACCOUNT
EHH, I ALREADY FOLLOW LIKE 3 DIFFERENT SHIBES
WELL, THIS ONE GREETS HIS OWNER WITH A ZUCCHINI EVERYDA–
OK FINE, I FOLLOWED
I HAVEN'T EVEN TOLD YOU THE NAME.
I FOLLOWED IT.

GOLDFISH MEMORY

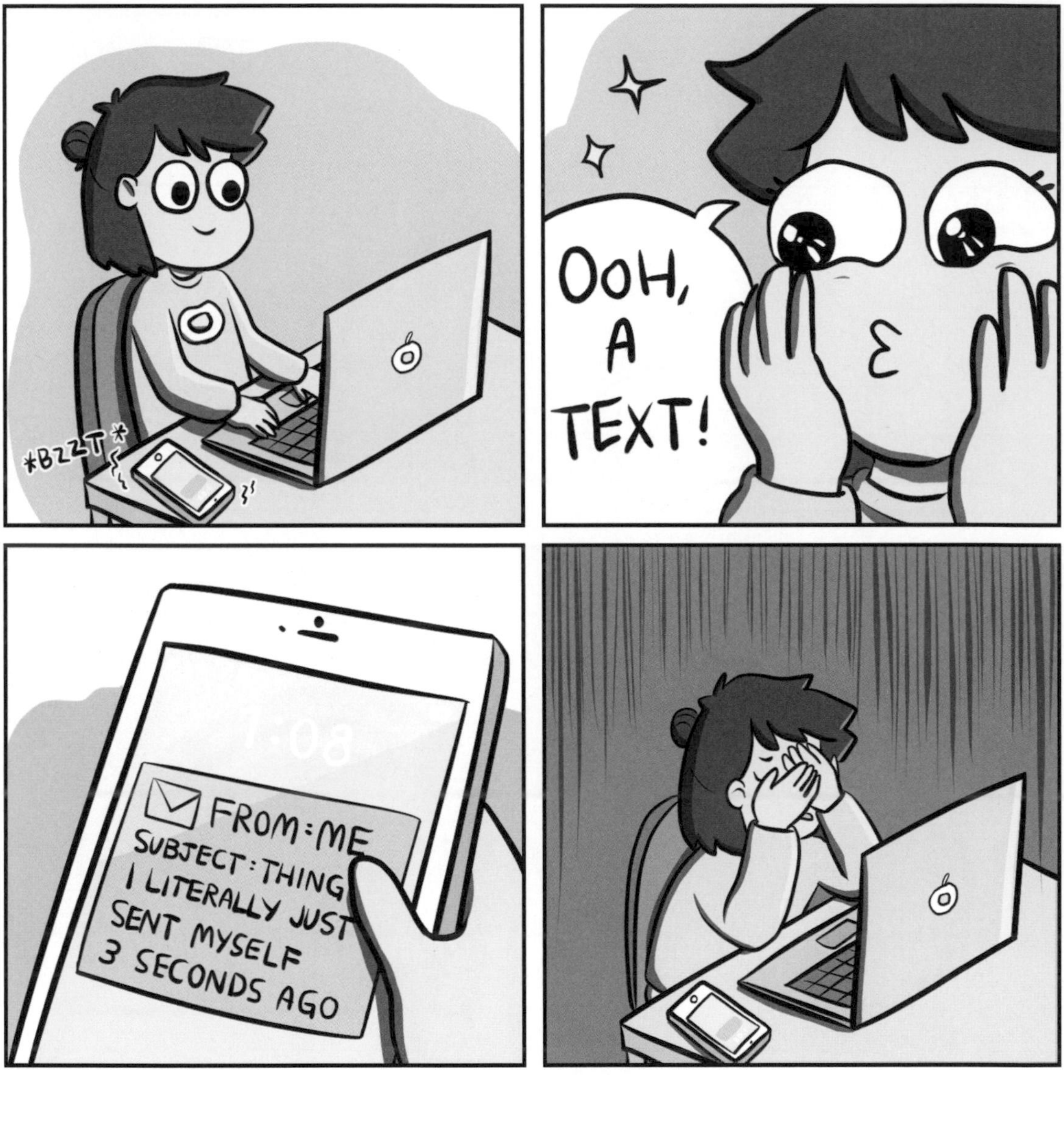
BZZT
OOH, A TEXT!
FROM: ME
SUBJECT: THING I LITERALLY JUST SENT MYSELF 3 SECONDS AGO

SPLOOT

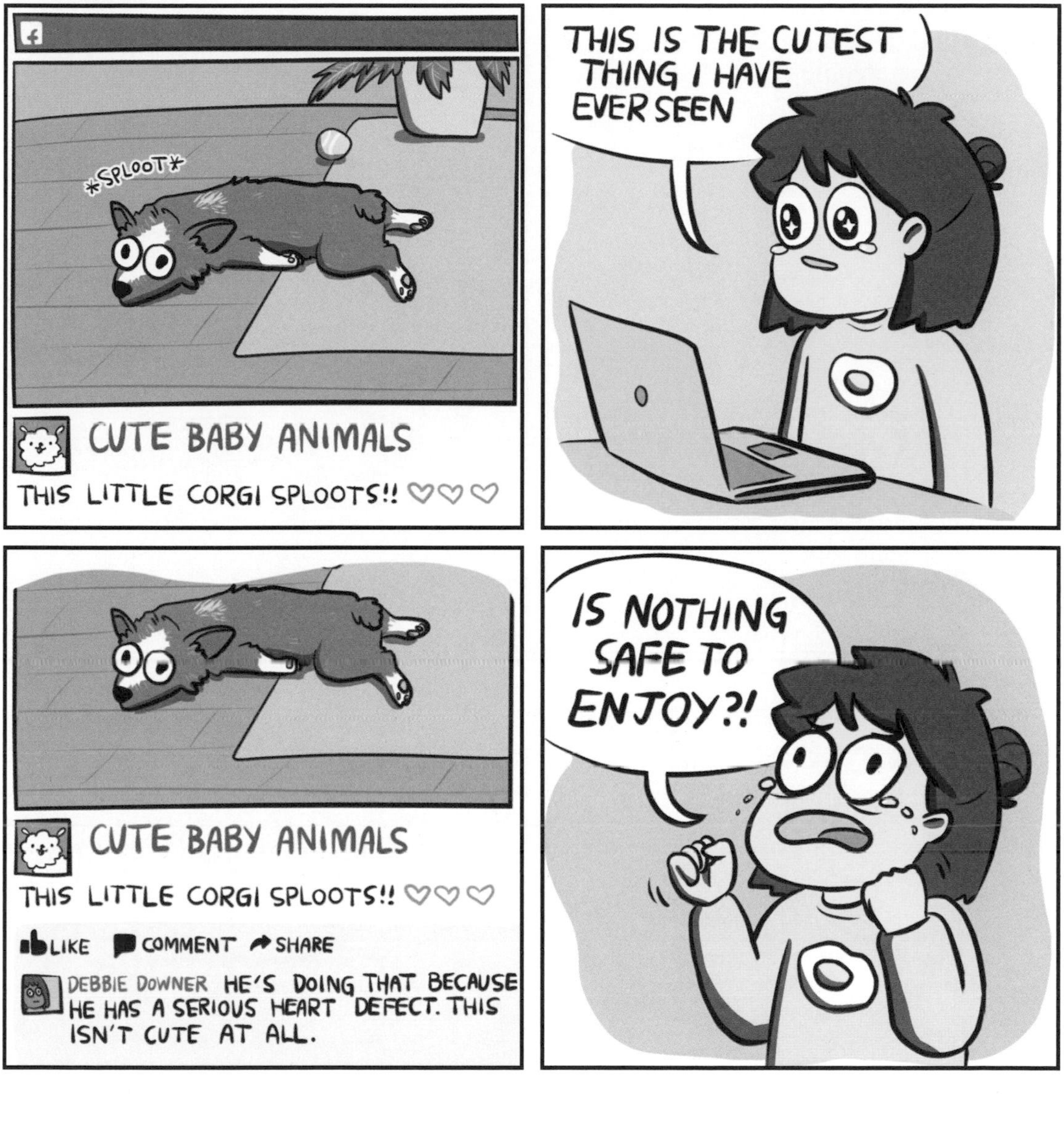
SPLOOT
CUTE BABY ANIMALS
THIS LITTLE CORGI SPLOOTS!!
THIS IS THE CUTEST THING I HAVE EVER SEEN
CUTE BABY ANIMALS
THIS LITTLE CORGI SPLOOTS!!
LIKE COMMENT SHARE
DEBBIE DOWNER HE'S DOING THAT BECAUSE HE HAS A SERIOUS HEART DEFECT. THIS ISN'T CUTE AT ALL.
IS NOTHING SAFE TO ENJOY?!

FOOD BLOGGER

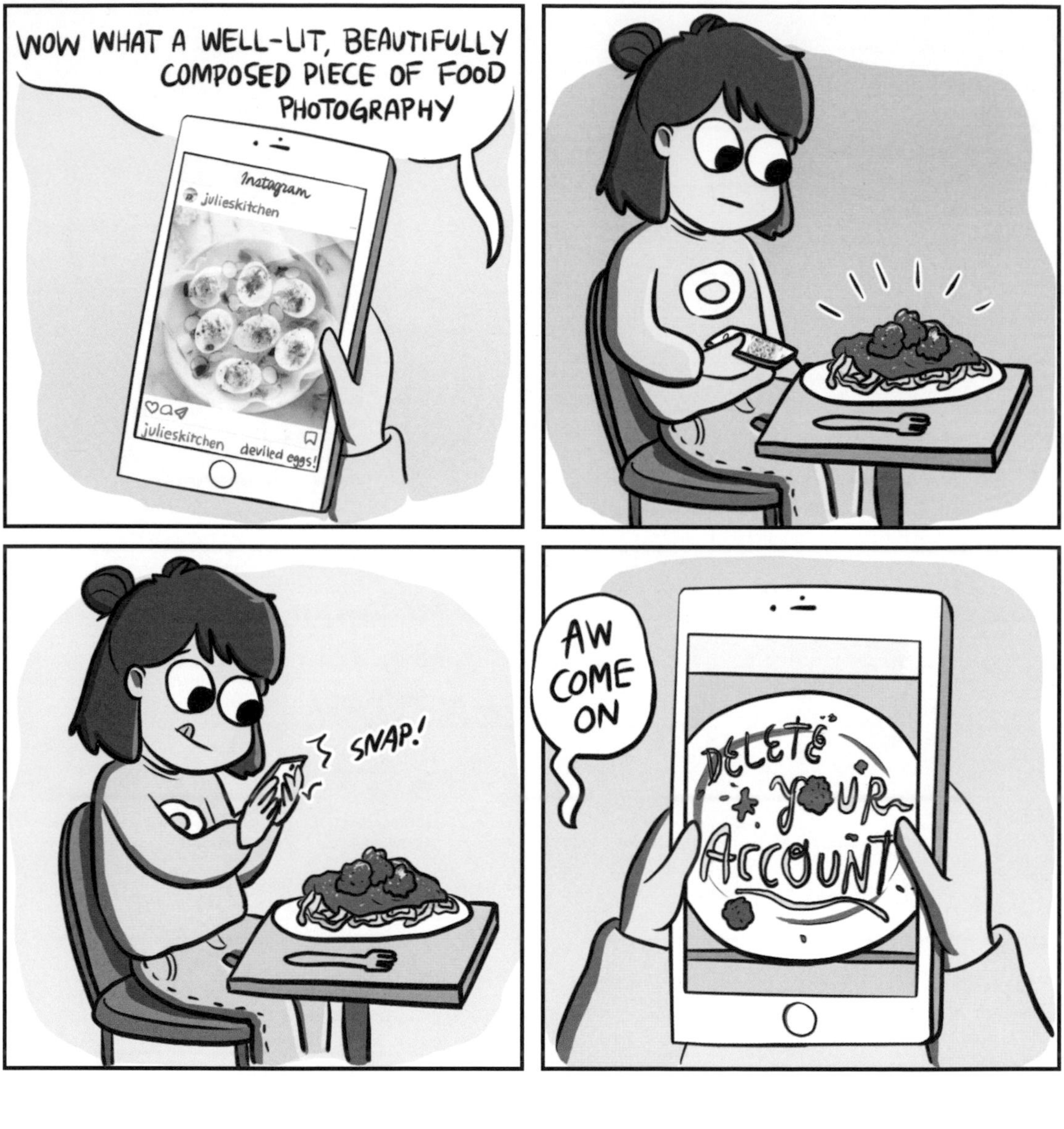
WOW WHAT A WELL-LIT, BEAUTIFULLY COMPOSED PIECE OF FOOD PHOTOGRAPHY
Instagram
julieskitchen
julieskitchen deviled eggs!
SNAP!
AW COME ON
DELETE YOUR ACCOUNT

KILL TWO BIRDS WITH ONE STONE

THE ONLY DESK I NEED

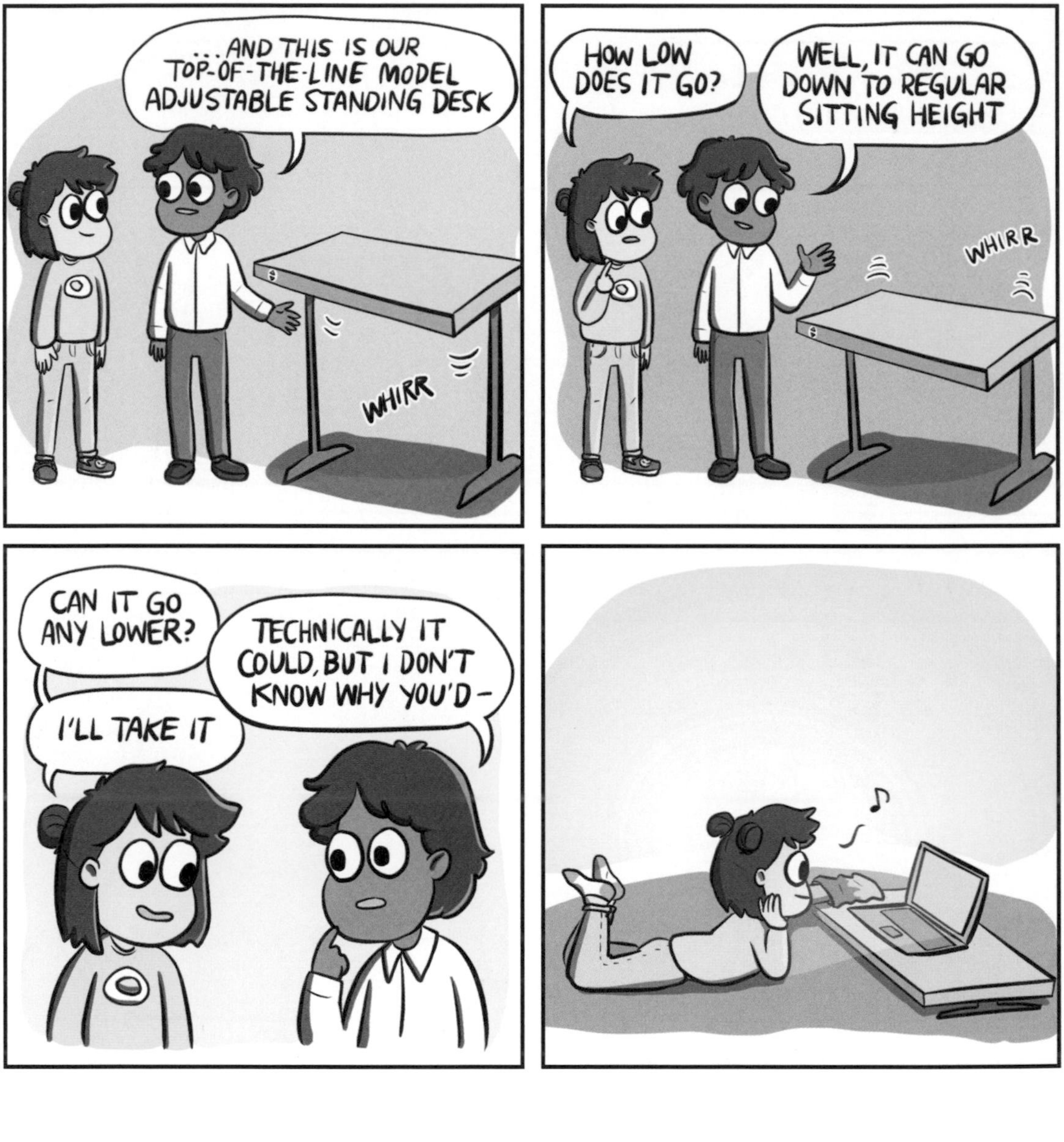

...AND THIS IS OUR TOP-OF-THE-LINE MODEL ADJUSTABLE STANDING DESK
WHIRR
HOW LOW DOES IT GO?
WELL, IT CAN GO DOWN TO REGULAR SITTING HEIGHT
WHIRR
CAN IT GO ANY LOWER?
TECHNICALLY IT COULD, BUT I DON'T KNOW WHY YOU'D-
I'LL TAKE IT

COMMUTE JAMS

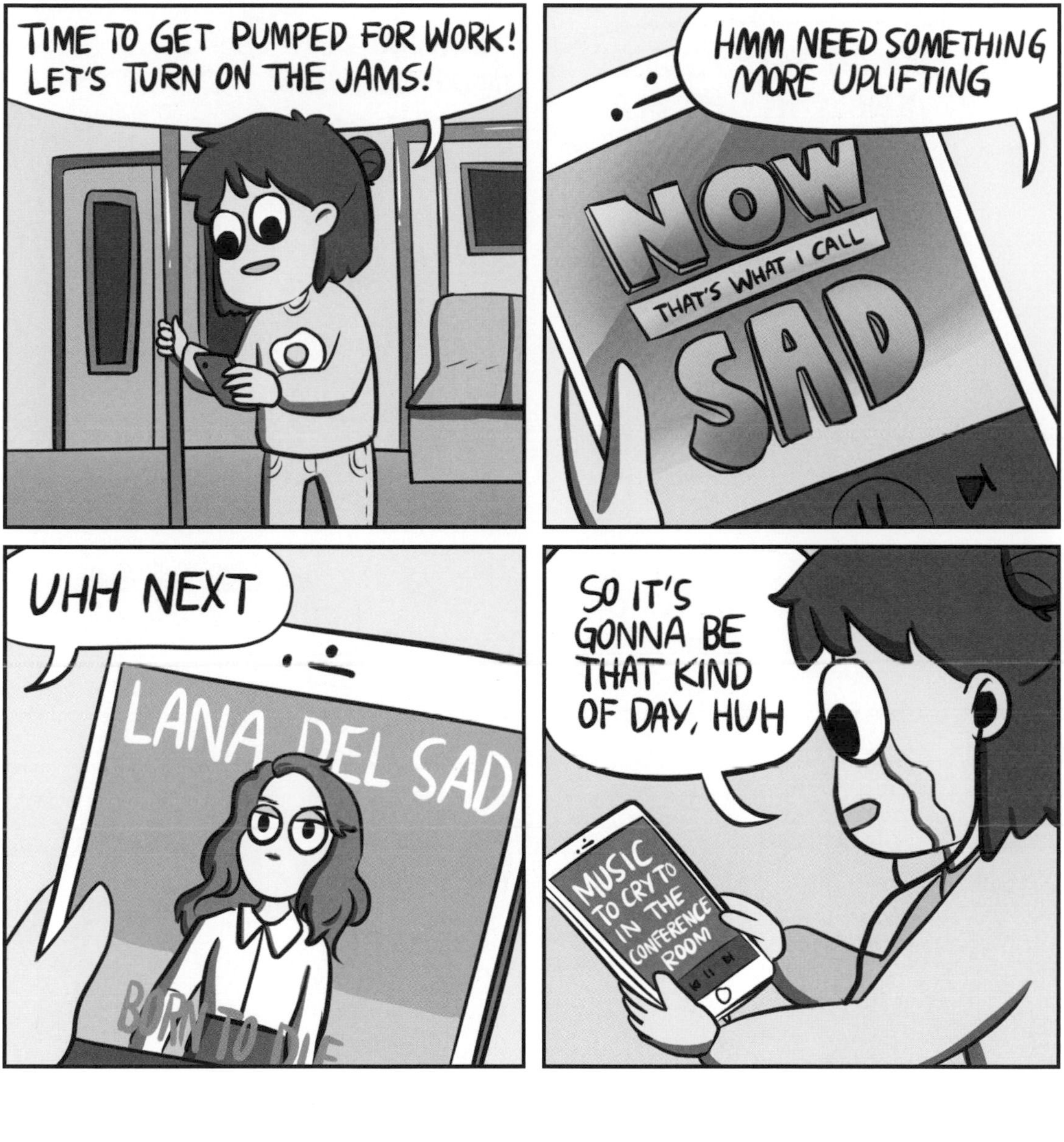
TIME TO GET PUMPED FOR WORK! LET'S TURN ON THE JAMS!
HMM NEED SOMETHING MORE UPLIFTING
NOW
THAT'S WHAT I CALL
SAD
UHH NEXT
LANA DEL SAD
SO IT'S GONNA BE THAT KIND OF DAY, HUH
MUSIC TO CRY TO IN THE CONFERENCE ROOM

ONE-UP

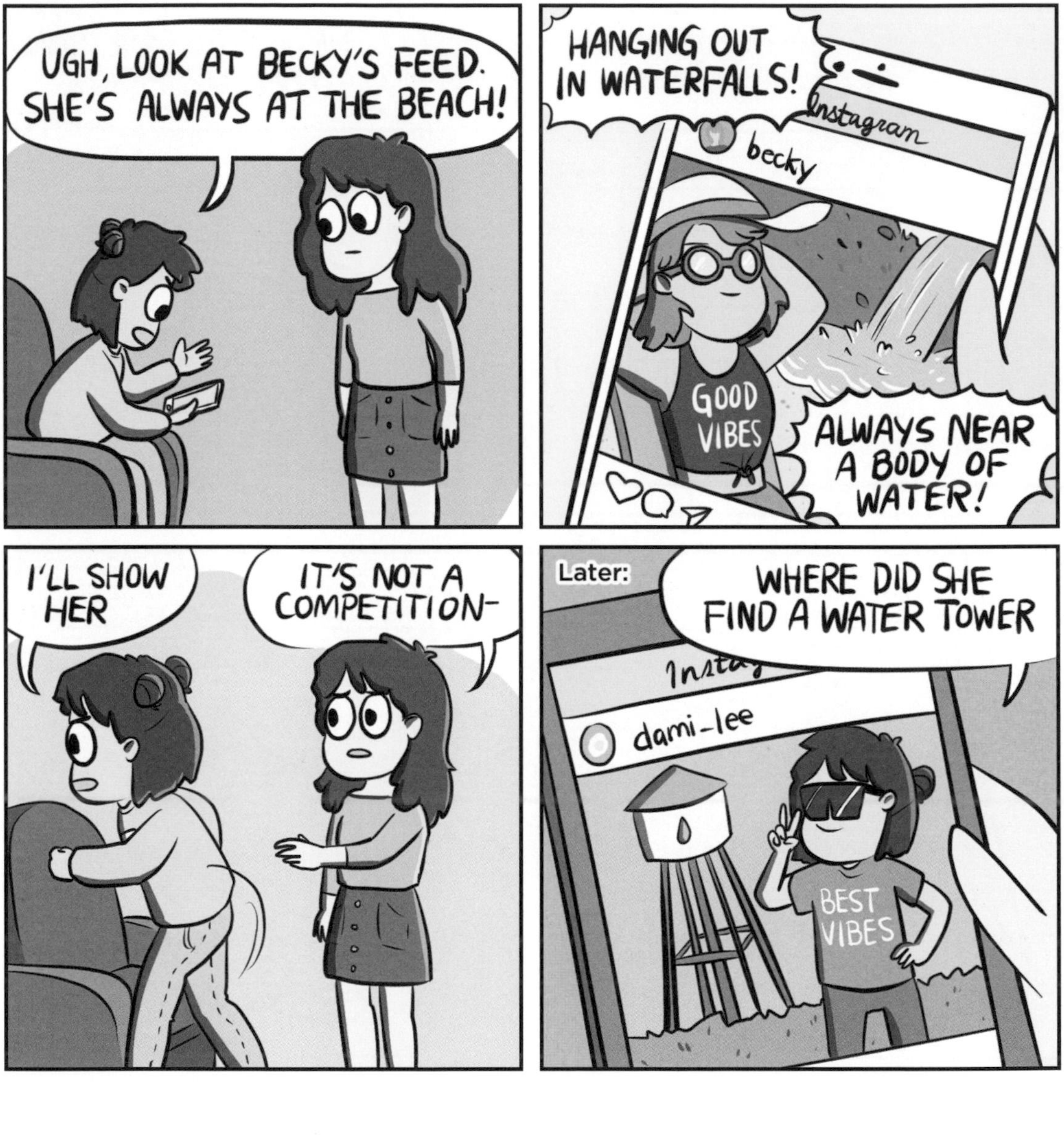
UGH, LOOK AT BECKY'S FEED. SHE'S ALWAYS AT THE BEACH!
HANGING OUT IN WATERFALLS!
Instagram
becky
GOOD VIBES
ALWAYS NEAR A BODY OF WATER!
I'LL SHOW HER
IT'S NOT A COMPETITION-
Later:
WHERE DID SHE FIND A WATER TOWER
dami_lee
BEST VIBES

REARRANGING MY MIND

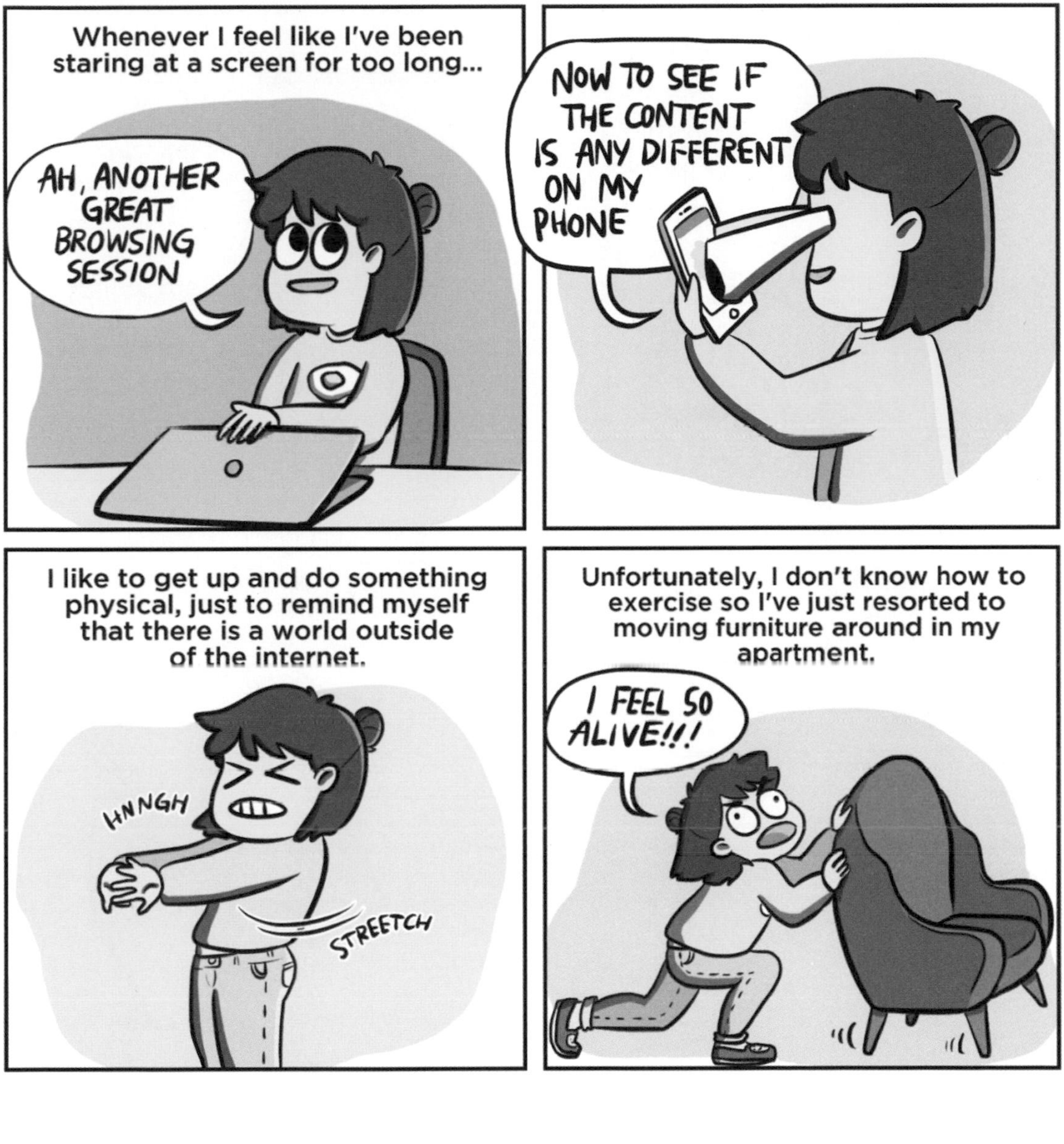
Whenever I feel like I've been staring at a screen for too long...
AH, ANOTHER GREAT BROWSING SESSION
NOW TO SEE IF THE CONTENT IS ANY DIFFERENT ON MY PHONE
I like to get up and do something physical, just to remind myself that there is a world outside of the internet.
HNNGH
STREETCH
Unfortunately, I don't know how to exercise so I've just resorted to moving furniture around in my apartment.
I FEEL SO ALIVE!!!

A WELL-DESERVED BREAK

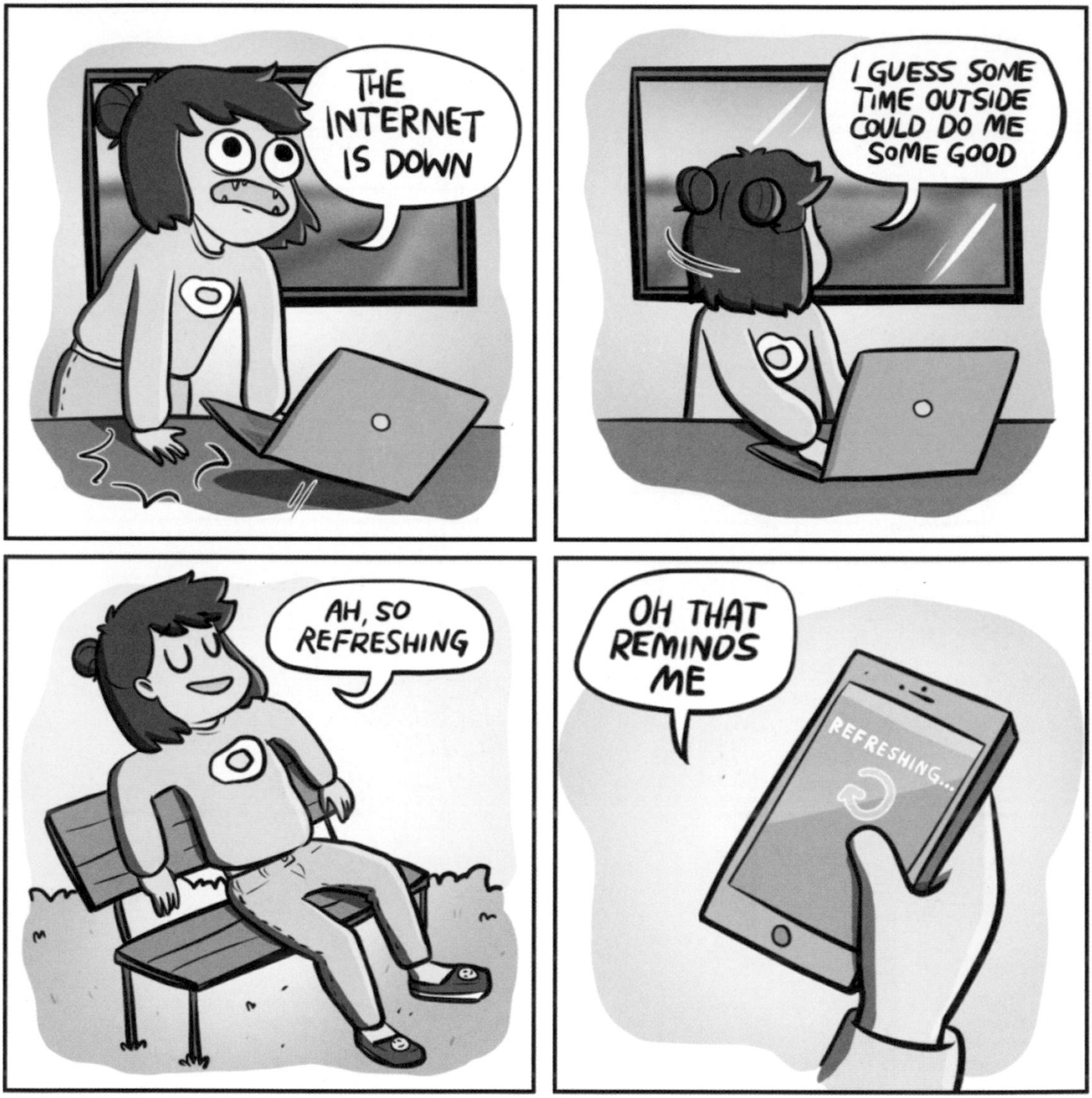
THE INTERNET IS DOWN
I GUESS SOME TIME OUTSIDE COULD DO ME SOME GOOD
AH, SO REFRESHING
OH THAT REMINDS ME
REFRESHING...

THE TRAP

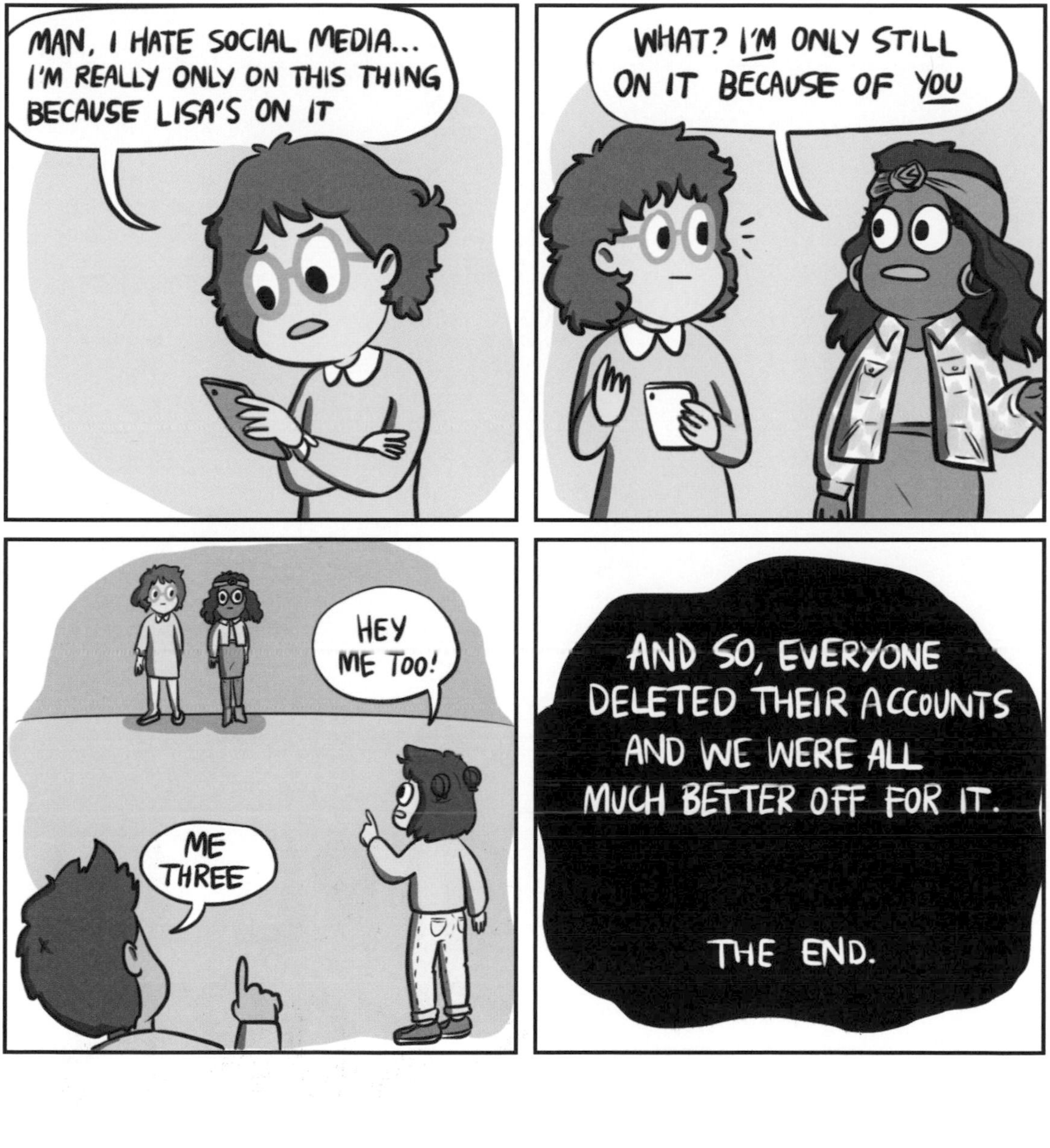

MAN, I HATE SOCIAL MEDIA... I'M REALLY ONLY ON THIS THING BECAUSE LISA'S ON IT
WHAT? I'M ONLY STILL ON IT BECAUSE OF YOU
HEY ME TOO!
ME THREE
AND SO, EVERYONE DELETED THEIR ACCOUNTS AND WE WERE ALL MUCH BETTER OFF FOR IT.
THE END.

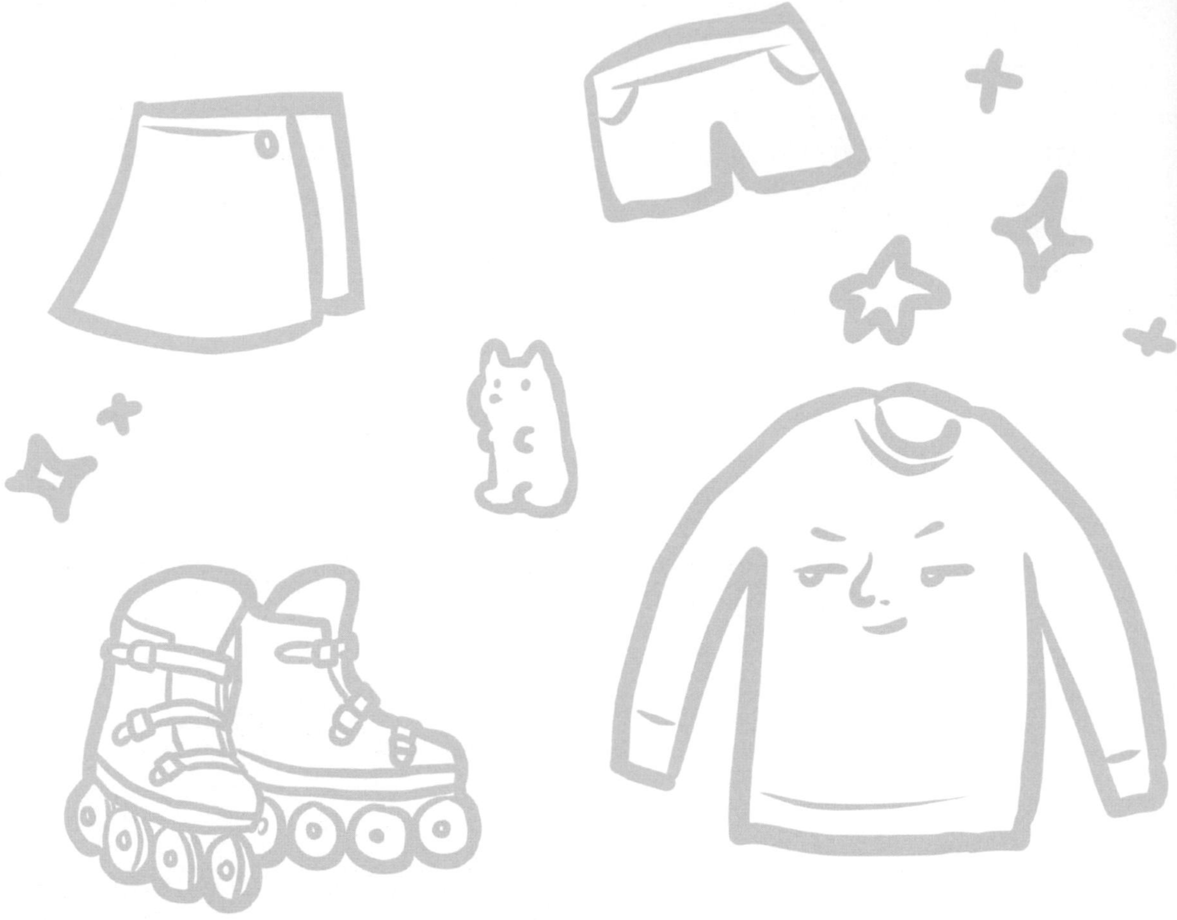

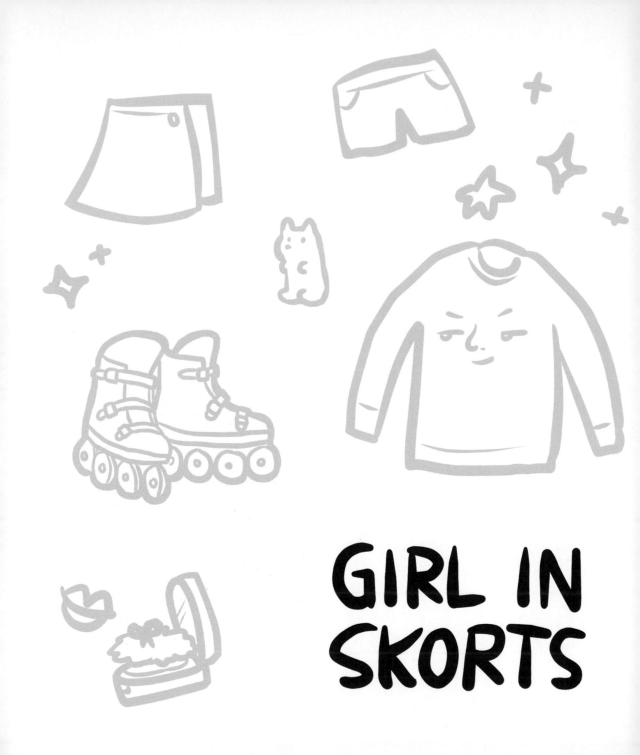

GIRL IN SKORTS

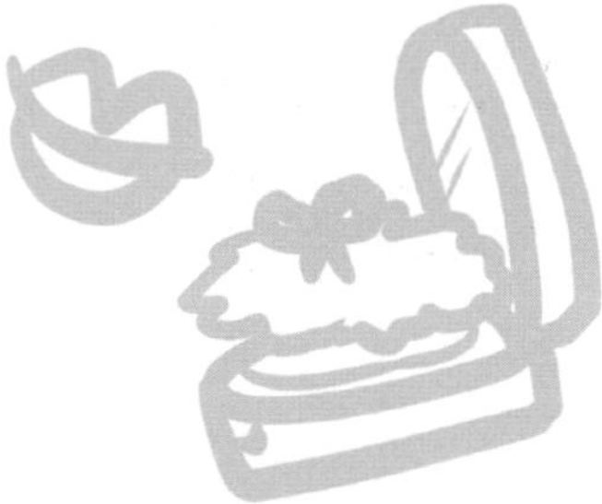

Nobody ever believes me when I tell them I was a tomboy. As the sedentary person I am today, I too, can hardly believe that I was once a ball of rambunctious energy constantly covered in bruises. My mom always had plans to dress me in ultra-feminine, ruffly dresses, which would get trashed the minute I stepped outside. So we compromised. For much of my formative years, I wore skorts. Many, many skorts.

The skorts always felt like a metaphor. Girlhood is a series of endless compromises, where girls are always having to find the line between what's expected of us and what we really want. Like, I want to be able to keep shopping at Forever 21, but the Lord had other plans for me by aging me to 28.

Skorts, like women, are complex. They're more than they appear. Though they have the exterior look of a skirt, it's as if they're whispering, "I've got a secret, and the secret is that the shorts underneath afford me a forgiving free range of motion with my legs."

Strained metaphors aside, it's actually a lot of fun being a girl! You can play around with makeup, you can film yourself playing around with makeup, and most importantly, you can get that sweet YouTube money from filming yourself play around with makeup. The most satisfying victories come from doing what you were told you can't do. Personally, I have been mostly driven by spite for all of my achievements. You just have to find what works for you.

WONDER WOMAN

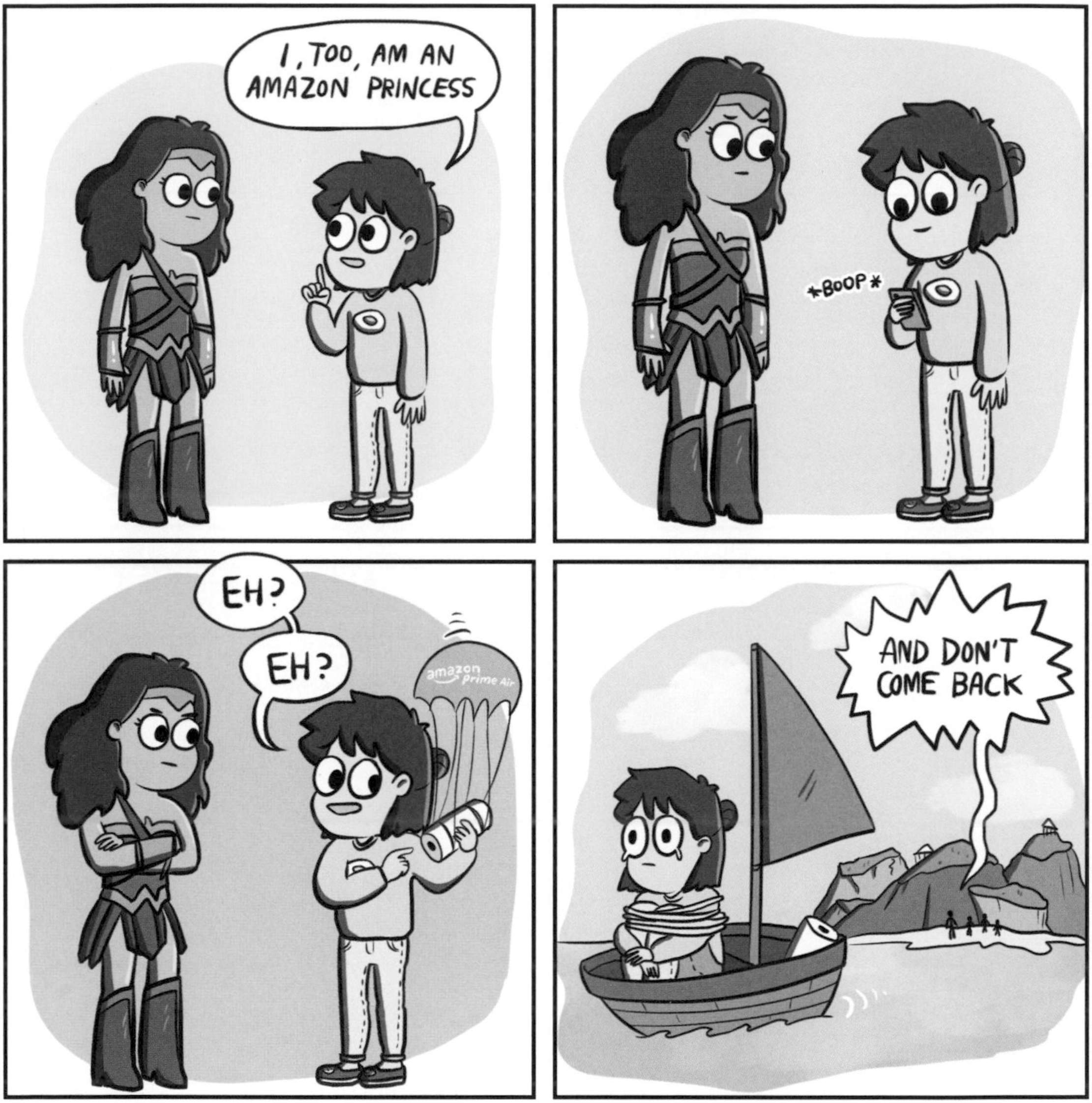
I, TOO, AM AN AMAZON PRINCESS
BOOP
EH?
EH?
amazon Prime Air
AND DON'T COME BACK

WHAT TO WEAR

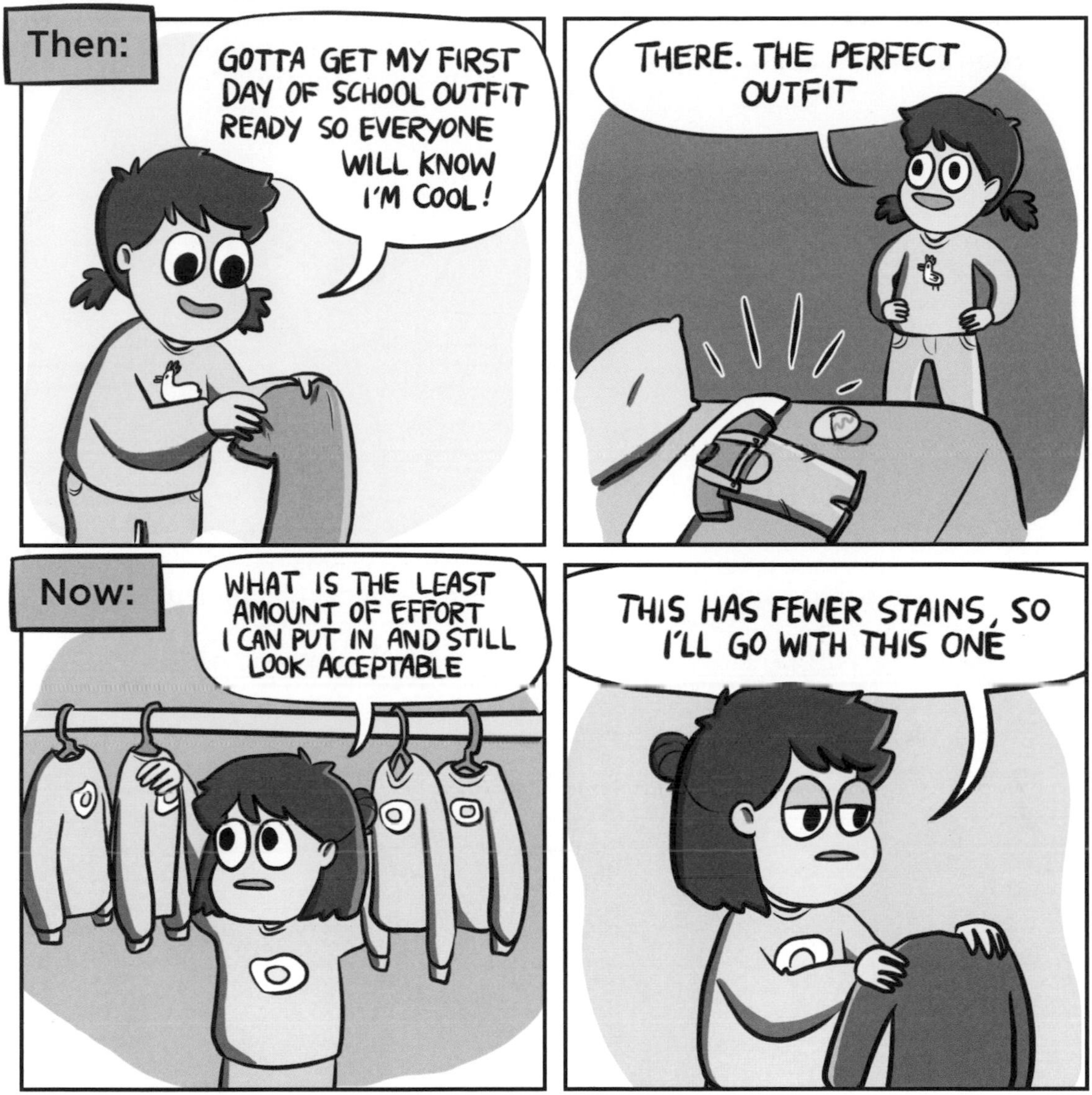

Then:
GOTTA GET MY FIRST DAY OF SCHOOL OUTFIT READY SO EVERYONE WILL KNOW I'M COOL!
THERE. THE PERFECT OUTFIT
Now:
WHAT IS THE LEAST AMOUNT OF EFFORT I CAN PUT IN AND STILL LOOK ACCEPTABLE
THIS HAS FEWER STAINS, SO I'LL GO WITH THIS ONE

CROP TOPS

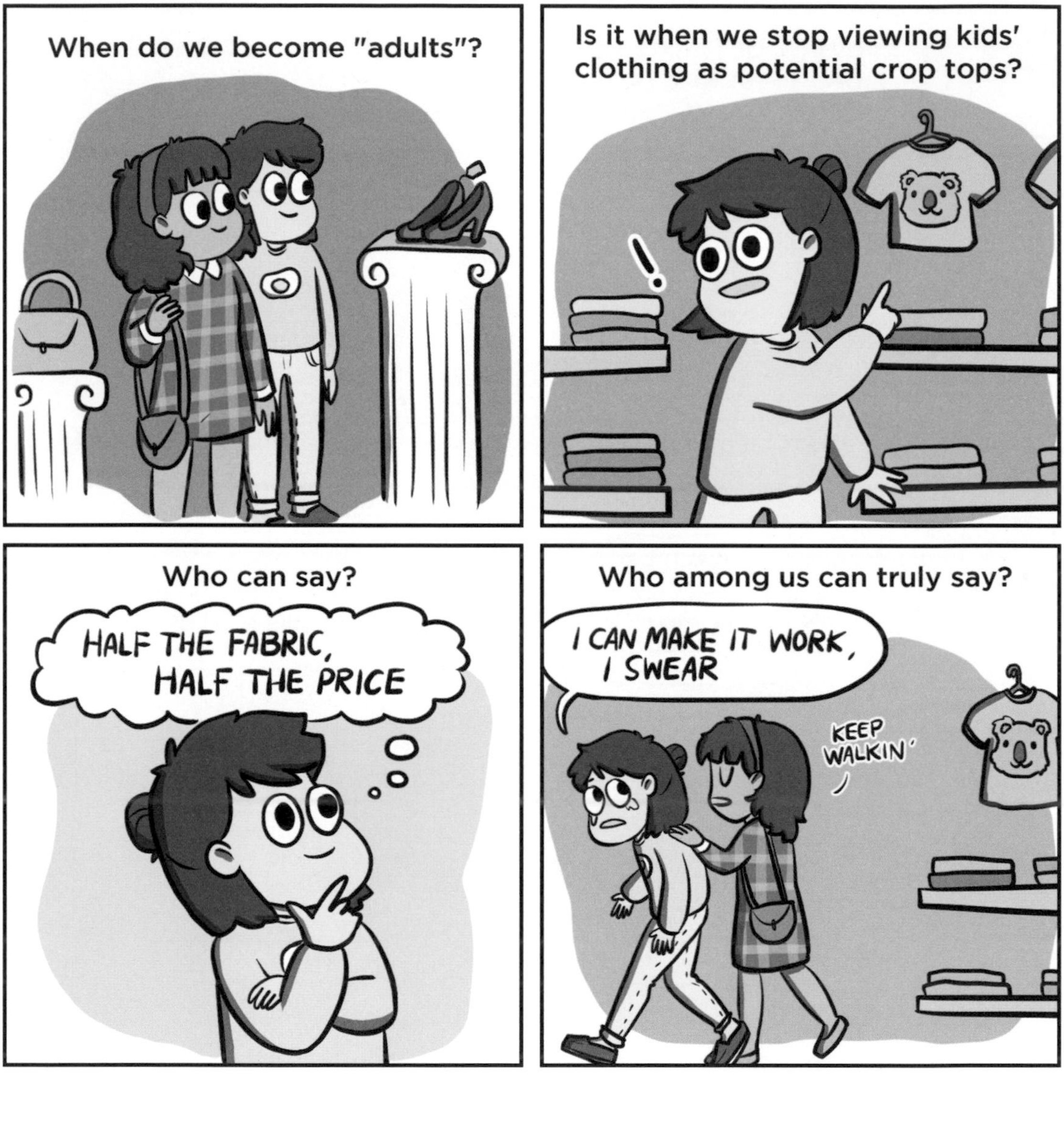
When do we become "adults"?
Is it when we stop viewing kids' clothing as potential crop tops?
!
Who can say?
HALF THE FABRIC, HALF THE PRICE
Who among us can truly say?
I CAN MAKE IT WORK, I SWEAR
KEEP WALKIN'

BOYFRIEND MATERIAL

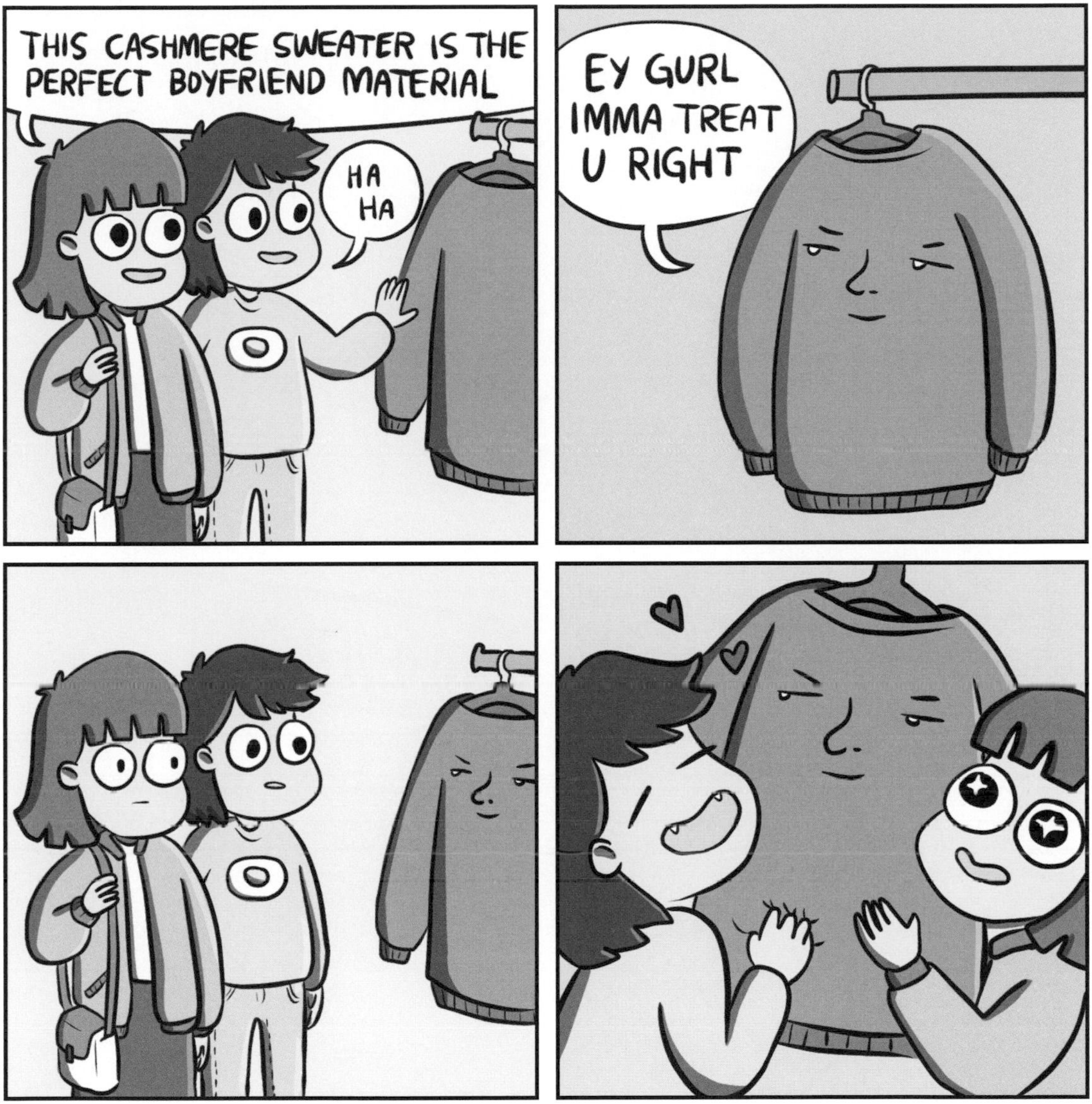

THIS CASHMERE SWEATER IS THE PERFECT BOYFRIEND MATERIAL
HA HA
EY GURL IMMA TREAT U RIGHT

NEVER TOO OLD

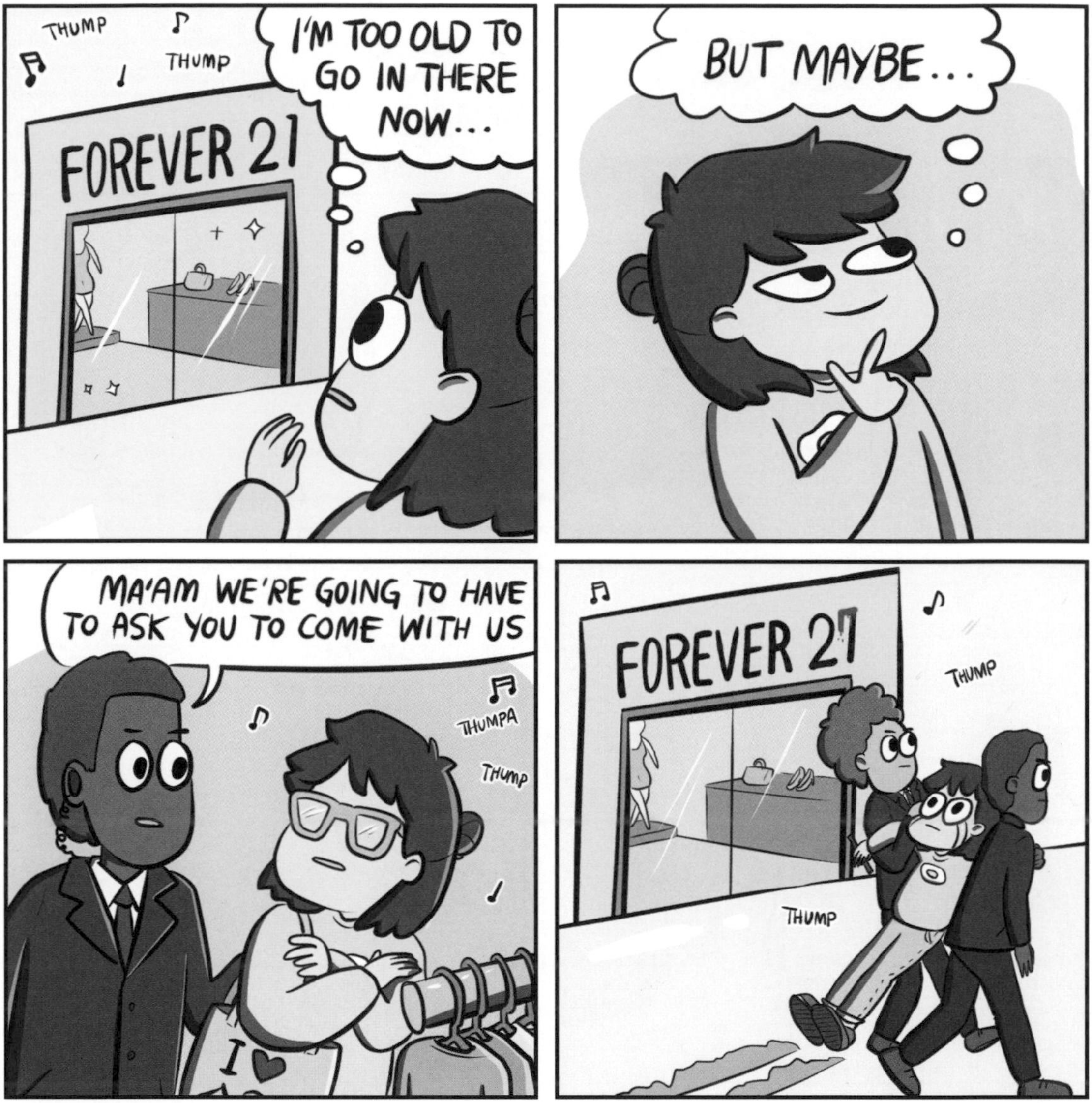
THUMP
THUMP
FOREVER 21
I'M TOO OLD TO GO IN THERE NOW...
BUT MAYBE...
MA'AM WE'RE GOING TO HAVE TO ASK YOU TO COME WITH US
THUMPA
THUMP
I ♥
FOREVER 21
THUMP
THUMP

AM I EVEN REAL

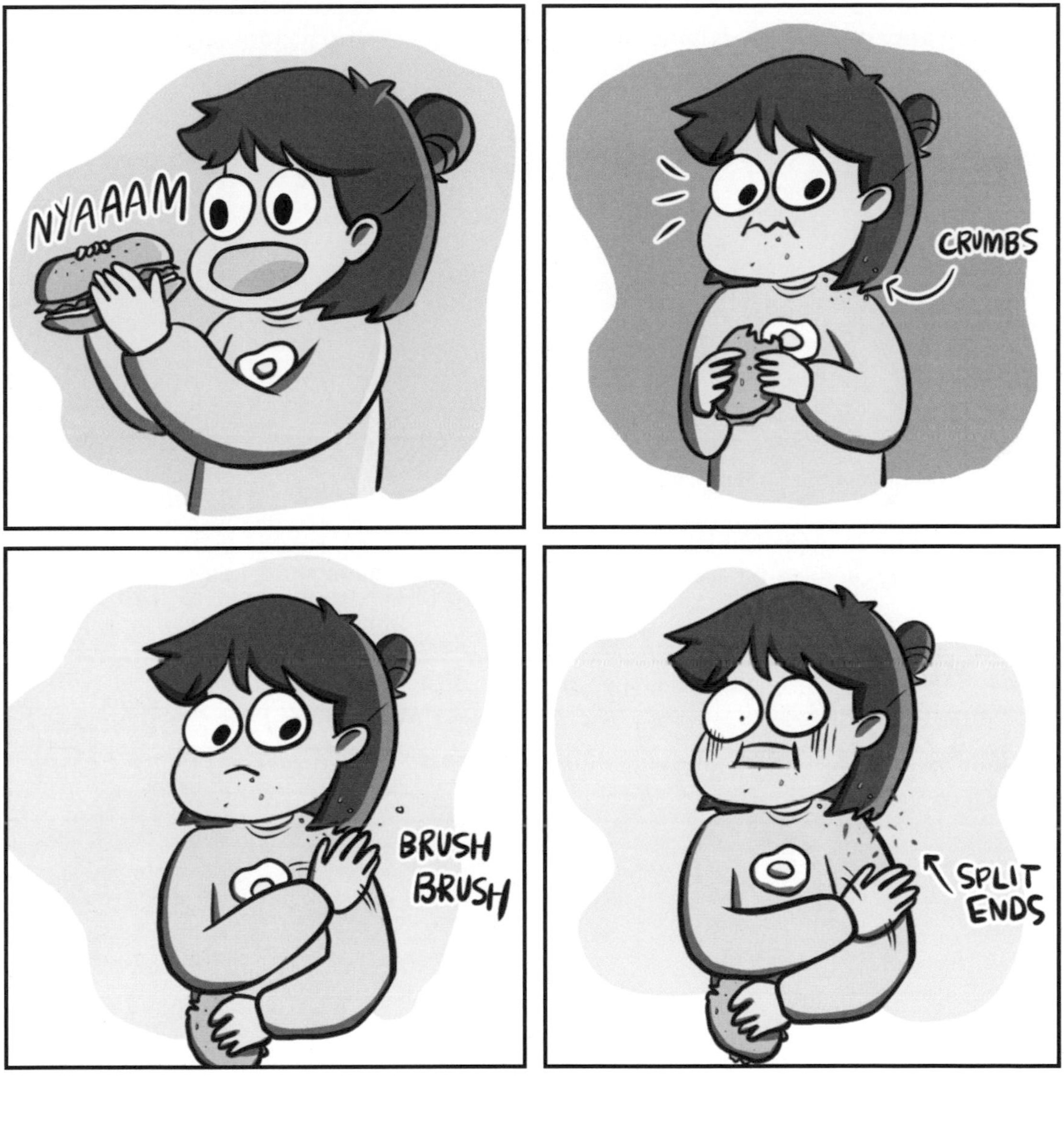
NYAAAM
CRUMBS
BRUSH BRUSH
SPLIT ENDS

STRESS PERM

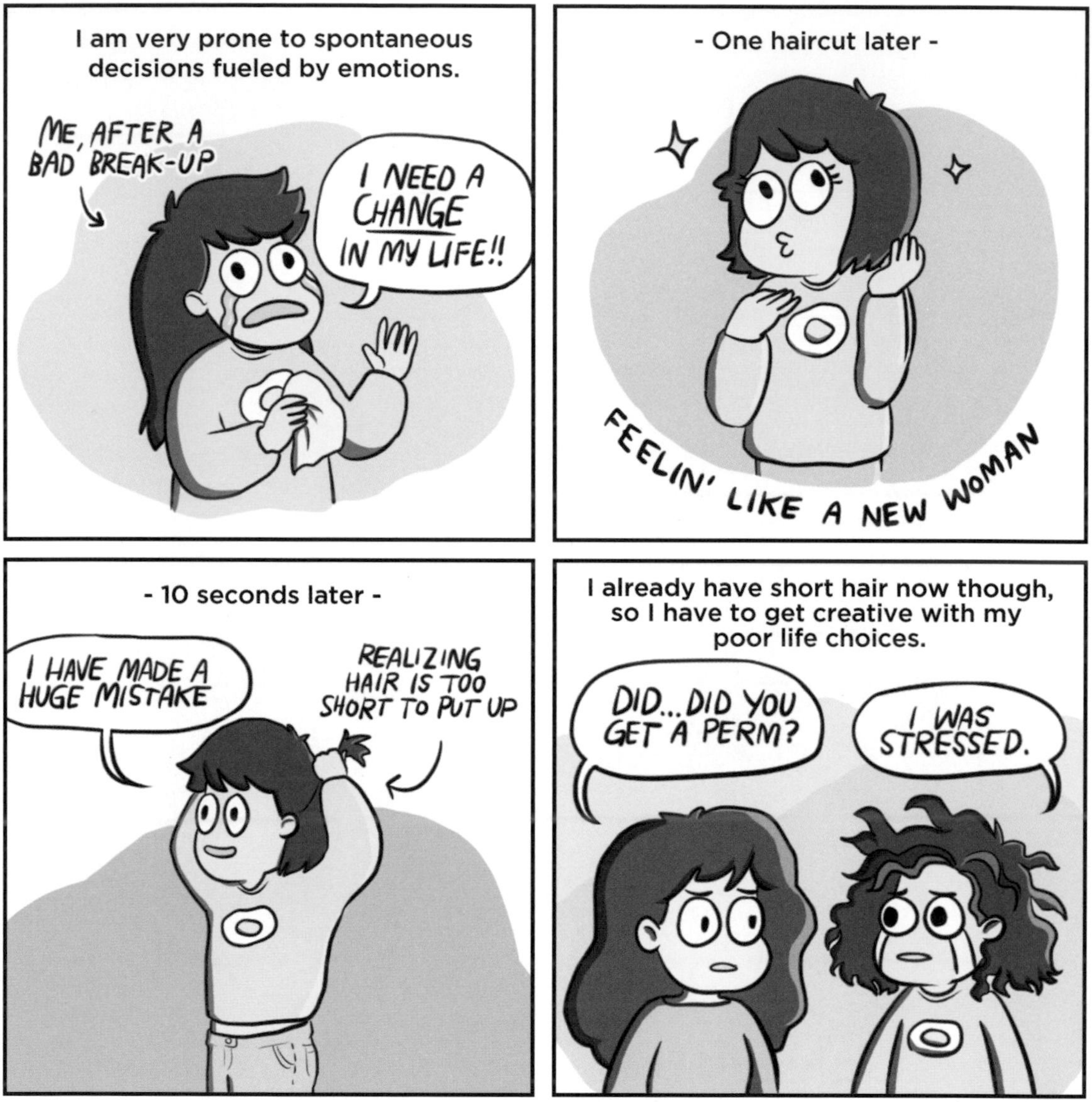
I am very prone to spontaneous decisions fueled by emotions.
ME, AFTER A BAD BREAK-UP
I NEED A CHANGE IN MY LIFE!!
- One haircut later -
FEELIN' LIKE A NEW WOMAN
- 10 seconds later -
I HAVE MADE A HUGE MISTAKE
REALIZING HAIR IS TOO SHORT TO PUT UP
I already have short hair now though, so I have to get creative with my poor life choices.
DID... DID YOU GET A PERM?
I WAS STRESSED.

THE DEFENSE

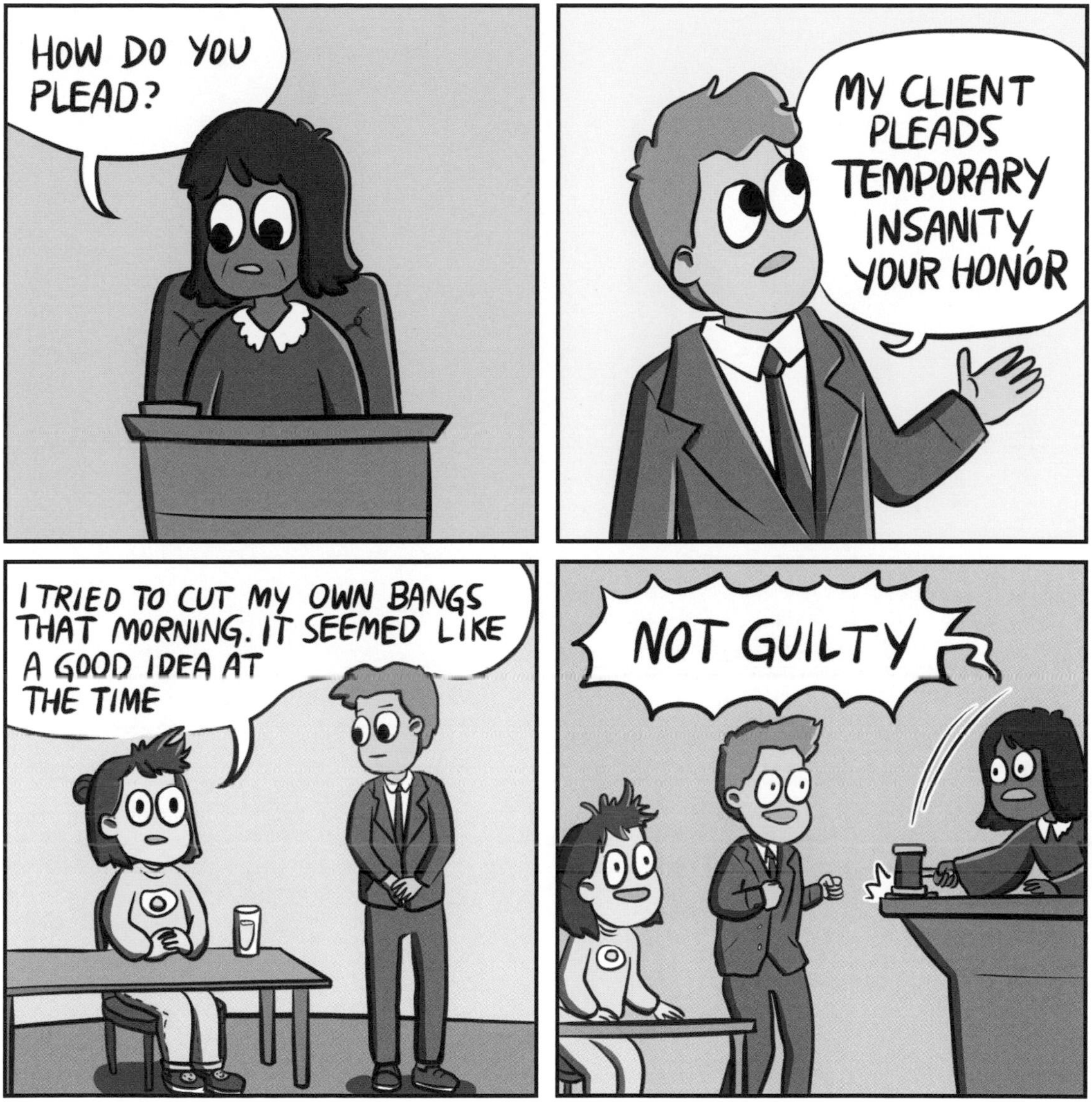
HOW DO YOU PLEAD?
MY CLIENT PLEADS TEMPORARY INSANITY YOUR HONOR
I TRIED TO CUT MY OWN BANGS THAT MORNING. IT SEEMED LIKE A GOOD IDEA AT THE TIME
NOT GUILTY

EMERGENCY

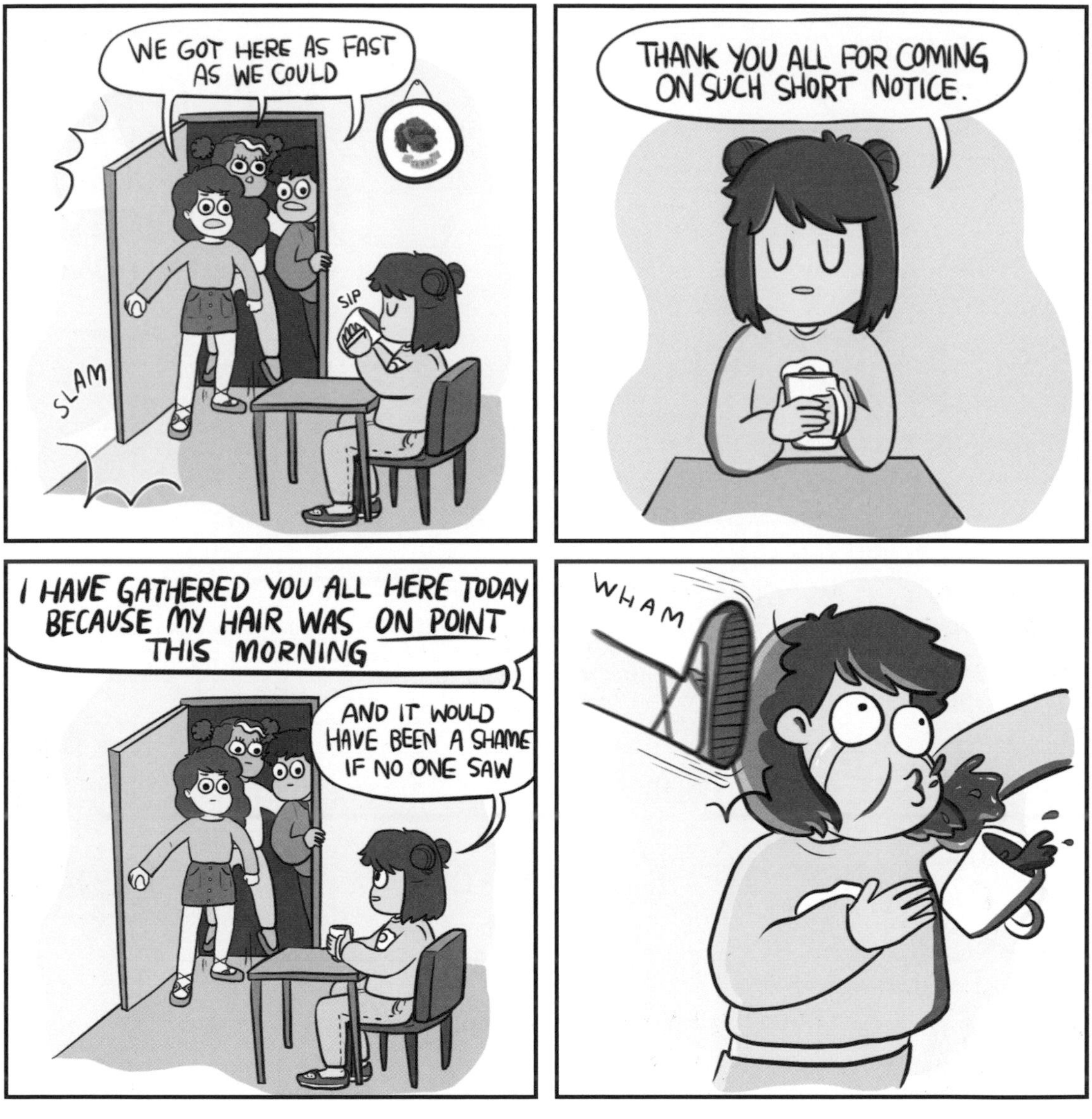

WE GOT HERE AS FAST AS WE COULD
SIP
SLAM
THANK YOU ALL FOR COMING ON SUCH SHORT NOTICE.
I HAVE GATHERED YOU ALL HERE TODAY BECAUSE MY HAIR WAS ON POINT THIS MORNING
AND IT WOULD HAVE BEEN A SHAME IF NO ONE SAW
WHAM

HAIR HORROR

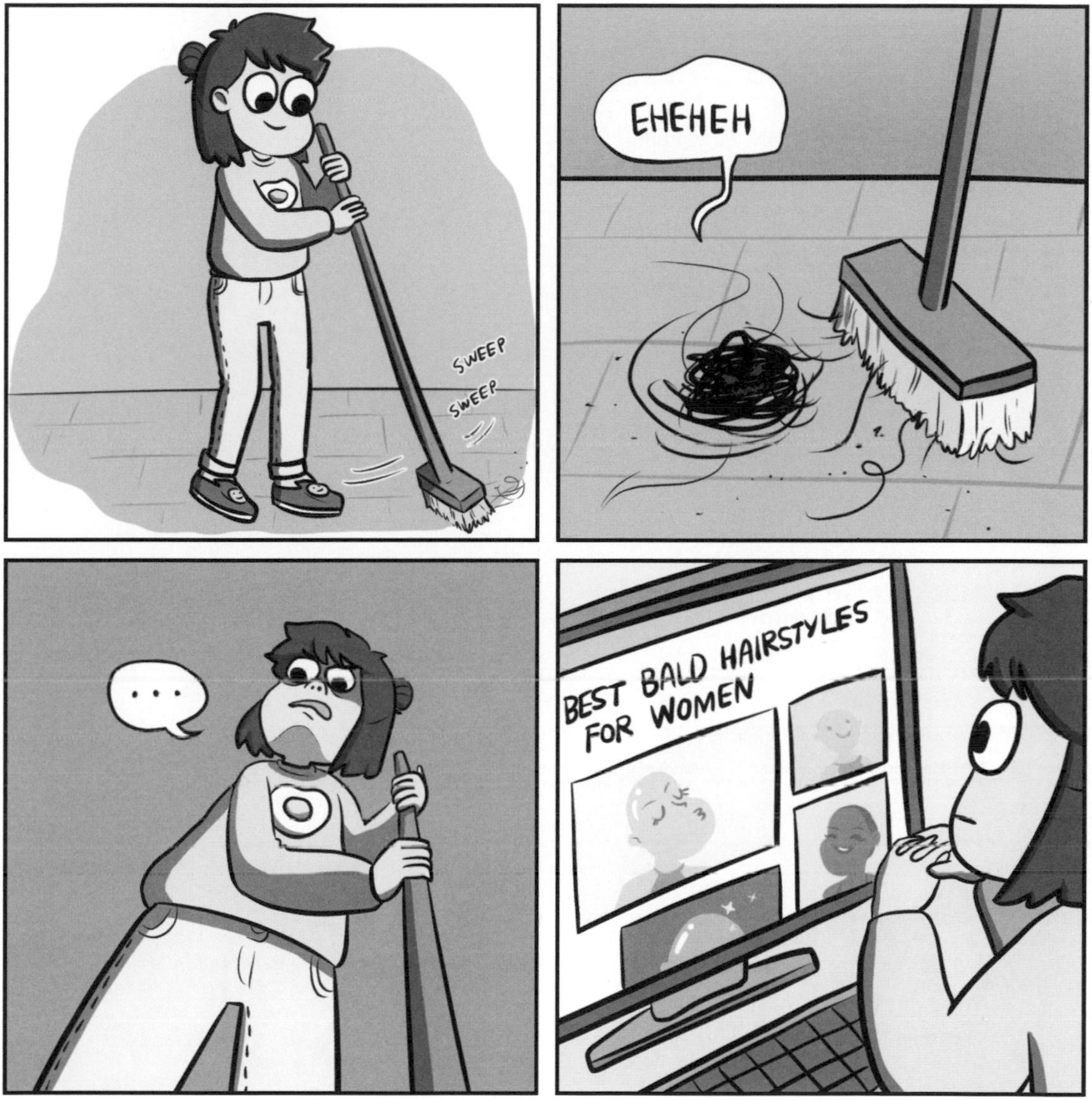
SWEEP
SWEEP
EHEHEH
...
BEST BALD HAIRSTYLES FOR WOMEN

THE PERKS OF BEING OLD

I have black hair, which means it's almost impossible to dye.

WHAT DO YOU WANT TO DO WITH YOUR HAIR?

I WANT TO DYE IT PASTEL PINK

OK YOU'LL HAVE TO BLEACH IT 5 TIMES AND IT'LL COST $400

YES OF COURSE WHATEVER IT TAKES

That's why I'm weirdly jealous of old people.

DAT SILVER HAIR... THE PERFECT BASE FOR DYEING HAIR

I'm really looking forward to my hair going gray, so I can dye it crazy colors.

A MAKE-UP TUTORIAL BY ME, A WITCH

GYM

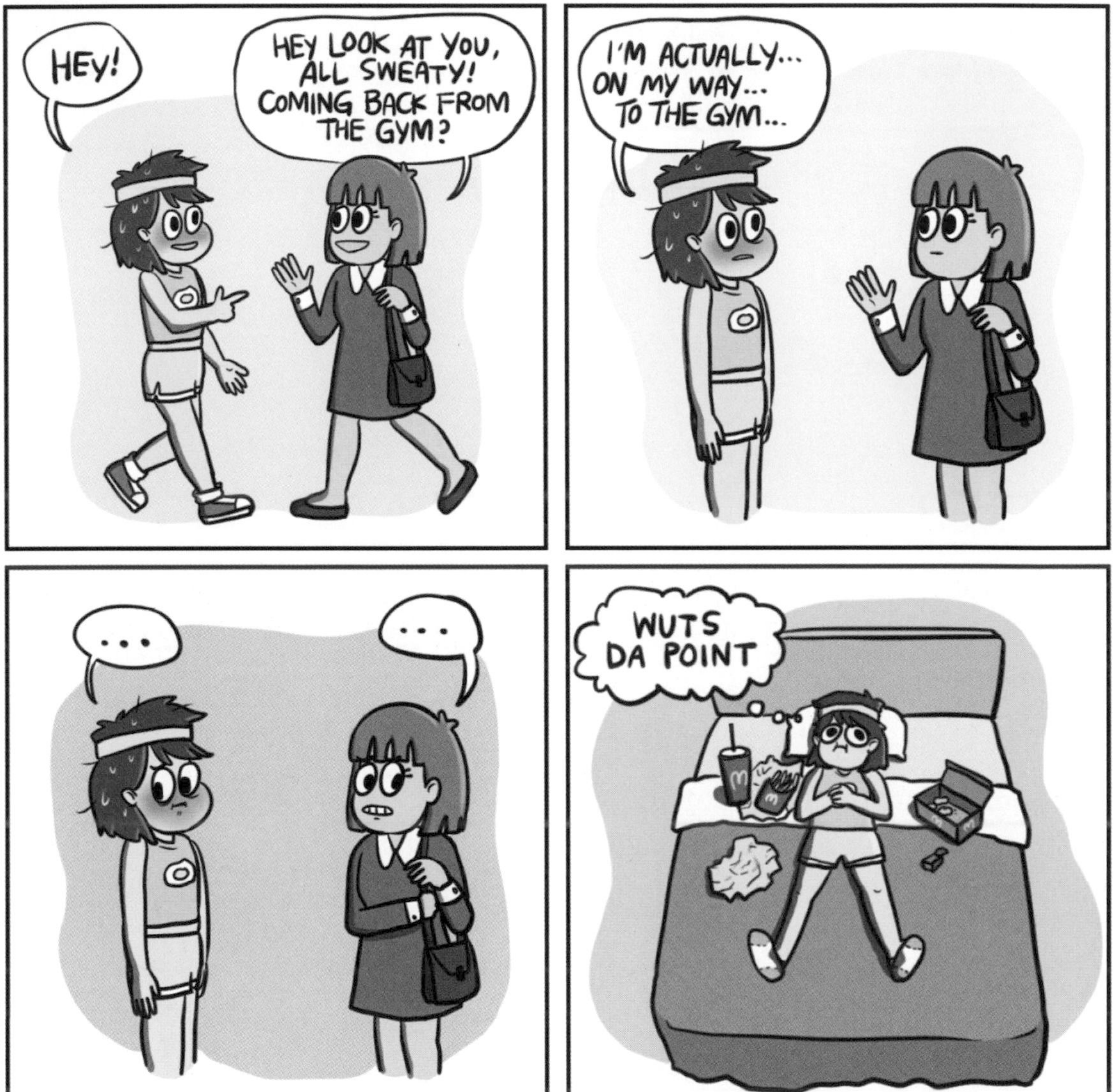
HEY!
HEY LOOK AT YOU, ALL SWEATY! COMING BACK FROM THE GYM?
I'M ACTUALLY... ON MY WAY... TO THE GYM...
...
...
WUTS DA POINT

GOOD KISSER

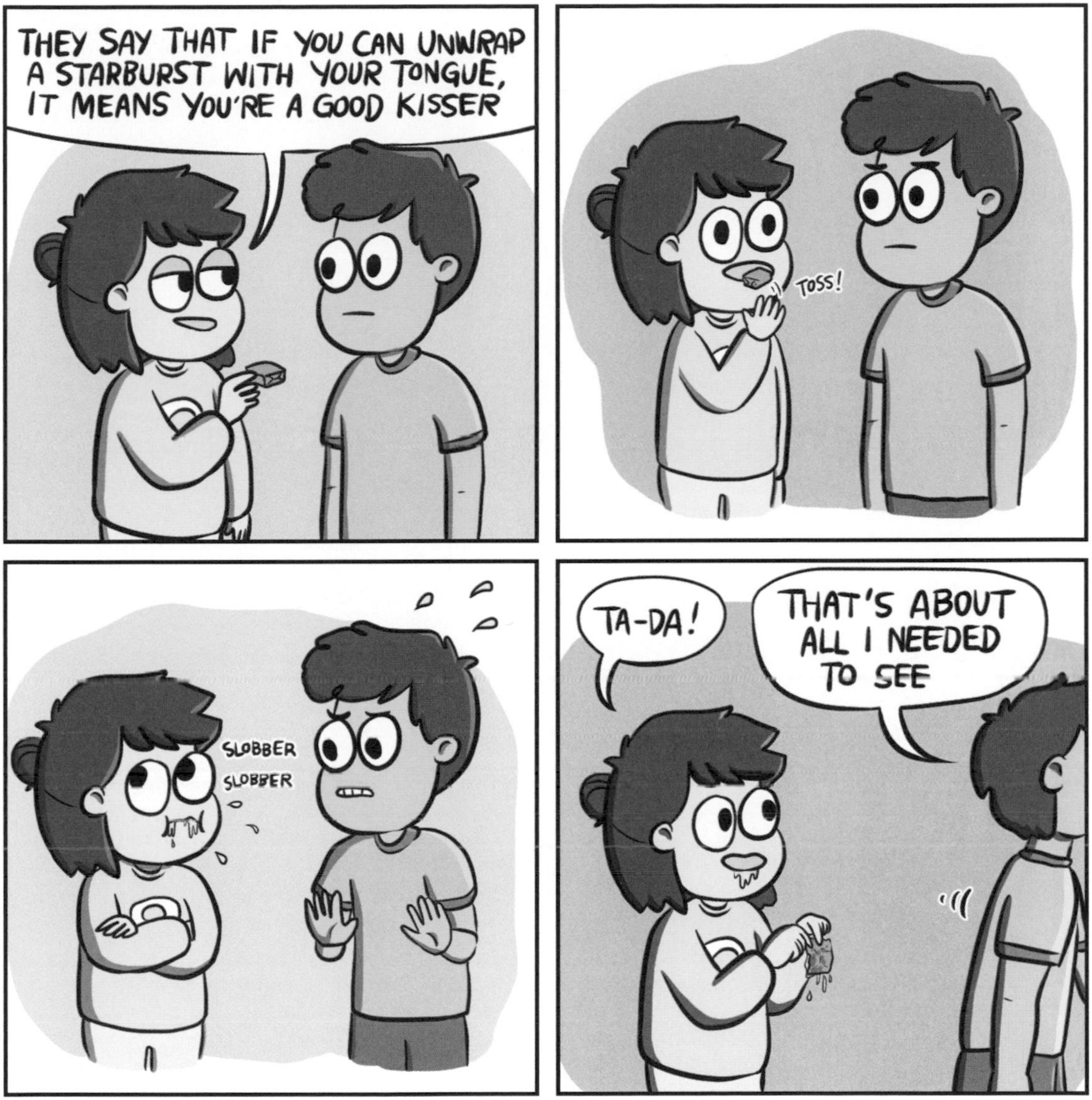
THEY SAY THAT IF YOU CAN UNWRAP A STARBURST WITH YOUR TONGUE, IT MEANS YOU'RE A GOOD KISSER
TOSS!
SLOBBER
SLOBBER
TA-DA!
THAT'S ABOUT ALL I NEEDED TO SEE

W.F.S.

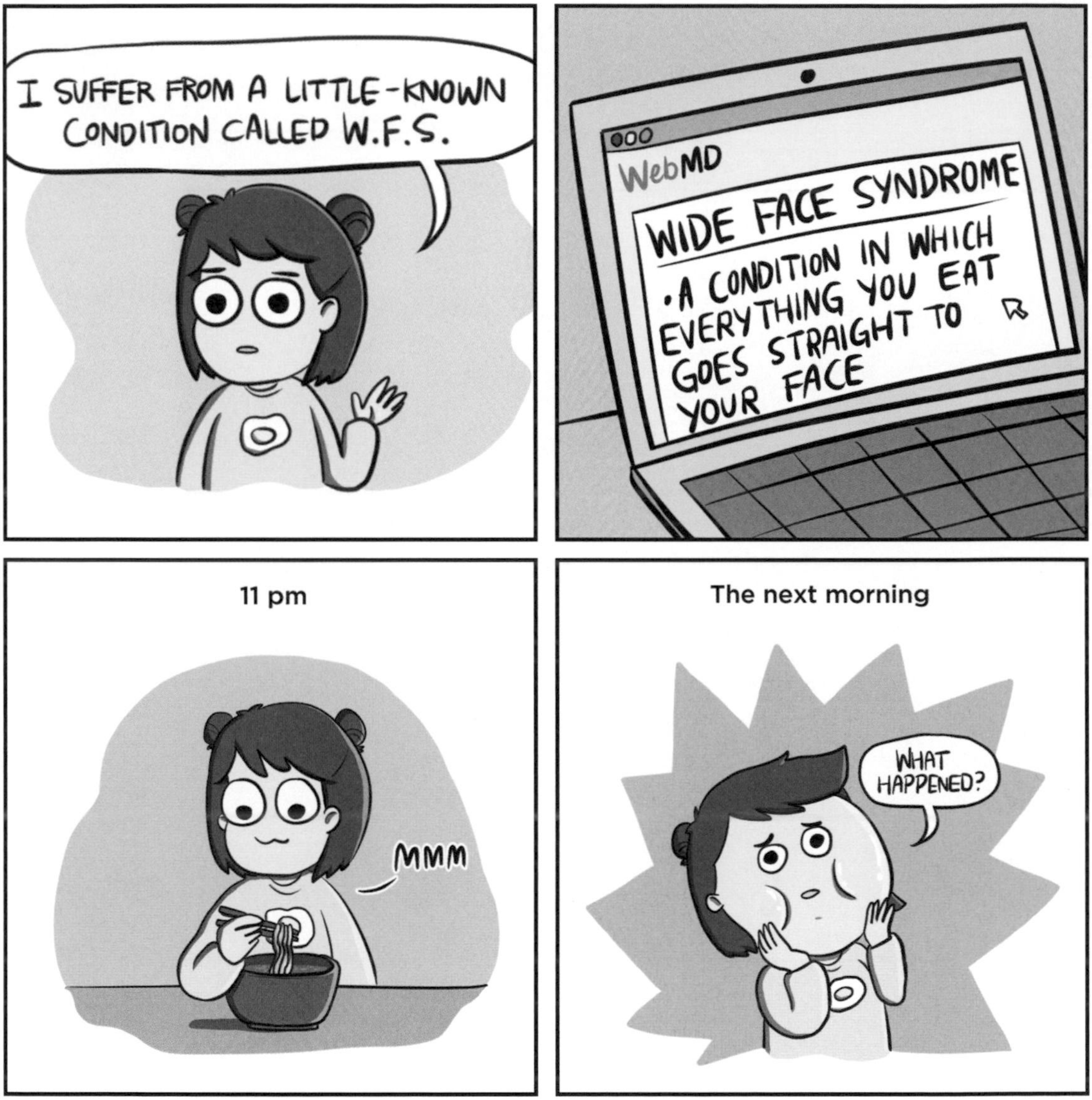

I SUFFER FROM A LITTLE-KNOWN CONDITION CALLED W.F.S.
WebMD
WIDE FACE SYNDROME
• A CONDITION IN WHICH EVERYTHING YOU EAT GOES STRAIGHT TO YOUR FACE
11 pm
MMM
The next morning
WHAT HAPPENED?

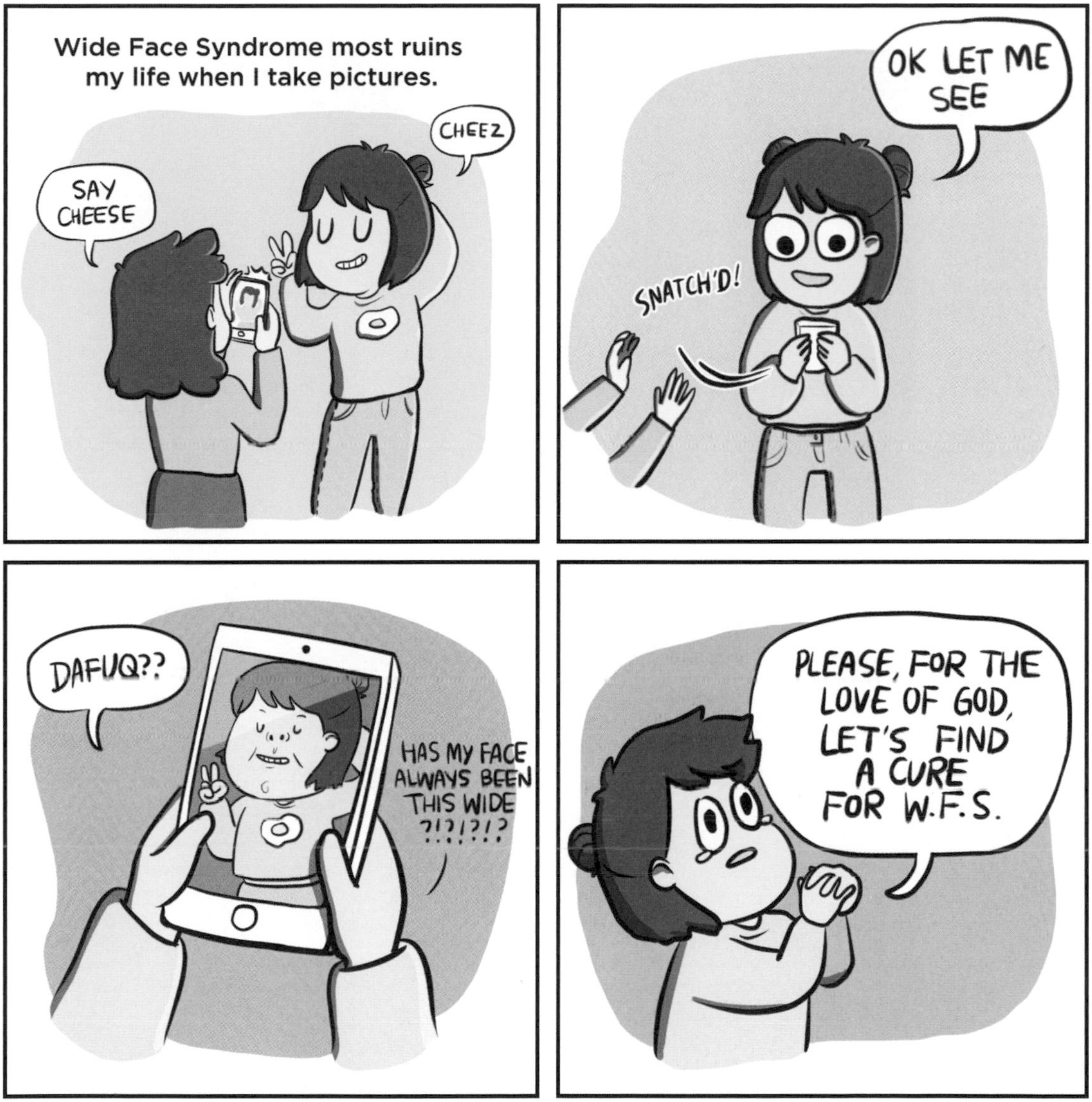
Wide Face Syndrome most ruins my life when I take pictures.
SAY CHEESE
CHEEZ
OK LET ME SEE
SNATCH'D!
DAFUQ??
HAS MY FACE ALWAYS BEEN THIS WIDE ?!?!?!?
PLEASE, FOR THE LOVE OF GOD, LET'S FIND A CURE FOR W.F.S.

MULTIVITAMINS

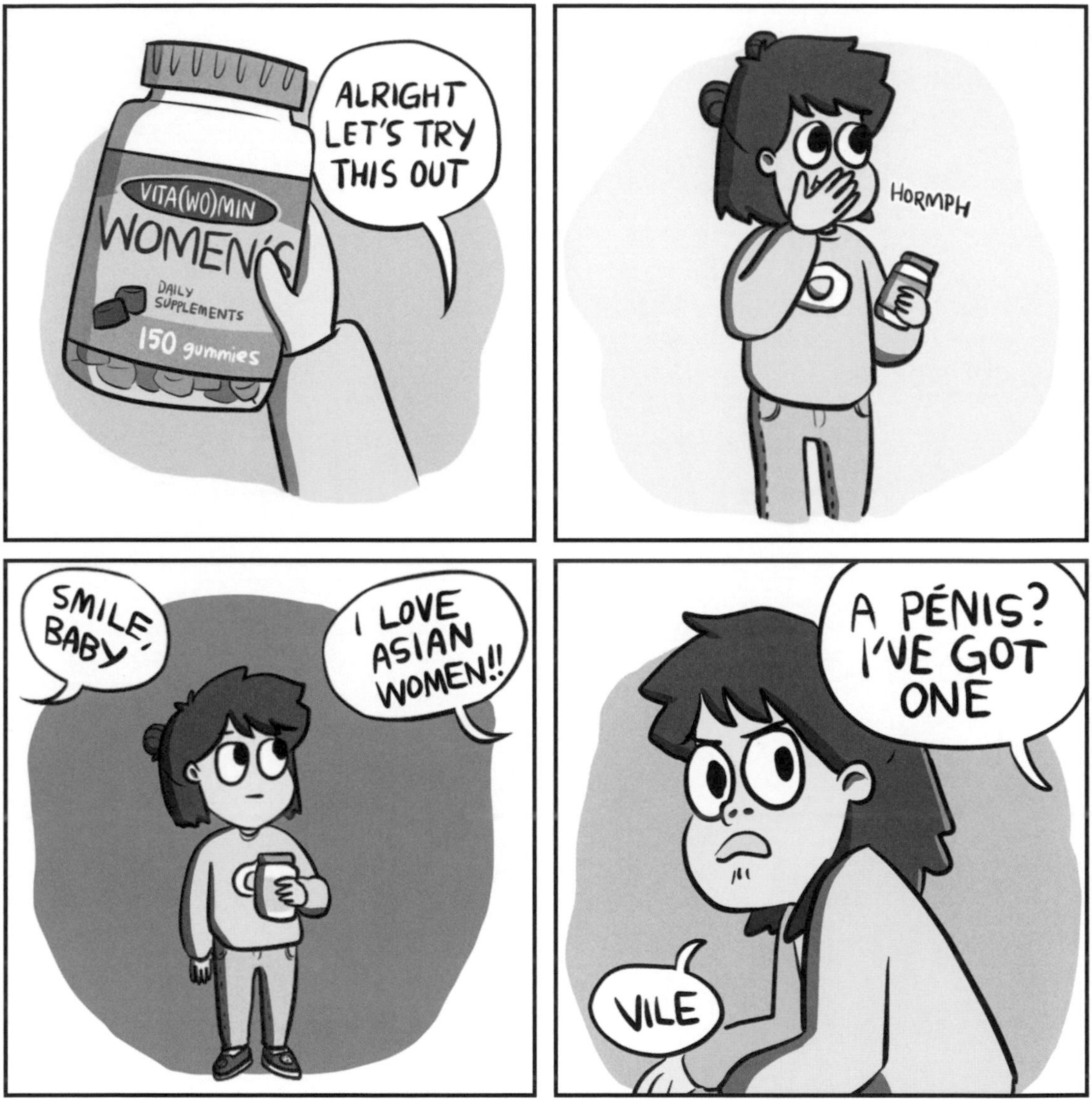
VITA(WO)MIN
WOMEN'S
DAILY SUPPLEMENTS
150 gummies
ALRIGHT LET'S TRY THIS OUT
HORMPH
SMILE, BABY
I LOVE ASIAN WOMEN!!
A PÉNIS? I'VE GOT ONE
VILE

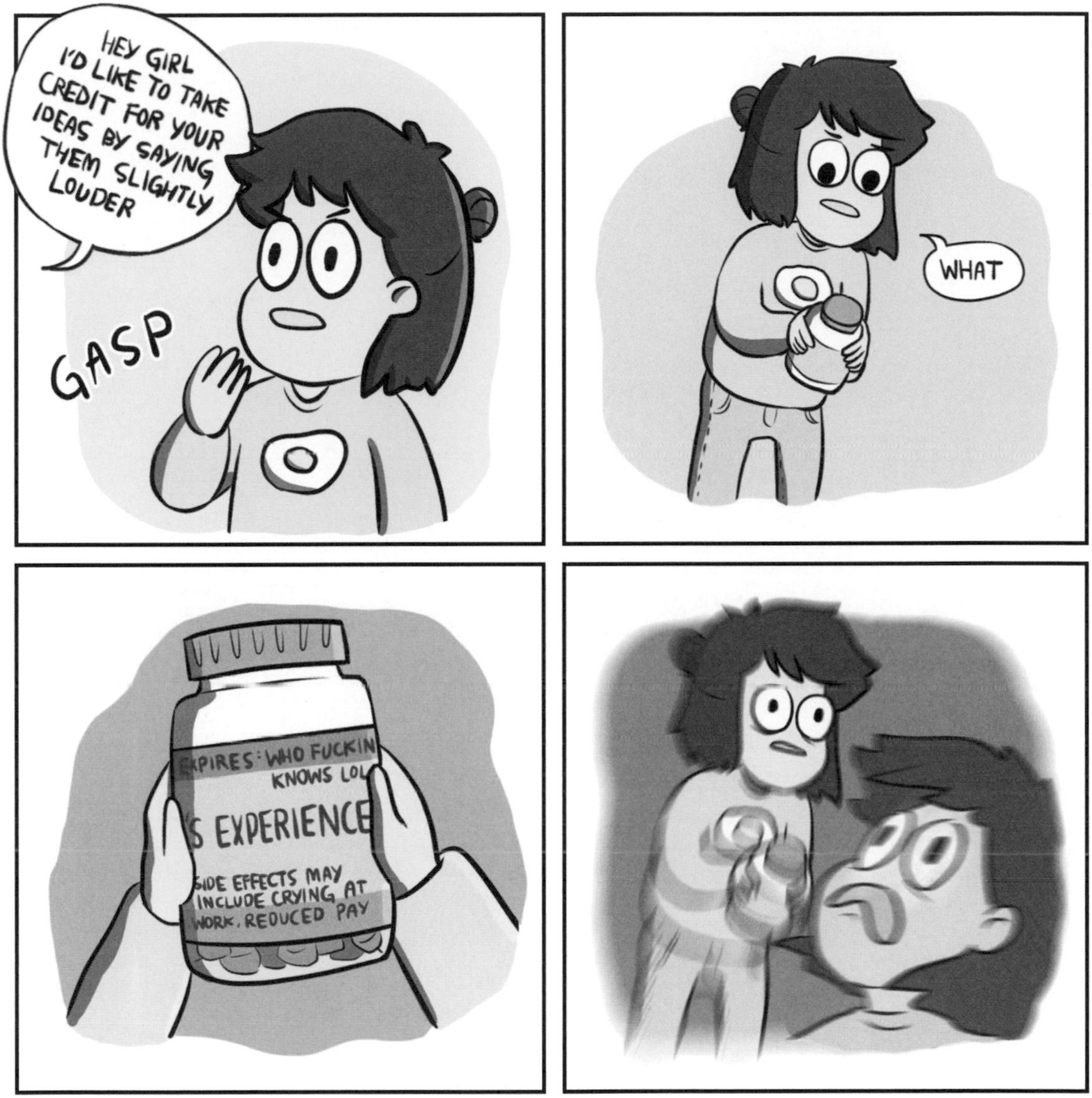
HEY GIRL I'D LIKE TO TAKE CREDIT FOR YOUR IDEAS BY SAYING THEM SLIGHTLY LOUDER
GASP
WHAT
PIRES: WHO FUCKIN KNOWS LOL
S EXPERIENCE
SIDE EFFECTS MAY INCLUDE CRYING AT WORK, REDUCED PAY

MODERN HANSEL AND GRETEL

BEWARE THE TIDES

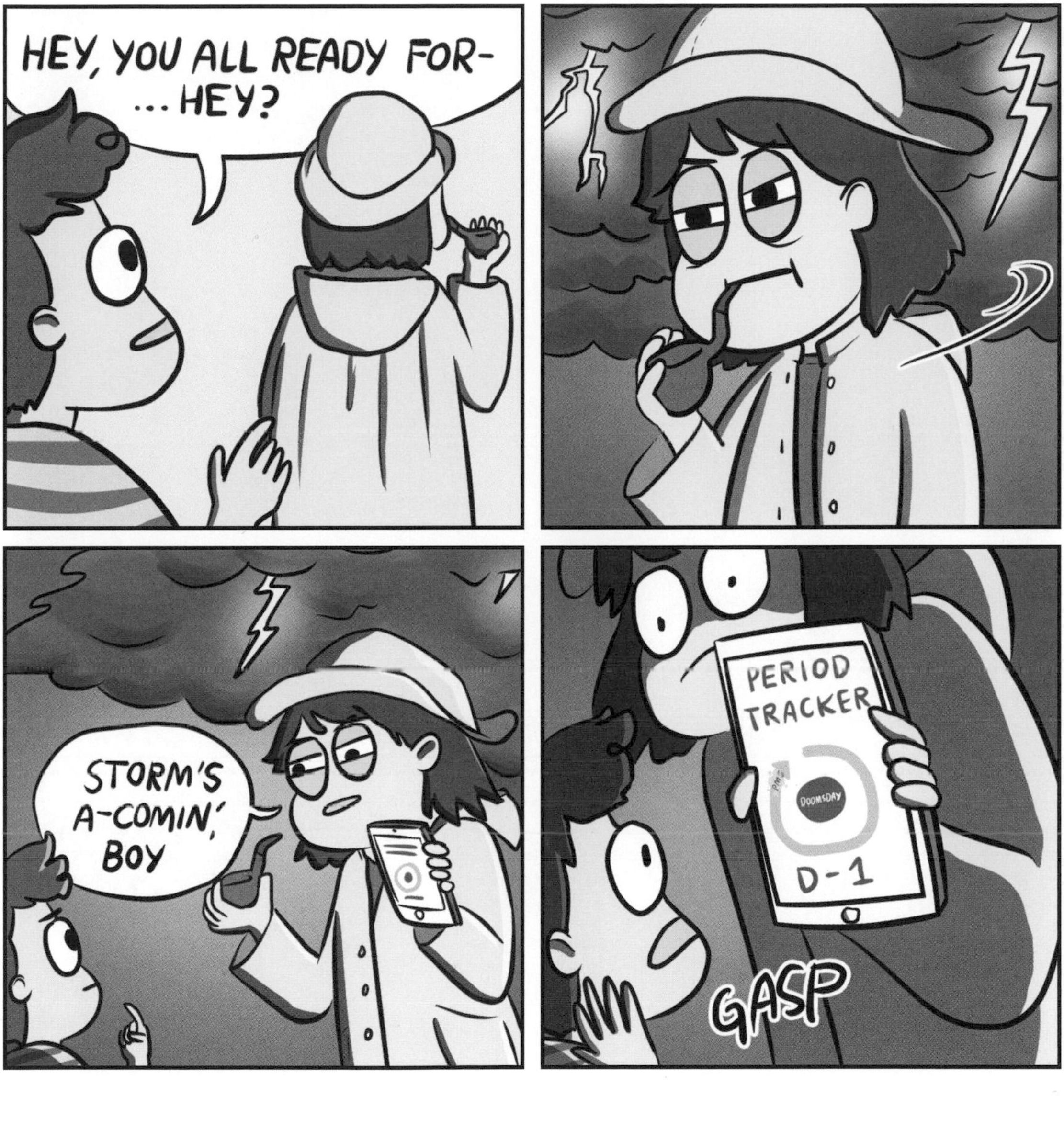
HEY, YOU ALL READY FOR- ... HEY?
STORM'S A-COMIN,' BOY
PERIOD TRACKER
DOOMSDAY
D-1
GASP

HAUNTED HOUSE

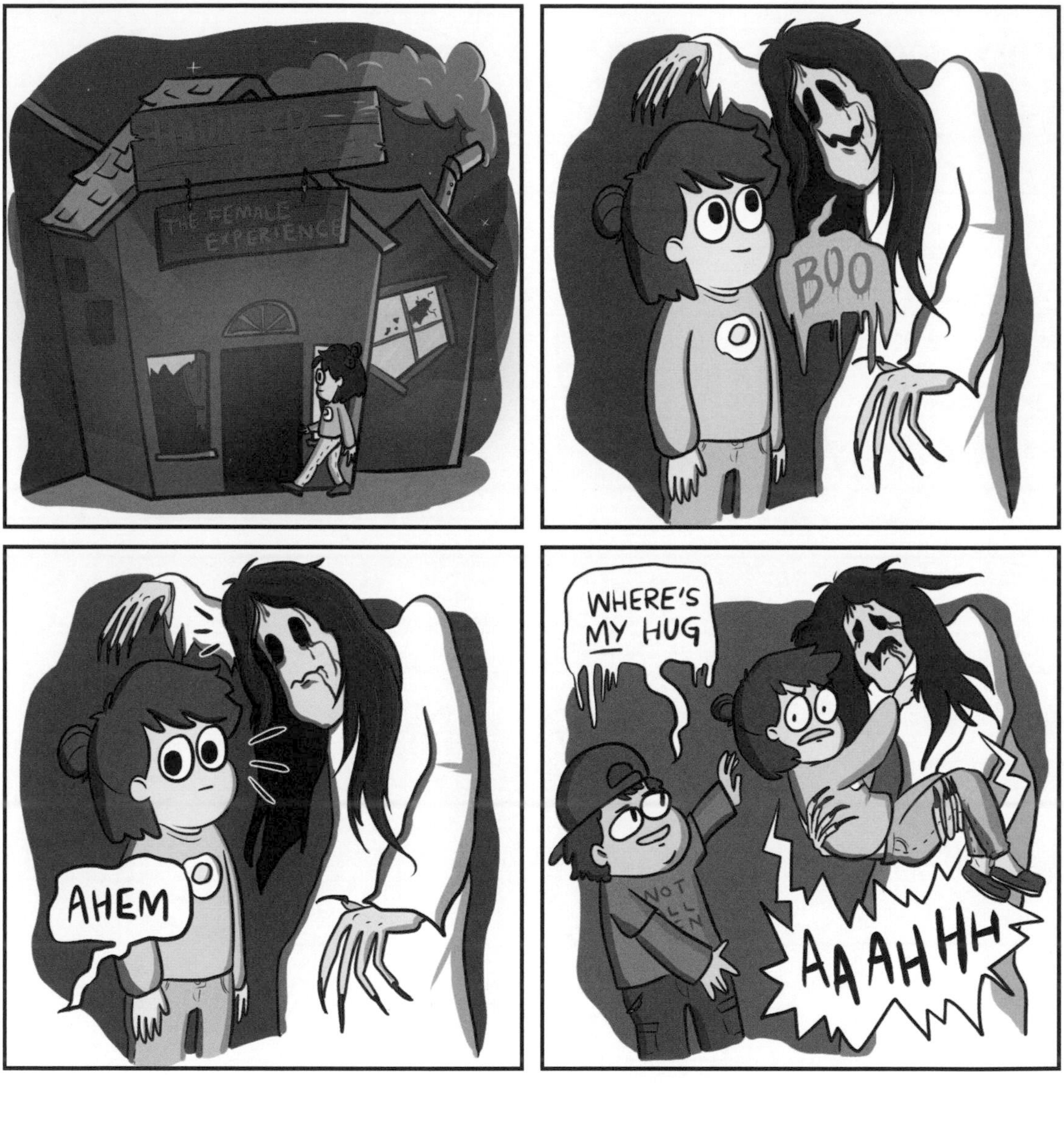
THE FEMALE EXPERIENCE
BOO
AHEM
WHERE'S MY HUG
AAAHHH

A GIRL WALKS HOME ALONE AT NIGHT

WHAT'S HER SECRET?

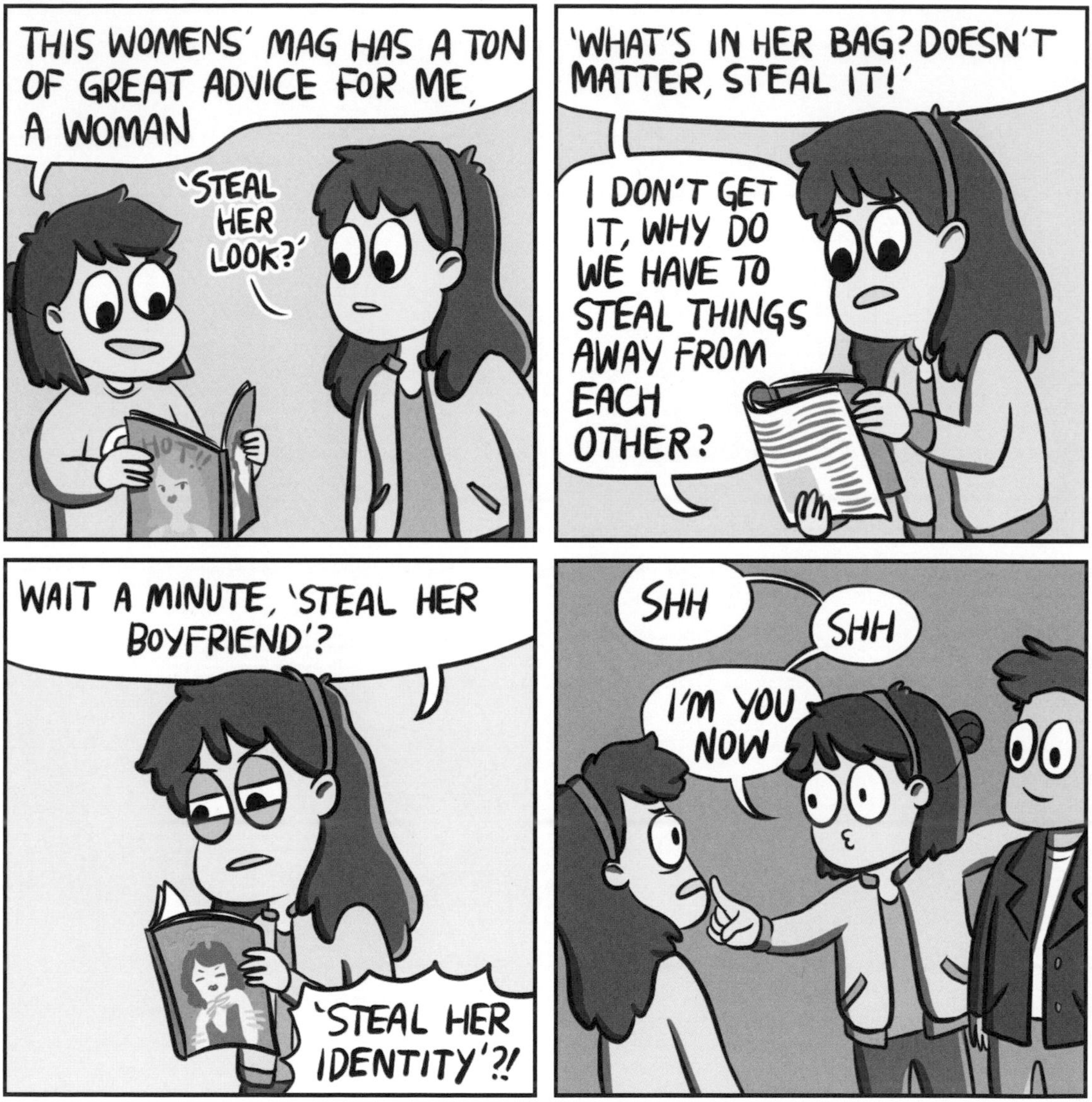
THIS WOMENS' MAG HAS A TON OF GREAT ADVICE FOR ME, A WOMAN
'STEAL HER LOOK?'
HOT!!
'WHAT'S IN HER BAG? DOESN'T MATTER, STEAL IT!'
I DON'T GET IT, WHY DO WE HAVE TO STEAL THINGS AWAY FROM EACH OTHER?
WAIT A MINUTE, 'STEAL HER BOYFRIEND'?
'STEAL HER IDENTITY'?!
SHH
SHH
I'M YOU NOW

YEARBOOK MEMORIES

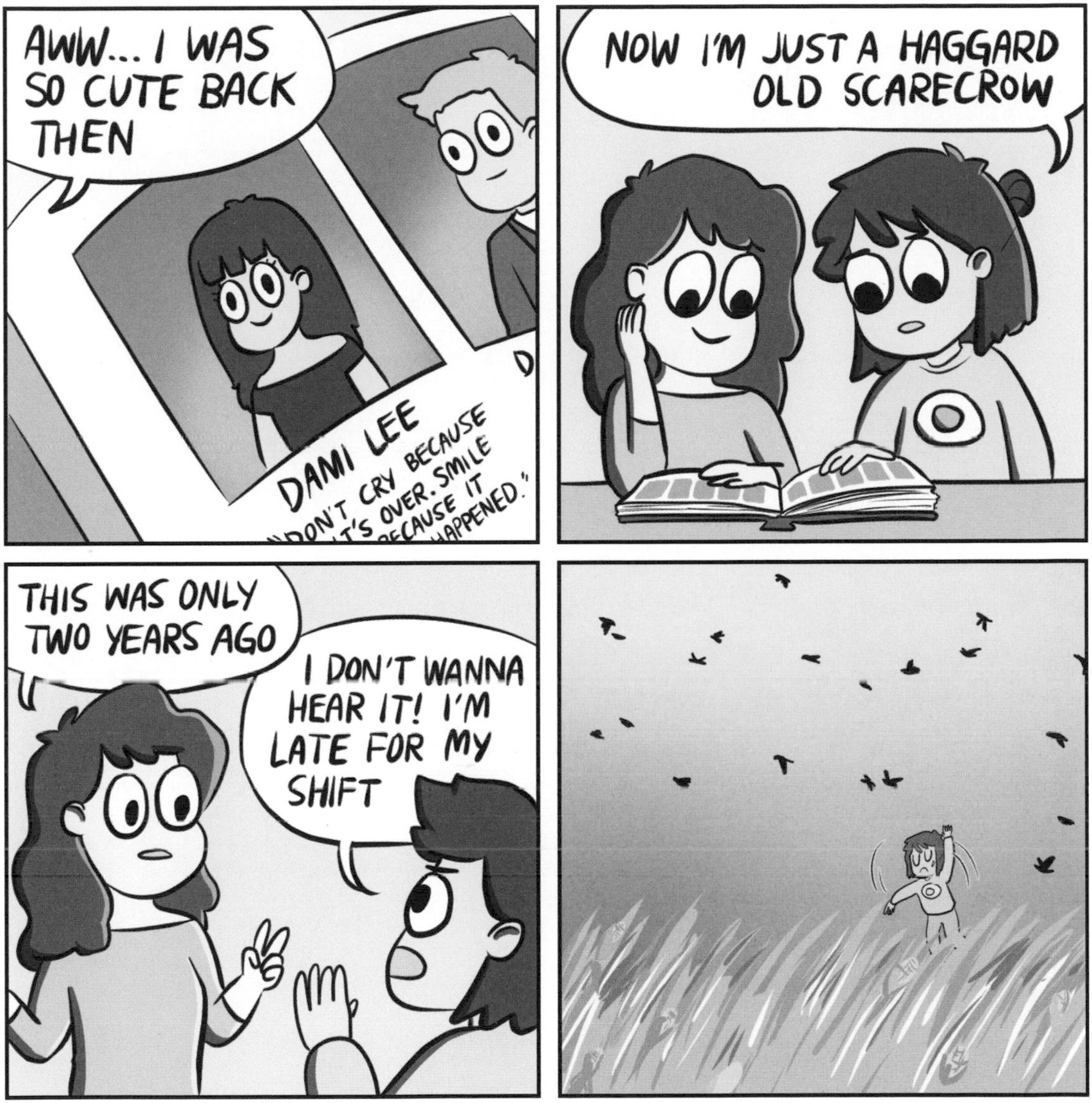
AWW... I WAS SO CUTE BACK THEN
DAMI LEE
"DON'T CRY BECAUSE
T'S OVER. SMILE
ECAUSE IT
HAPPENED."
NOW I'M JUST A HAGGARD OLD SCARECROW
THIS WAS ONLY TWO YEARS AGO
I DON'T WANNA HEAR IT! I'M LATE FOR MY SHIFT

UNFINISHED BUSINESS

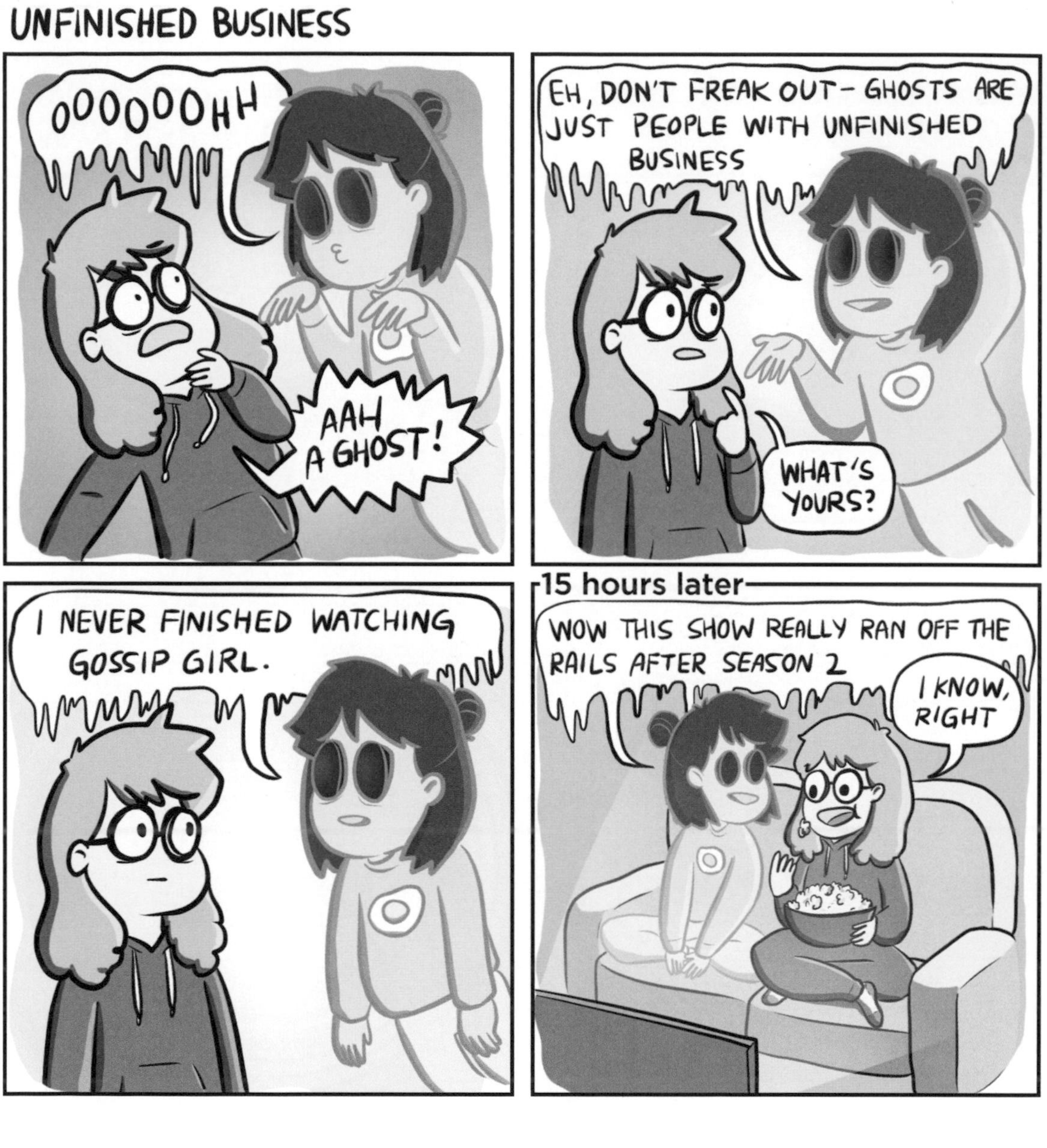
OOOOOOOHH
AAH A GHOST!
EH, DON'T FREAK OUT- GHOSTS ARE JUST PEOPLE WITH UNFINISHED BUSINESS
WHAT'S YOURS?
I NEVER FINISHED WATCHING GOSSIP GIRL.
15 hours later
WOW THIS SHOW REALLY RAN OFF THE RAILS AFTER SEASON 2
I KNOW, RIGHT

LABELS

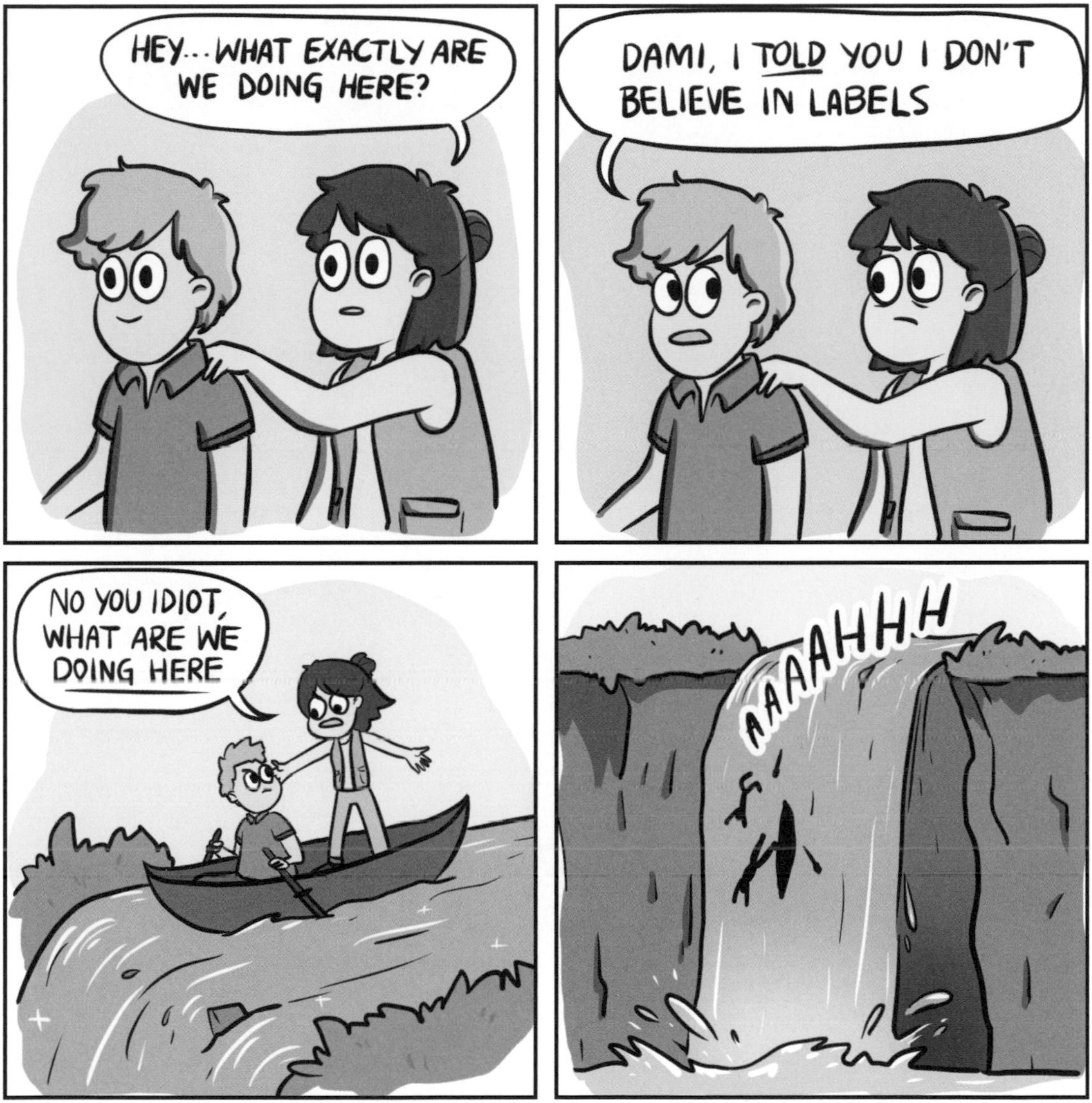
HEY... WHAT EXACTLY ARE WE DOING HERE?
DAMI, I TOLD YOU I DON'T BELIEVE IN LABELS
NO YOU IDIOT, WHAT ARE WE DOING HERE
AAAAHHHH

K BYE

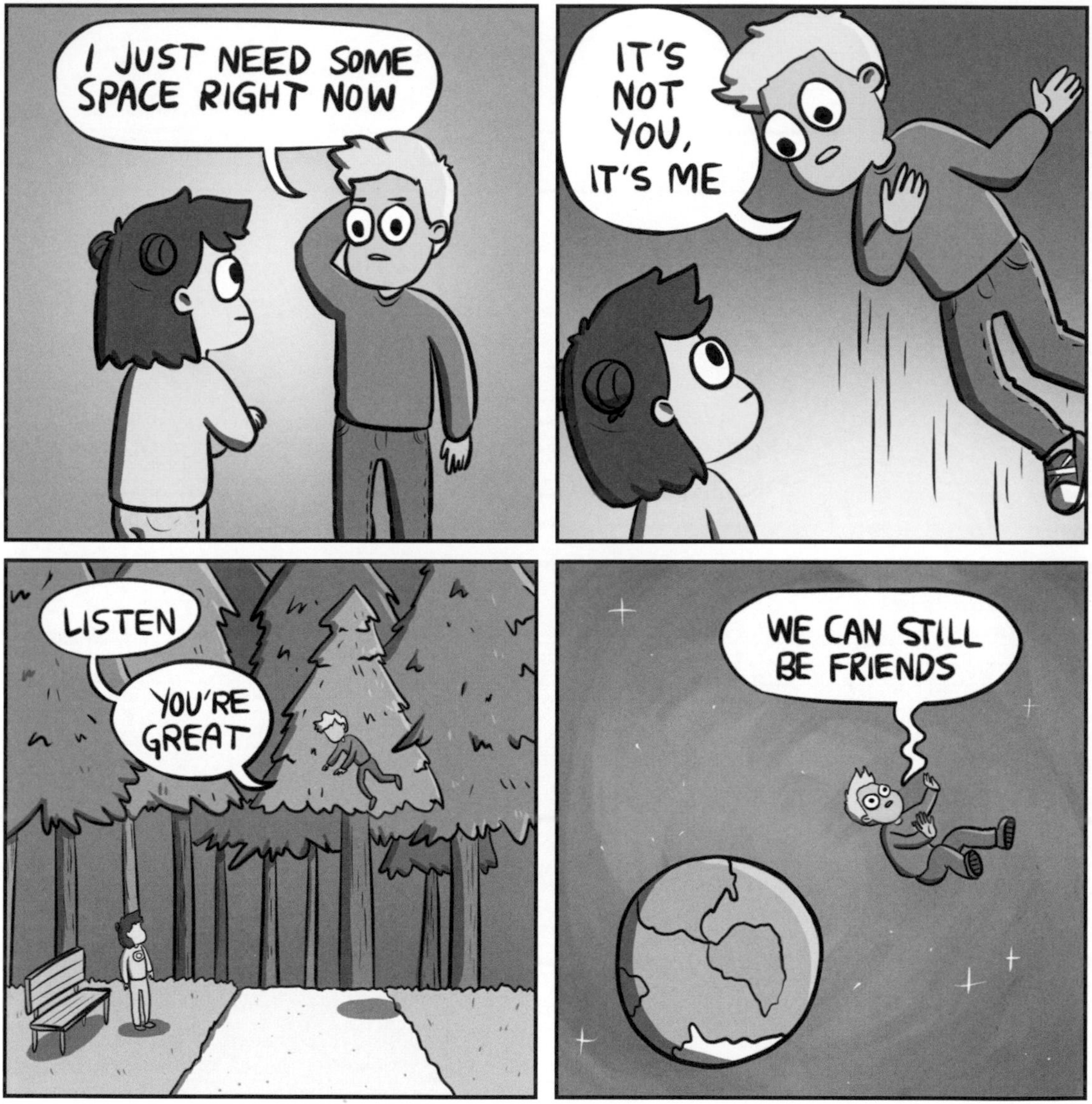

I JUST NEED SOME SPACE RIGHT NOW
IT'S NOT YOU, IT'S ME
LISTEN
YOU'RE GREAT
WE CAN STILL BE FRIENDS

DINING ALONE

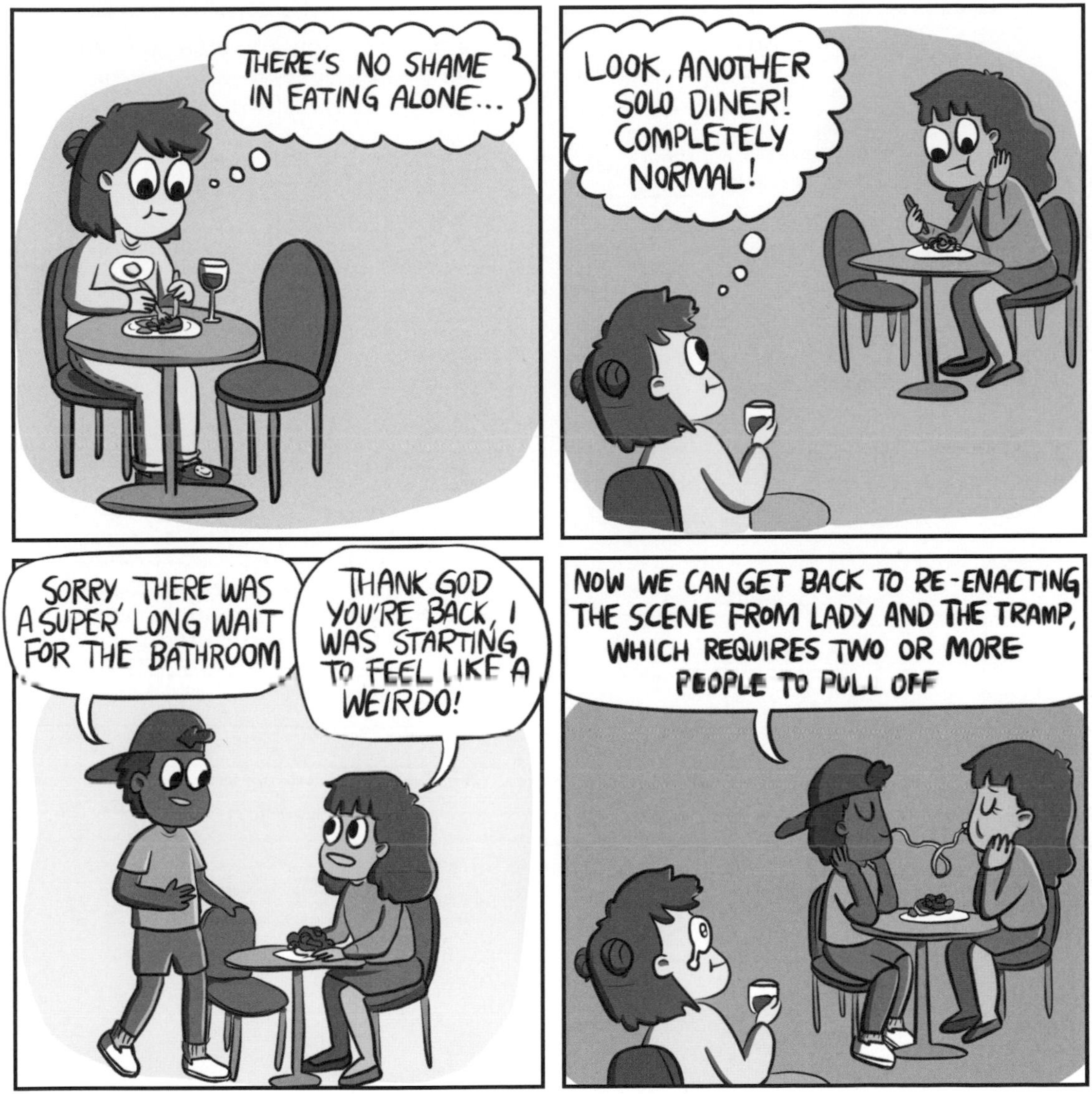
THERE'S NO SHAME IN EATING ALONE...
LOOK, ANOTHER SOLO DINER! COMPLETELY NORMAL!
SORRY, THERE WAS A SUPER' LONG WAIT FOR THE BATHROOM
THANK GOD YOU'RE BACK, I WAS STARTING TO FEEL LIKE A WEIRDO!
NOW WE CAN GET BACK TO RE-ENACTING THE SCENE FROM LADY AND THE TRAMP, WHICH REQUIRES TWO OR MORE PEOPLE TO PULL OFF

HOW TO DEAL WITH HEARTBREAK

98

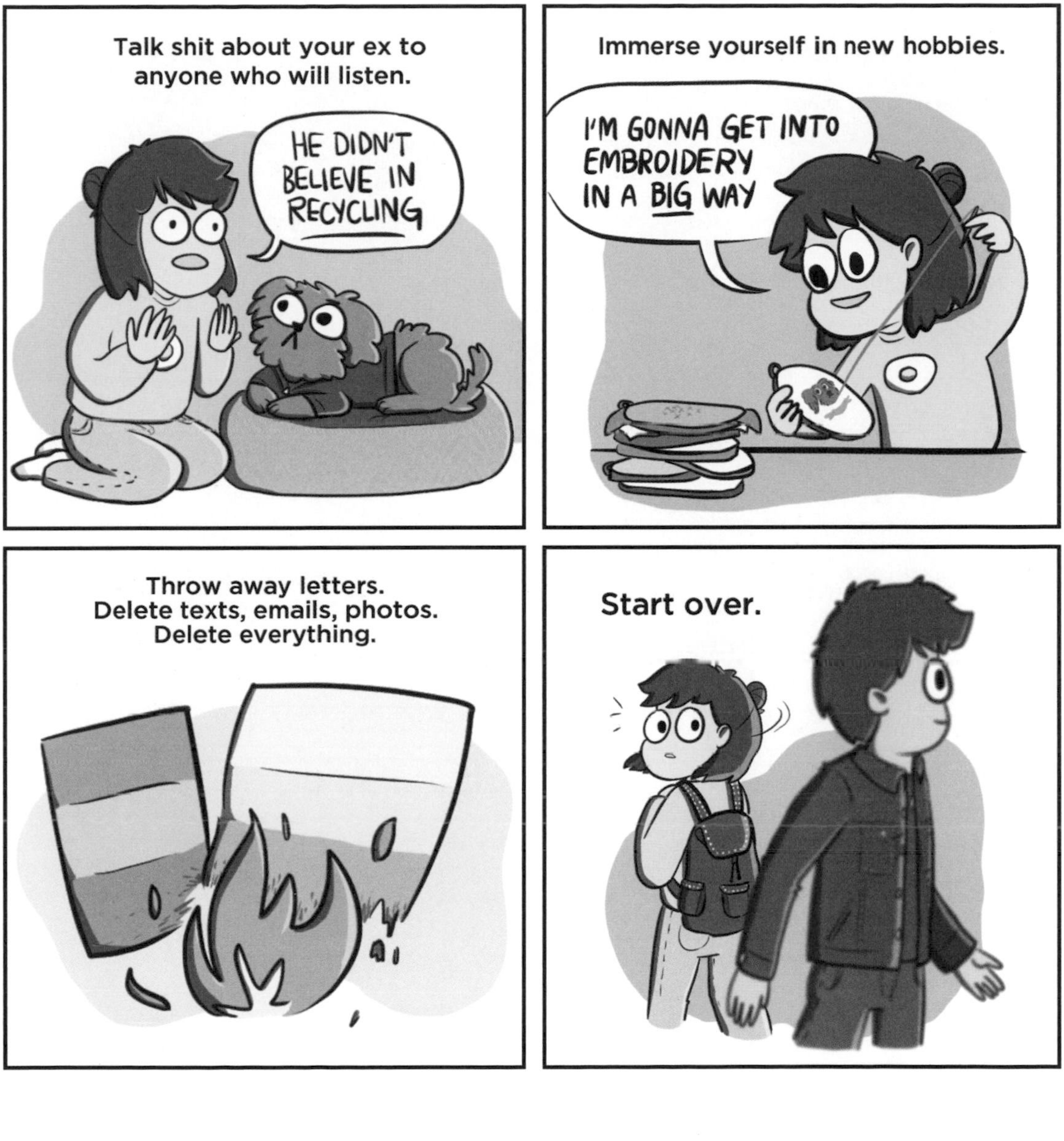
Talk shit about your ex to anyone who will listen.
HE DIDN'T BELIEVE IN RECYCLING
Immerse yourself in new hobbies.
I'M GONNA GET INTO EMBROIDERY IN A BIG WAY
Throw away letters. Delete texts, emails, photos. Delete everything.
Start over.

DATING 101

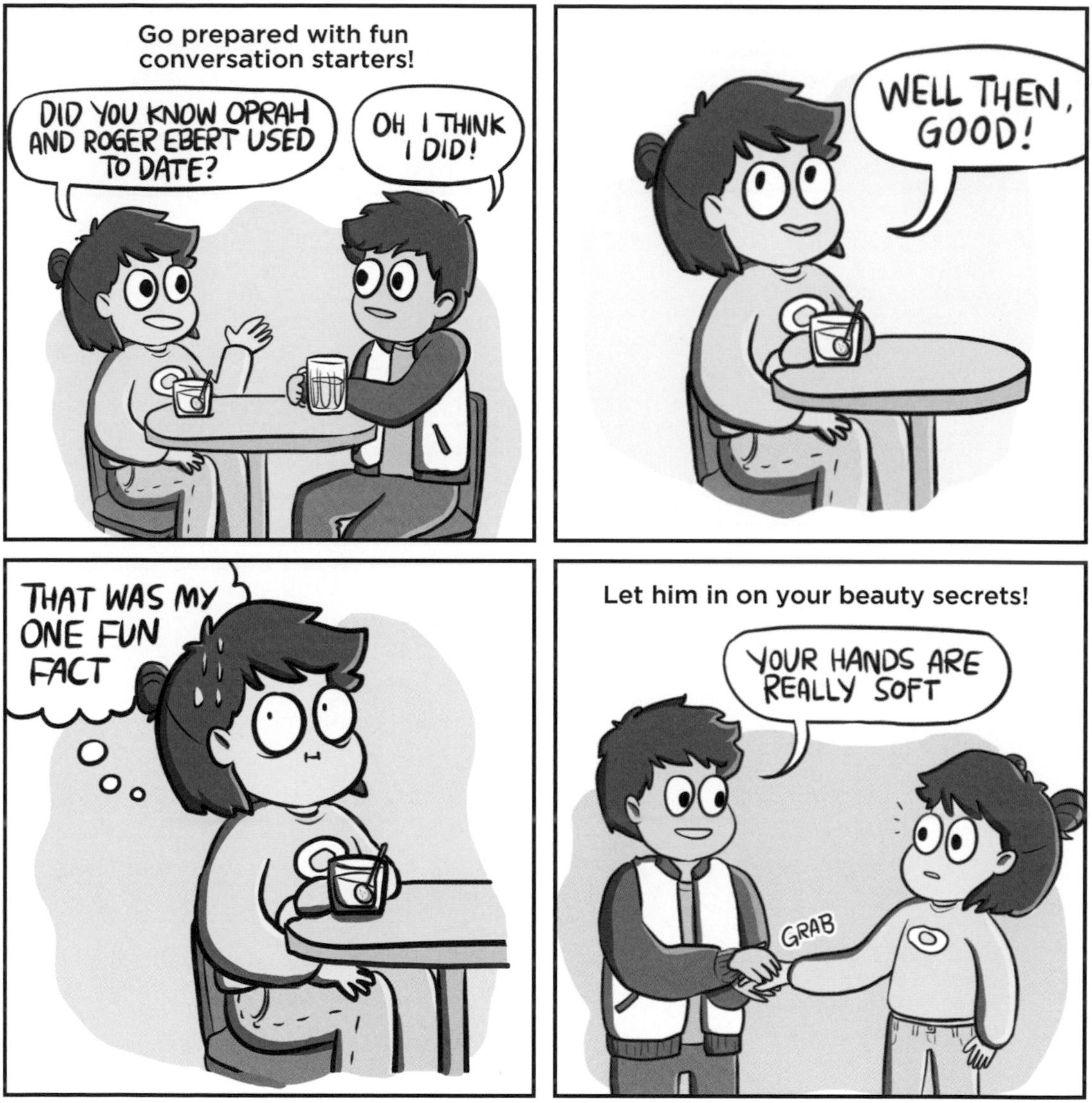
Go prepared with fun conversation starters!
DID YOU KNOW OPRAH AND ROGER EBERT USED TO DATE?
OH I THINK I DID!
WELL THEN, GOOD!
THAT WAS MY ONE FUN FACT
Let him in on your beauty secrets!
YOUR HANDS ARE REALLY SOFT
GRAB

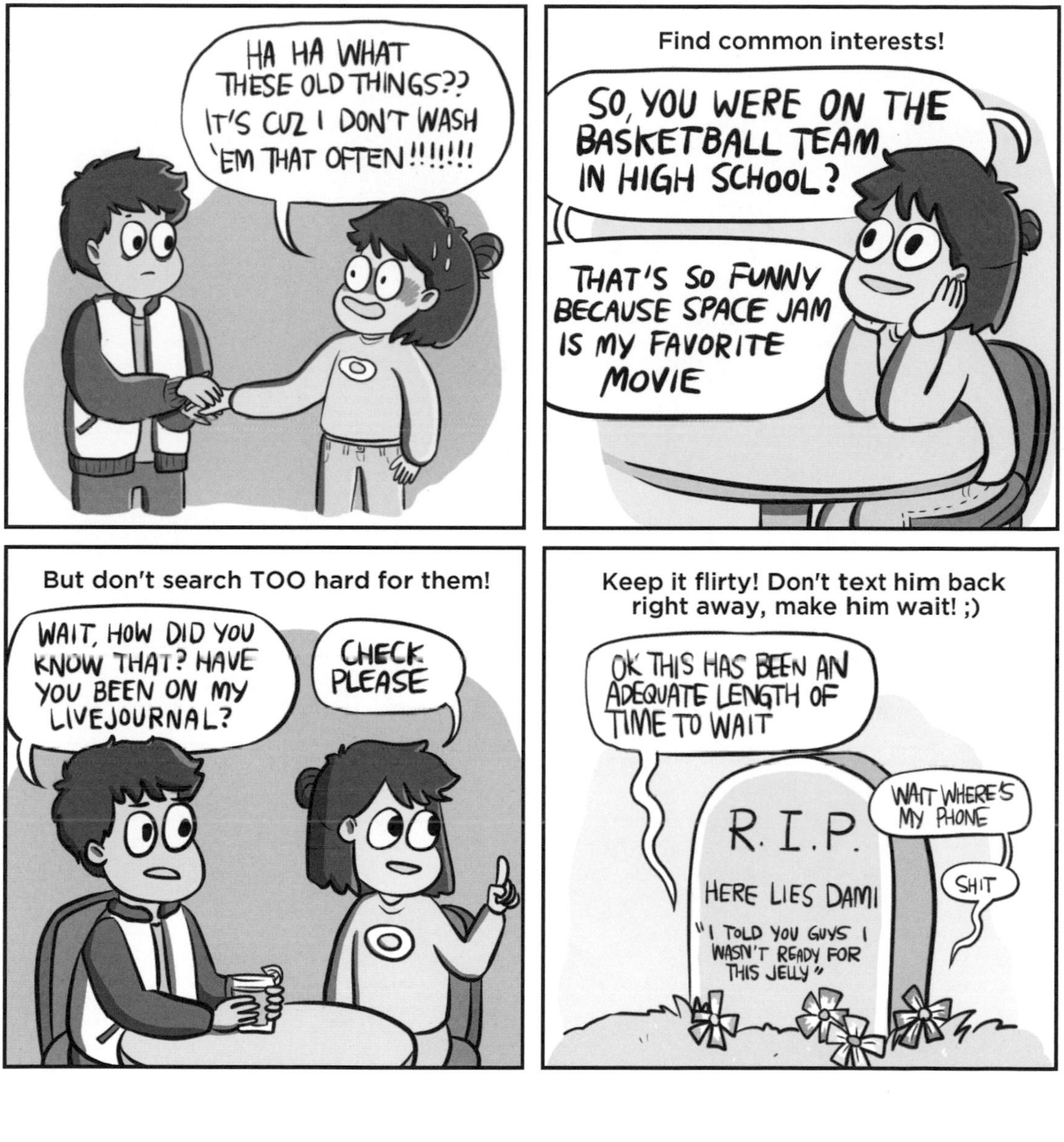
HA HA WHAT THESE OLD THINGS?? IT'S CUZ I DON'T WASH 'EM THAT OFTEN!!!!!!!
Find common interests!
SO, YOU WERE ON THE BASKETBALL TEAM IN HIGH SCHOOL?
THAT'S SO FUNNY BECAUSE SPACE JAM IS MY FAVORITE MOVIE
But don't search TOO hard for them!
WAIT, HOW DID YOU KNOW THAT? HAVE YOU BEEN ON MY LIVEJOURNAL?
CHECK PLEASE
Keep it flirty! Don't text him back right away, make him wait! ;)
OK THIS HAS BEEN AN ADEQUATE LENGTH OF TIME TO WAIT
R.I.P.
HERE LIES DAMI
"I TOLD YOU GUYS I WASN'T READY FOR THIS JELLY"
WAIT WHERE'S MY PHONE
SHIT

BAD FOODS TO EAT ON A FIRST DATE

NOT LIKE THE OTHERS

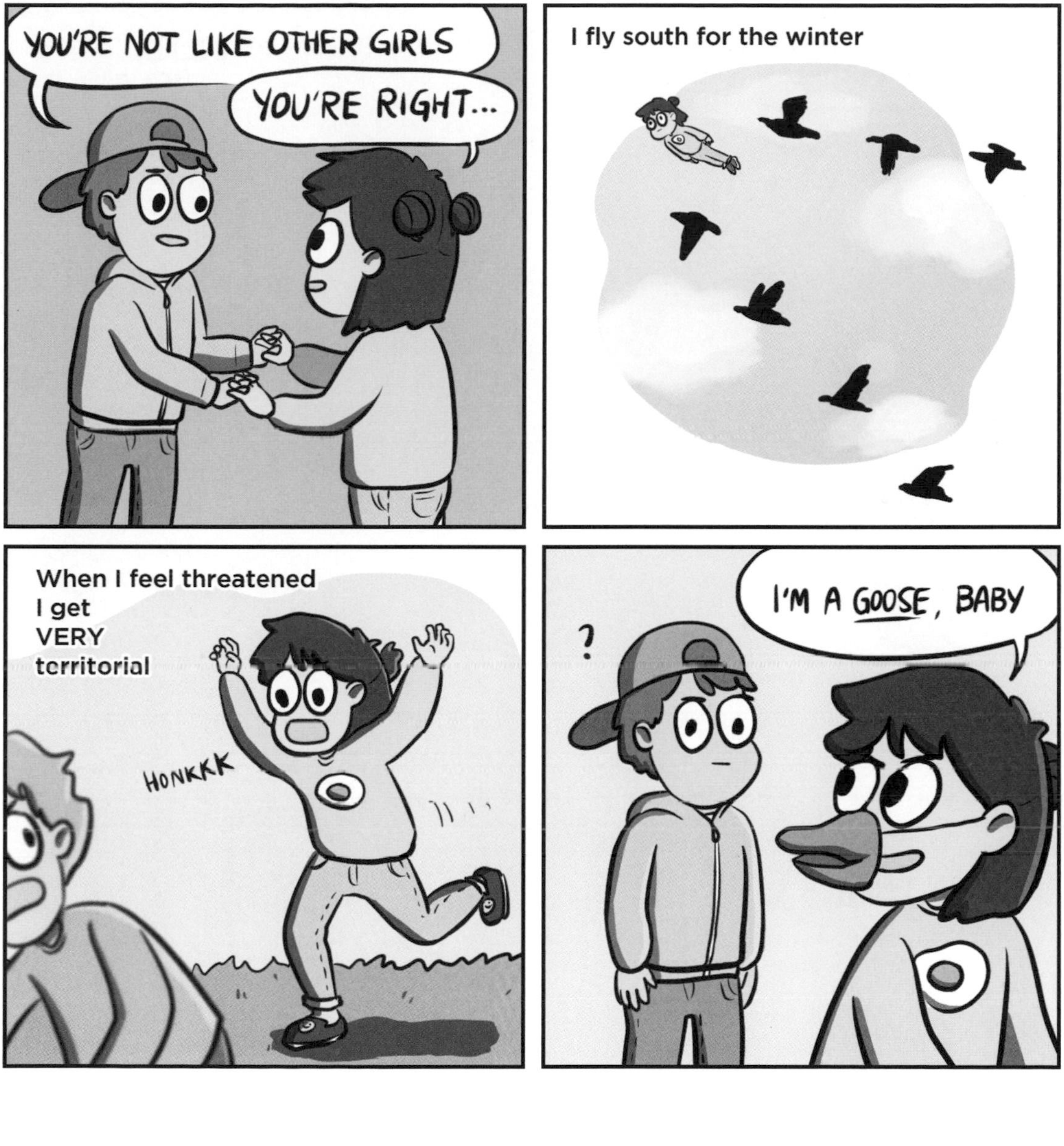
YOU'RE NOT LIKE OTHER GIRLS
YOU'RE RIGHT...
I fly south for the winter
When I feel threatened
I get
VERY
territorial
HONKKK
?
I'M A GOOSE, BABY

SEAL THE DEAL

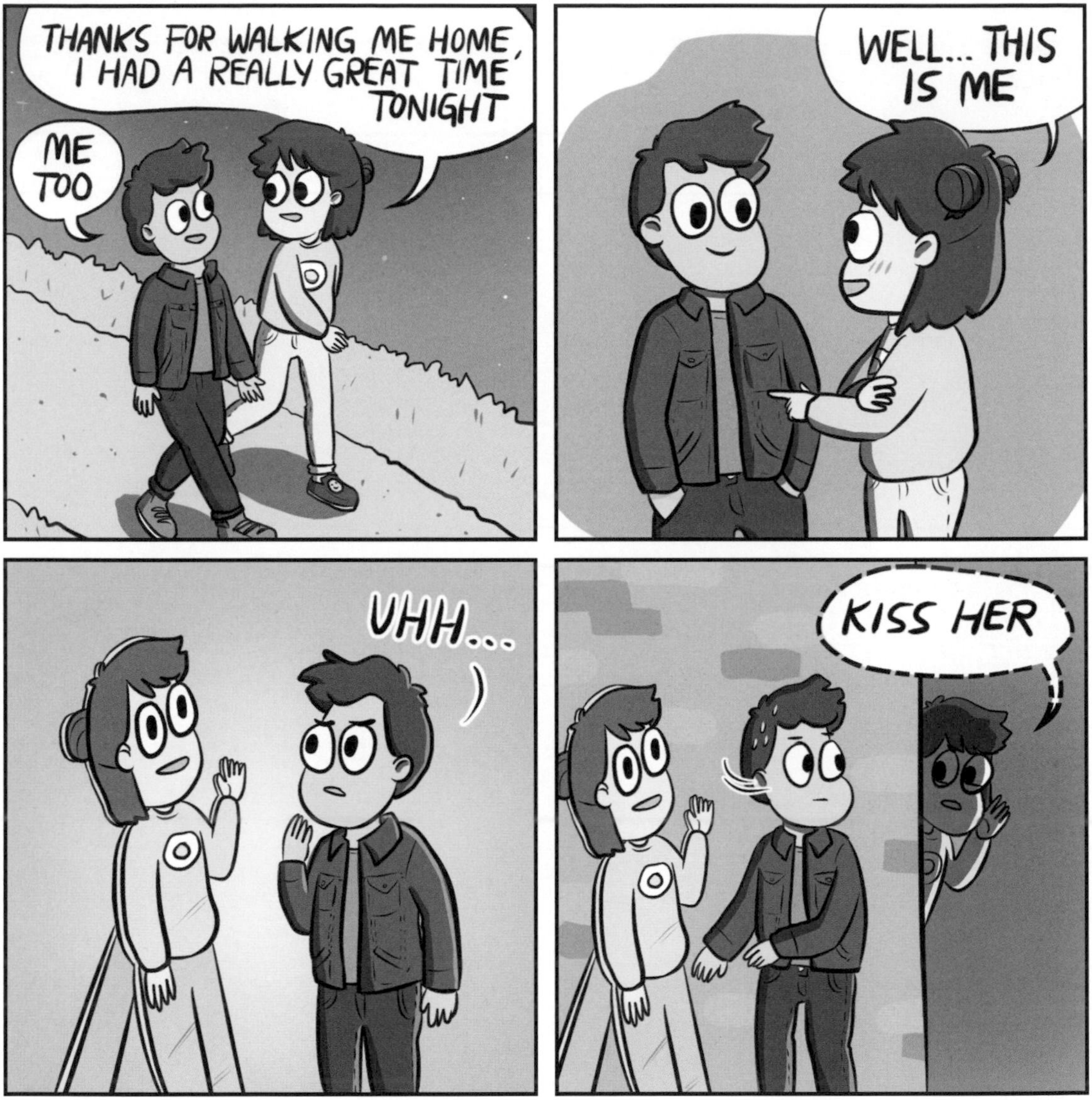
THANKS FOR WALKING ME HOME, I HAD A REALLY GREAT TIME TONIGHT
ME TOO
WELL... THIS IS ME
UHH...
KISS HER

MARKS OF LOVE

You can usually tell when someone's in love. It's written all over their face.

Or literally shown all over their face with marks of love.

OH THESE OL' THANGS?

These marks are telling of our closest relationships.

I JUST WANT THESE MARKS TO FADE BY THE TIME I GET TO WORK.

COME BACK TO BED, BABE

SIGH

I'VE GOT RECEIPTS

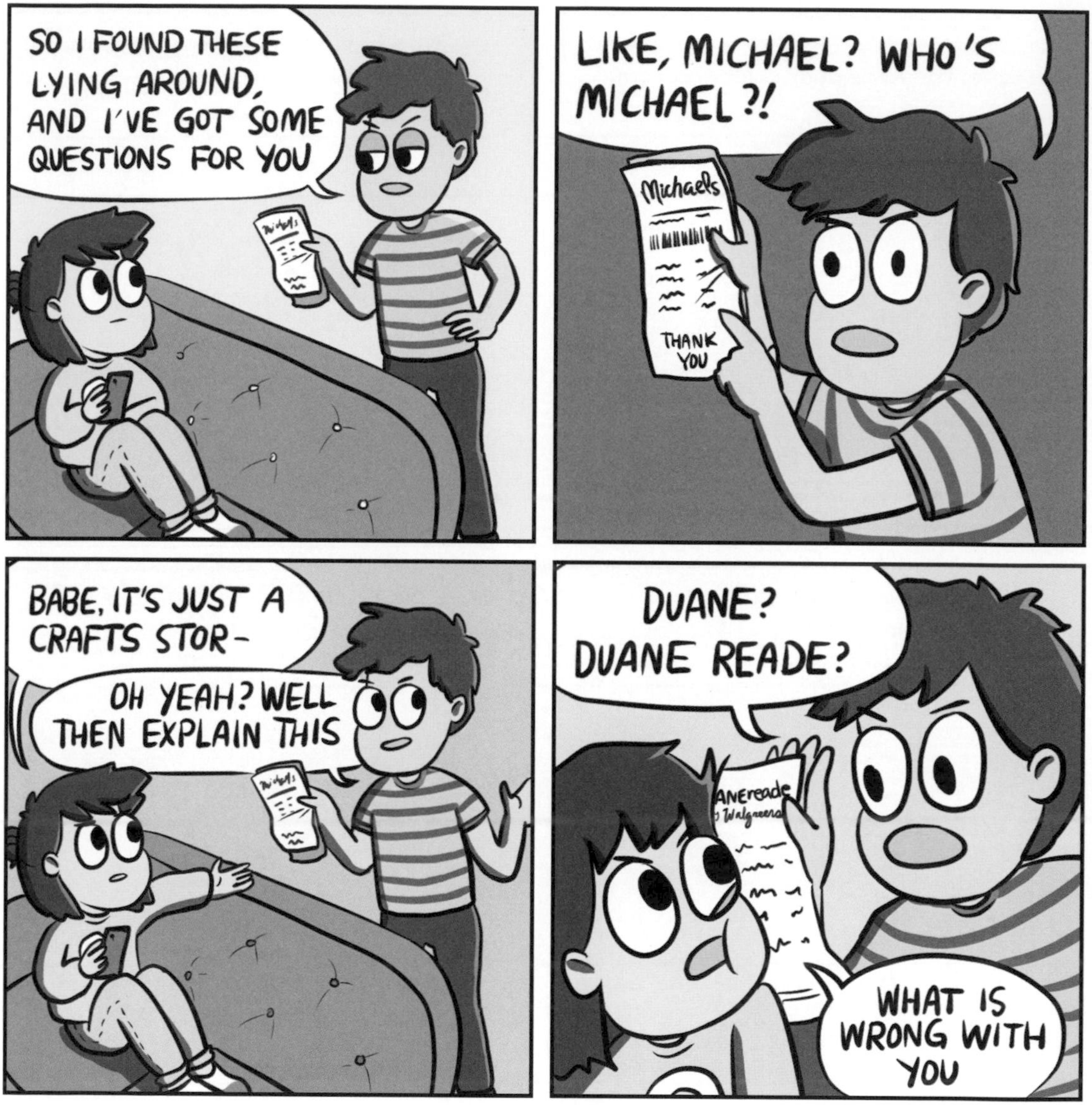
SO I FOUND THESE LYING AROUND, AND I'VE GOT SOME QUESTIONS FOR YOU
LIKE, MICHAEL? WHO'S MICHAEL?!
Michaels
THANK YOU
BABE, IT'S JUST A CRAFTS STOR-
OH YEAH? WELL THEN EXPLAIN THIS
DUANE? DUANE READE?
WHAT IS WRONG WITH YOU

WEEKEND GETAWAY

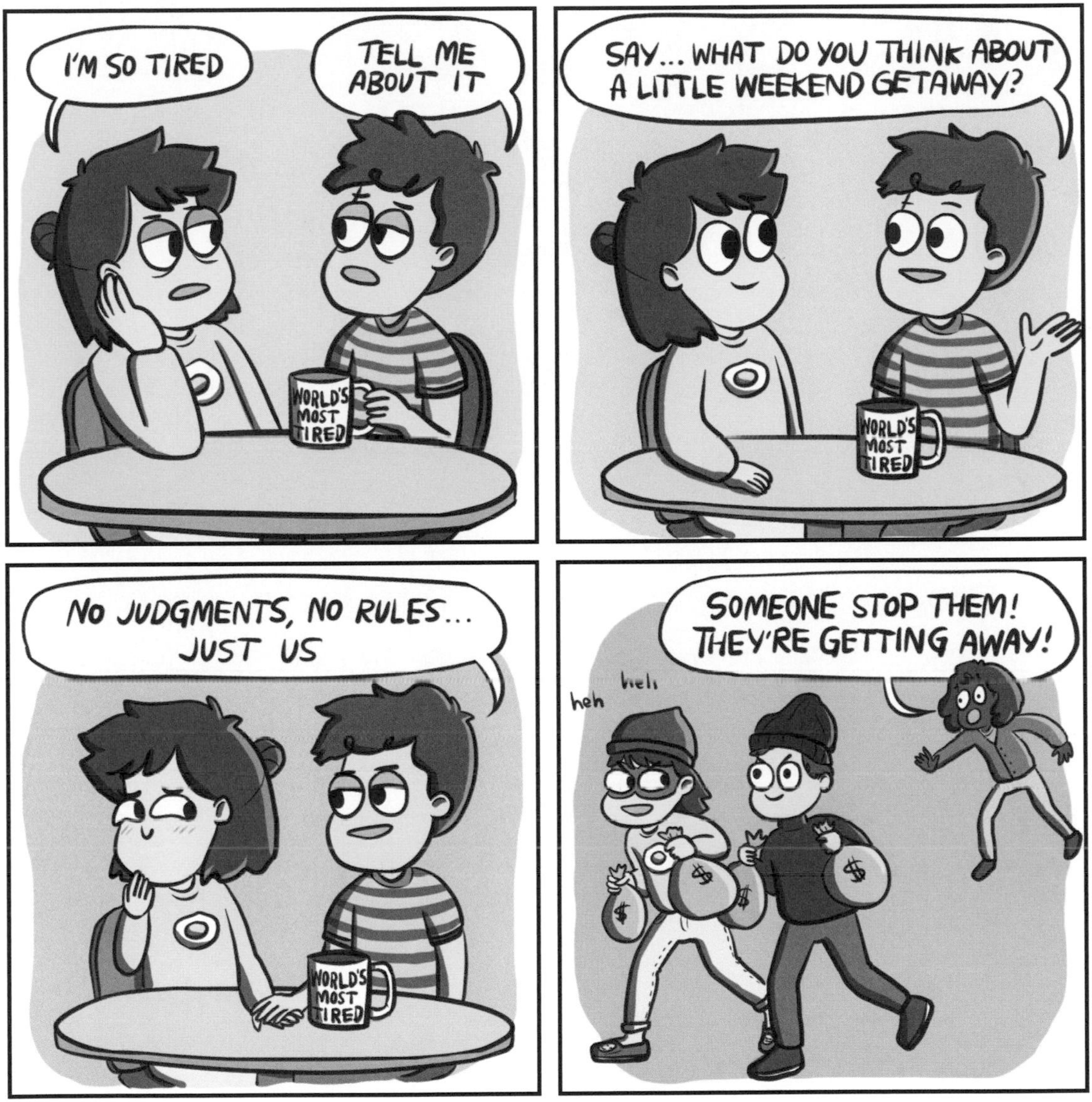
I'M SO TIRED
TELL ME ABOUT IT
WORLD'S MOST TIRED
SAY... WHAT DO YOU THINK ABOUT A LITTLE WEEKEND GETAWAY?
WORLD'S MOST TIRED
NO JUDGMENTS, NO RULES... JUST US
WORLD'S MOST TIRED
SOMEONE STOP THEM! THEY'RE GETTING AWAY!
heh
heh

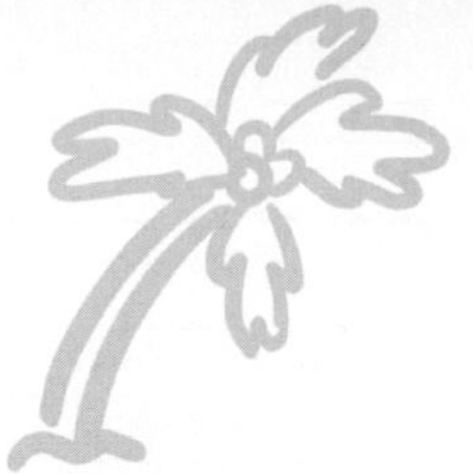

THE STATE OF THINGS NOW

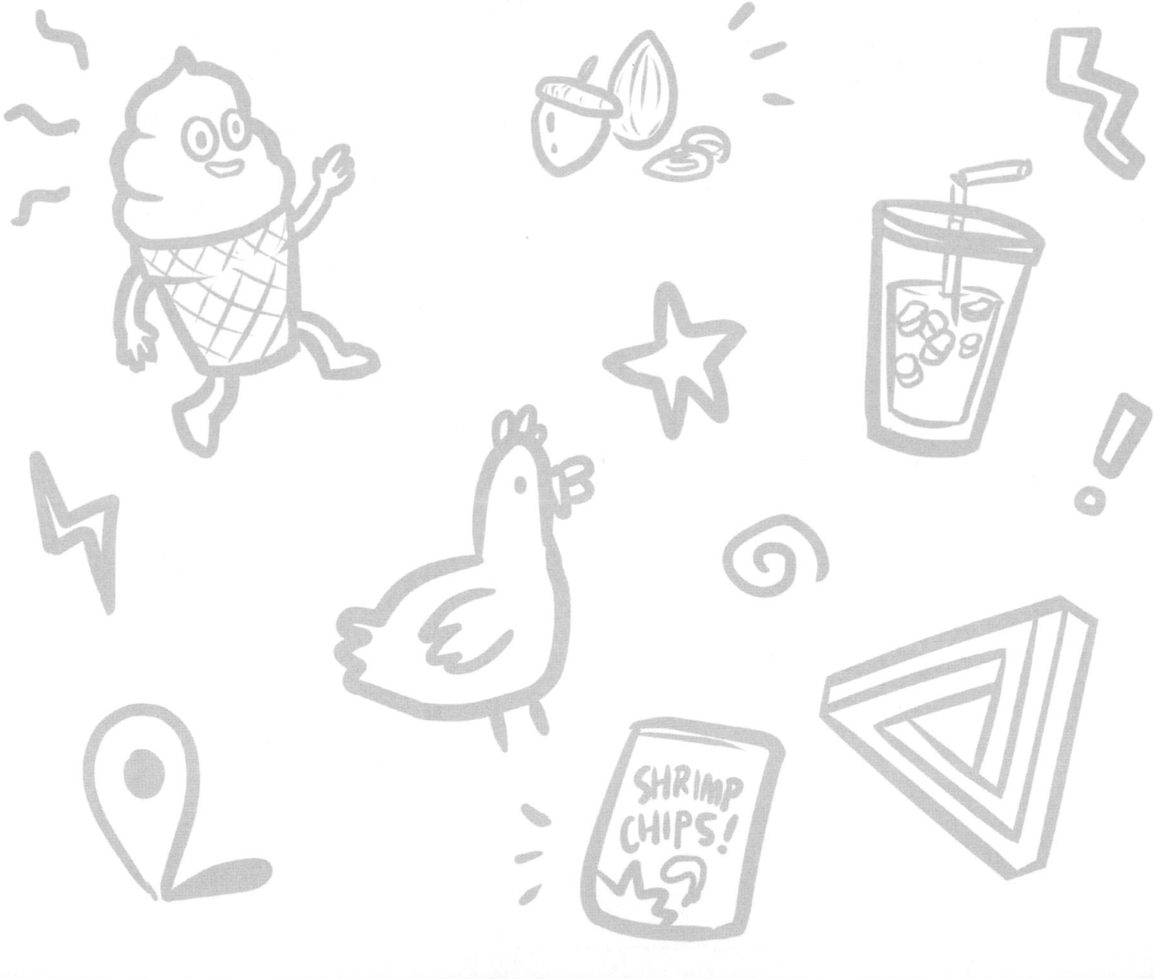
SHRIMP CHIPS!

Because I like to live on the edge, at least twice a week I will come home from work, and immediately have to start drawing, in a race against the clock to meet a comic deadline. This after-work crunch time happens to be when evening in New York aligns with daytime in Seoul. This means one thing: my mom will undoubtedly call or send me adorable photos of my growing baby niece.

When I lived in Korea, I always had FOMO looking at pictures of my friends' nights out; these days, whenever I'm cooped up in my apartment drawing, I get the fear that I'm missing out on being with my family back home. When I look at what I'm drawing on my screen, there is usually something very dumb on it, like an incredibly buff kangaroo.

But living so far away from my family has given me a whole new appreciation for them. It makes me wonder what kind of children I'll have, and what kind of mother I'll be. Will I be a fun, cool mom, or will I be a literal helicopter parent? It's a lot to chew on. So these are comics about the state of things now, in which I balance my two jobs while daydreaming about the future, all while saving a little time for snacks. There's always time for snacking.

TIME DIFFERENCE

It can be hard living in a different country from your parents.

MA
PA
TEDDY
ME

The trickiest part is the 13-hour time difference.

+13

Sometimes I'll forget and accidentally text my mom when she's asleep.

WOOPS

It won't matter though, because she'll always respond.

3:43 AM
DAMI
DAMI
HI MOM
3:40 AM
3:42 AM
WHAT'S UP?

WHY DO I LIVE HERE

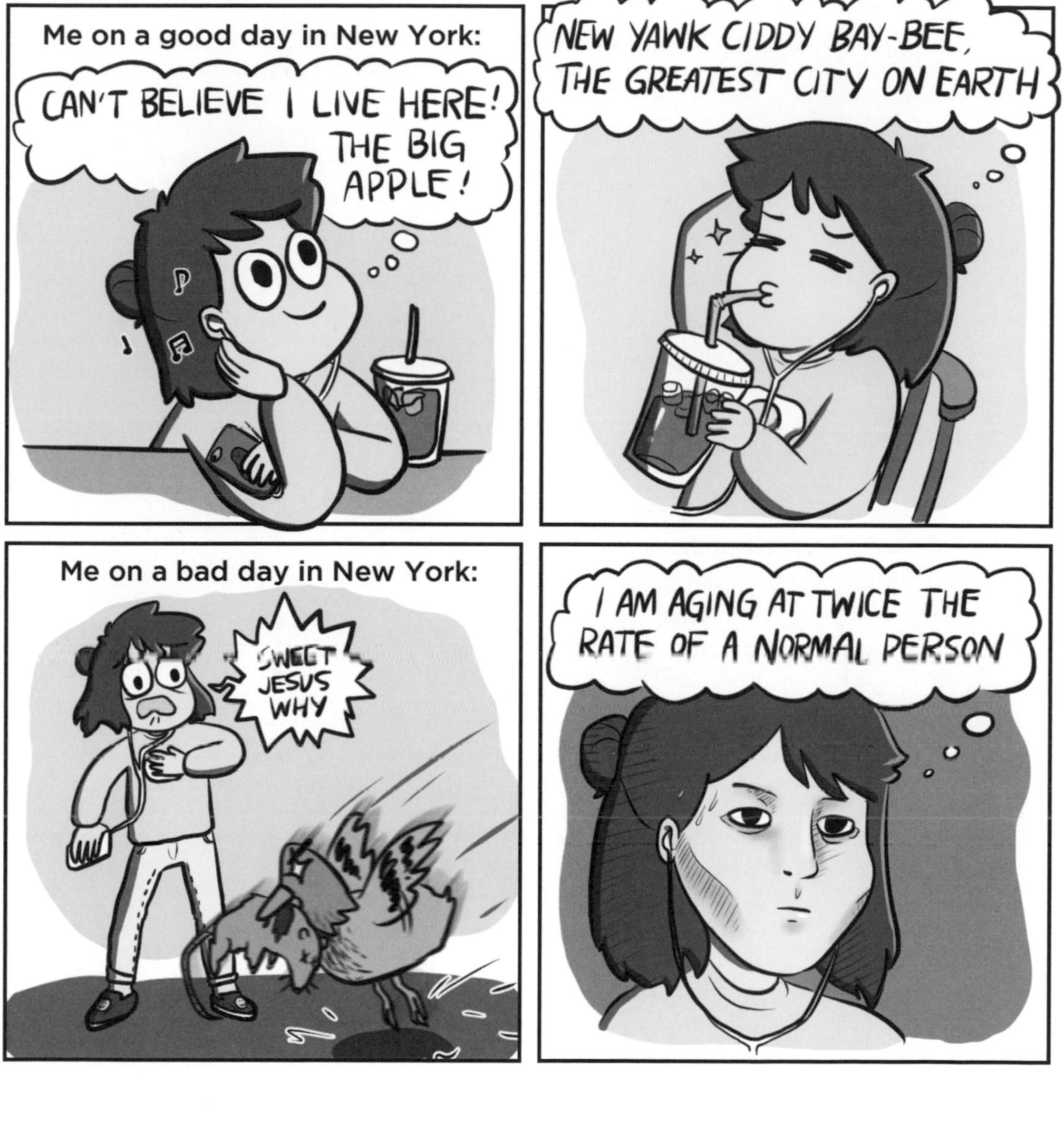

Me on a good day in New York:
CAN'T BELIEVE I LIVE HERE! THE BIG APPLE!
NEW YAWK CIDDY BAY-BEE, THE GREATEST CITY ON EARTH
Me on a bad day in New York:
SWEET JESUS WHY
I AM AGING AT TWICE THE RATE OF A NORMAL PERSON

CITY WORKOUT

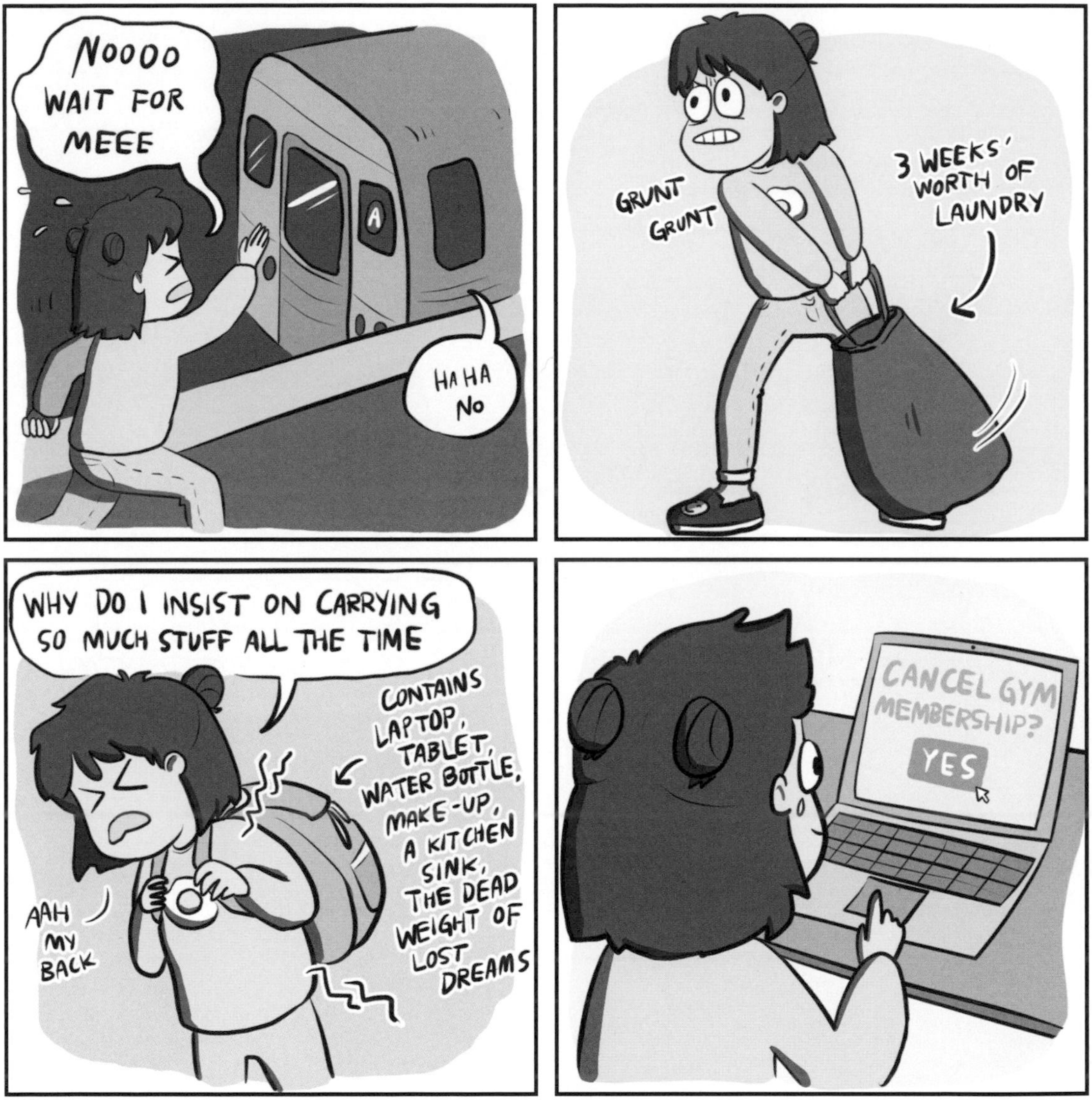

NOOOO WAIT FOR MEEE
HA HA NO
GRUNT GRUNT
3 WEEKS' WORTH OF LAUNDRY
WHY DO I INSIST ON CARRYING SO MUCH STUFF ALL THE TIME
CONTAINS LAPTOP, TABLET, WATER BOTTLE, MAKE-UP, A KITCHEN SINK, THE DEAD WEIGHT OF LOST DREAMS
AAH MY BACK
CANCEL GYM MEMBERSHIP?
YES

ADULTHOOD → SQUIRRELHOOD

When my company relocated, it pushed my commute to over an hour.

7:30 AM

NO BIG DEAL, JUST GOTTA WAKE UP 30 MINUTES EARLIER NOW!

It was harder to adjust to than expected.

8:53 AM

SO... HUNGRY

A lot harder.

DO YOU NEED TO SIT DOWN?

thank... you...

Now I carry nuts and berries to snack on in the subway so I don't faint from hunger.

CRUNCH CRUNCH

I'm embracing my new life as a squirrel.

IT'S TIME

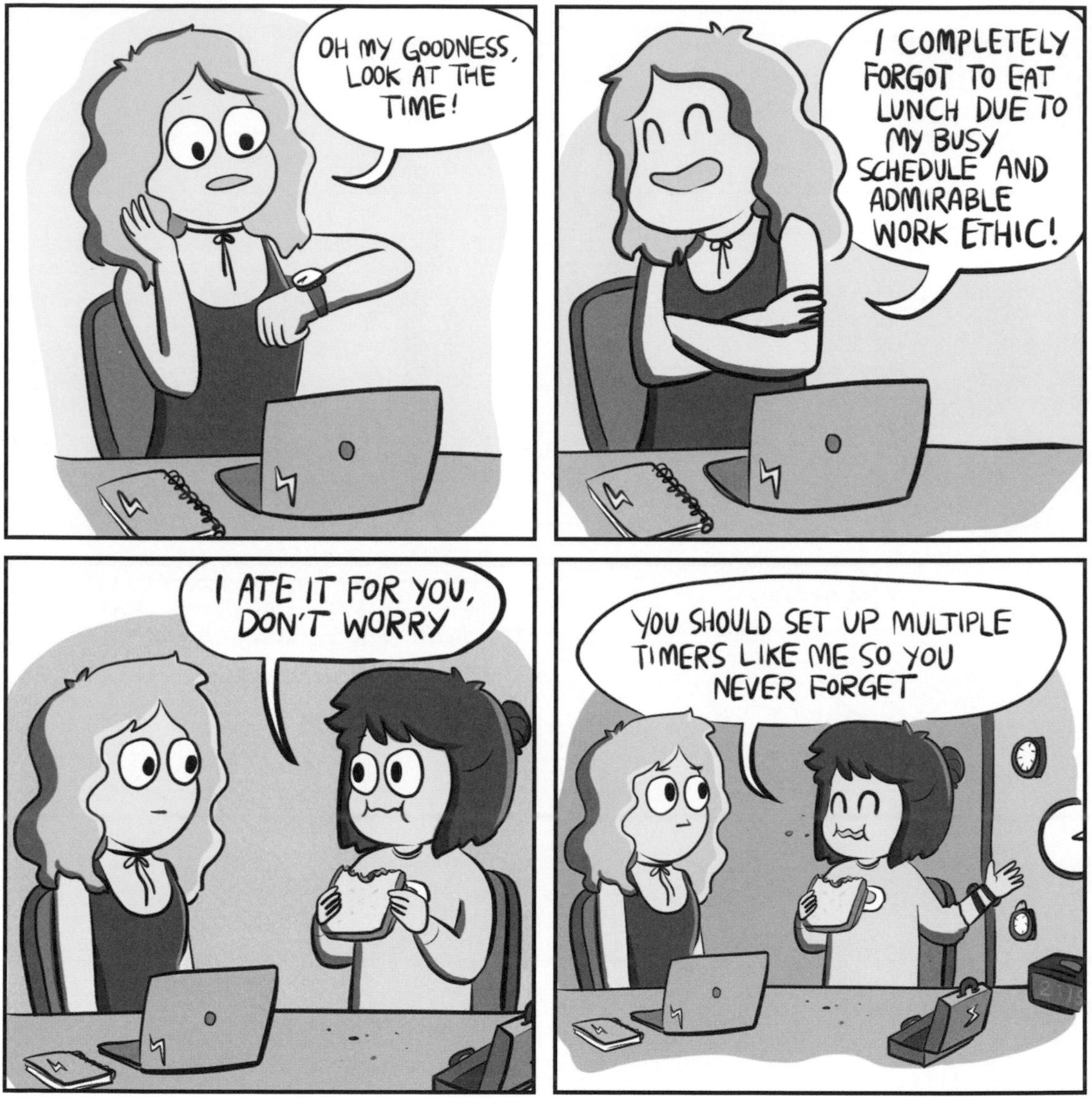

OH MY GOODNESS, LOOK AT THE TIME!
I COMPLETELY FORGOT TO EAT LUNCH DUE TO MY BUSY SCHEDULE AND ADMIRABLE WORK ETHIC!
I ATE IT FOR YOU, DON'T WORRY
YOU SHOULD SET UP MULTIPLE TIMERS LIKE ME SO YOU NEVER FORGET

OFFICE THRILLS

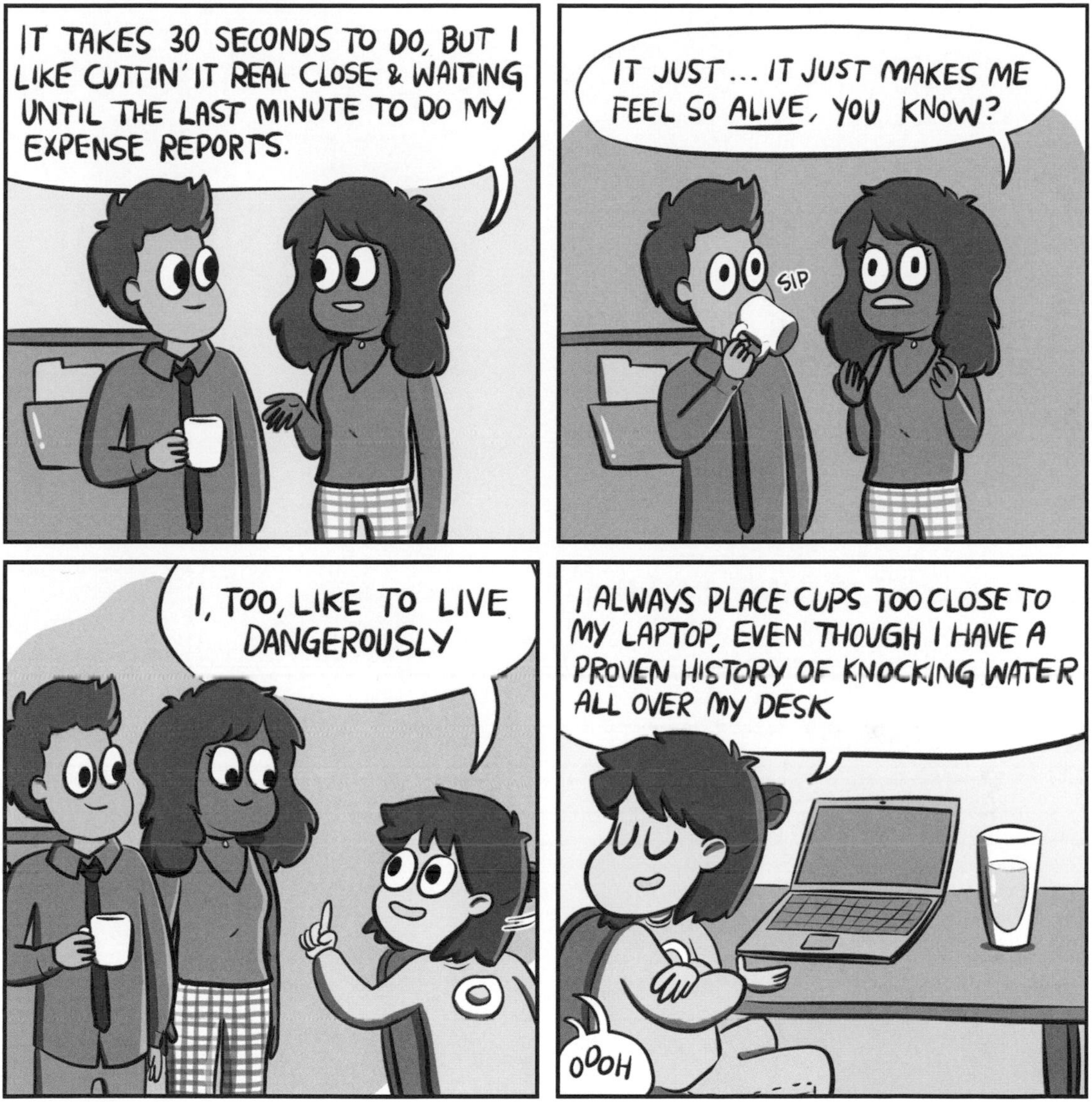

IT TAKES 30 SECONDS TO DO, BUT I LIKE CUTTIN' IT REAL CLOSE & WAITING UNTIL THE LAST MINUTE TO DO MY EXPENSE REPORTS.
IT JUST... IT JUST MAKES ME FEEL SO ALIVE, YOU KNOW?
SIP
I, TOO, LIKE TO LIVE DANGEROUSLY
I ALWAYS PLACE CUPS TOO CLOSE TO MY LAPTOP, EVEN THOUGH I HAVE A PROVEN HISTORY OF KNOCKING WATER ALL OVER MY DESK
OOOH

MOTIVATOR

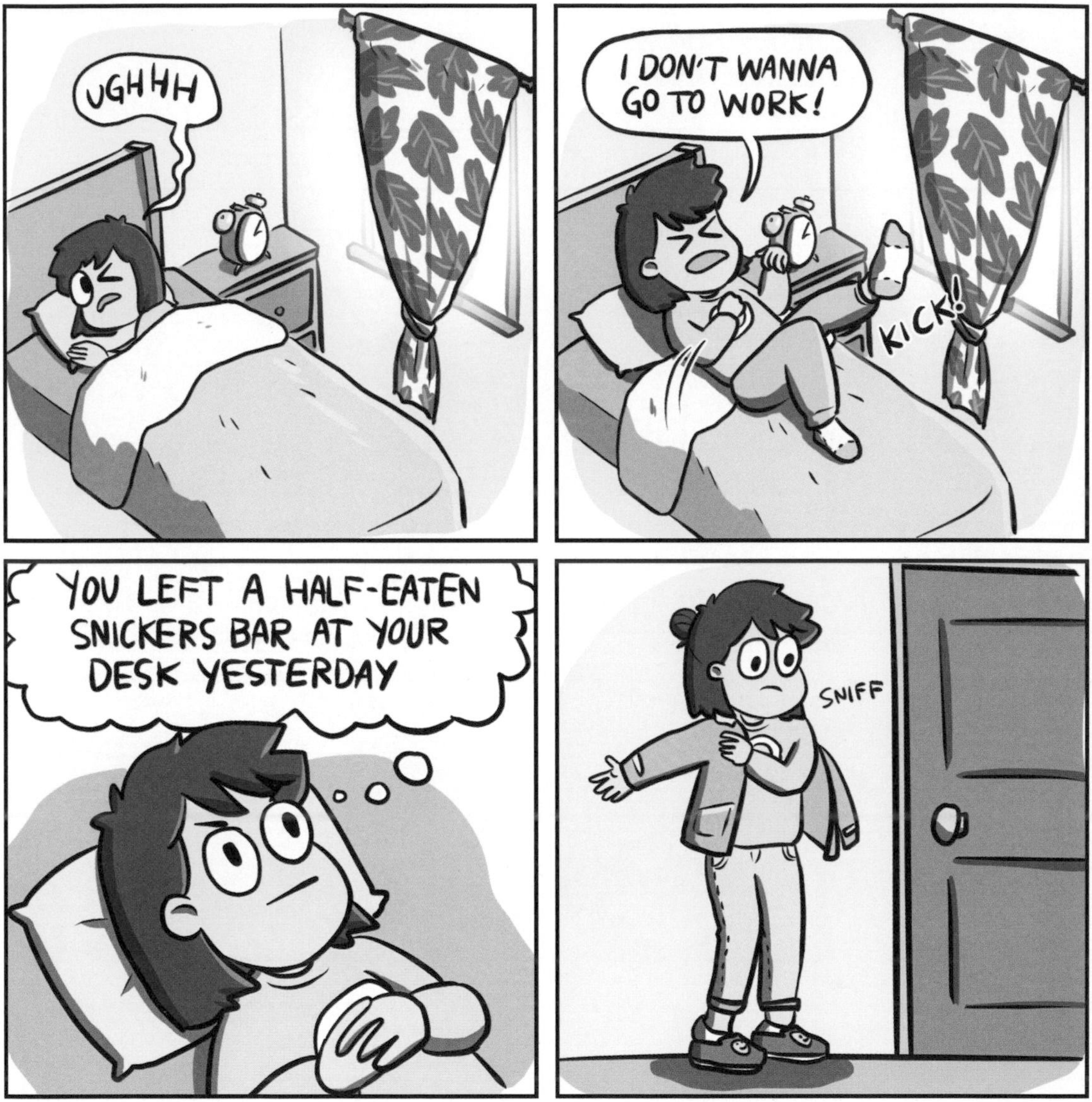
UGHHH
I DON'T WANNA GO TO WORK!
KICK!
YOU LEFT A HALF-EATEN SNICKERS BAR AT YOUR DESK YESTERDAY
SNIFF

PRETENDING NOT TO KNOW ENGLISH

VACATION MEMORIES

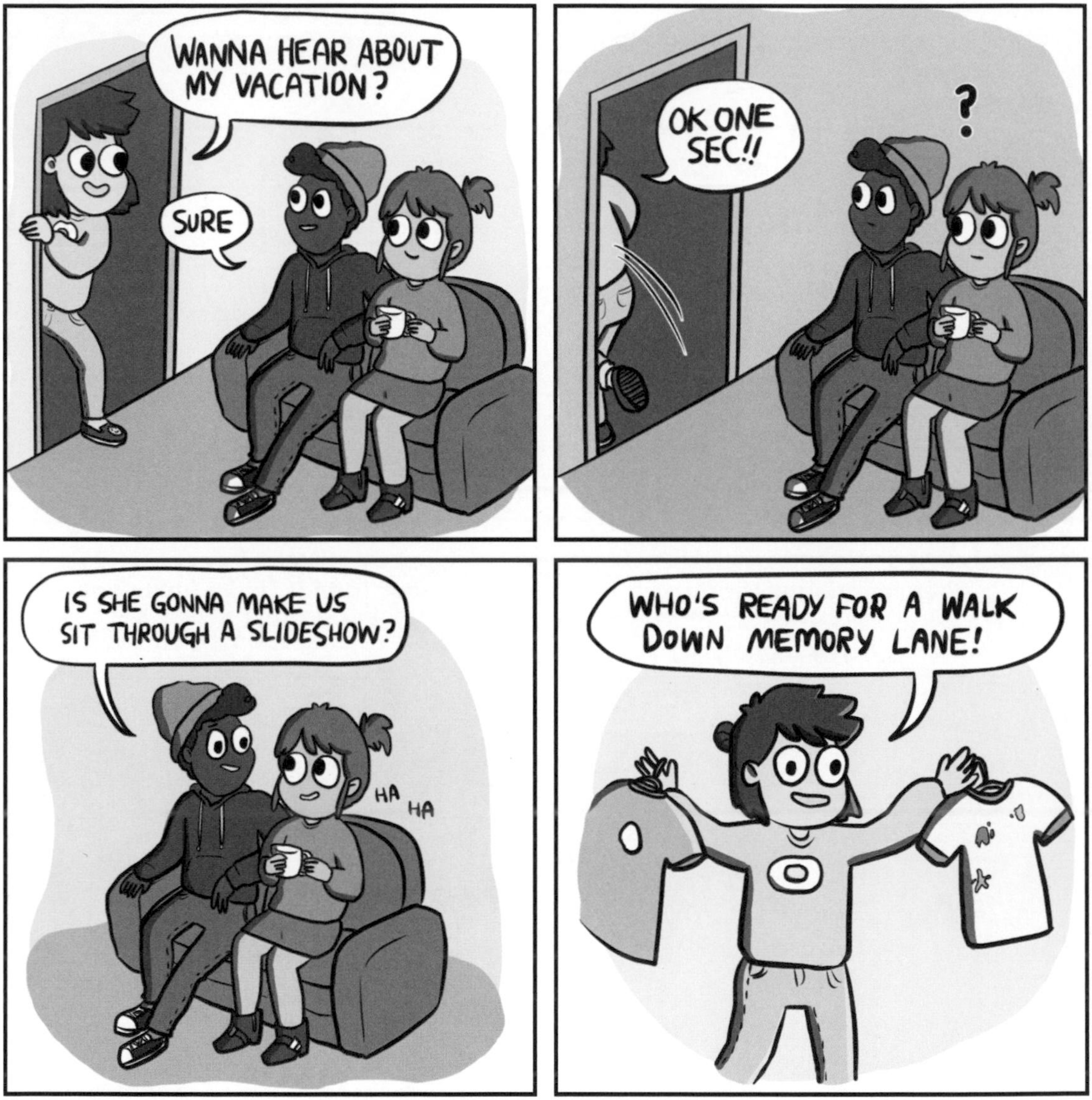
WANNA HEAR ABOUT MY VACATION?
SURE
OK ONE SEC!!
?
IS SHE GONNA MAKE US SIT THROUGH A SLIDESHOW?
HA HA
WHO'S READY FOR A WALK DOWN MEMORY LANE!

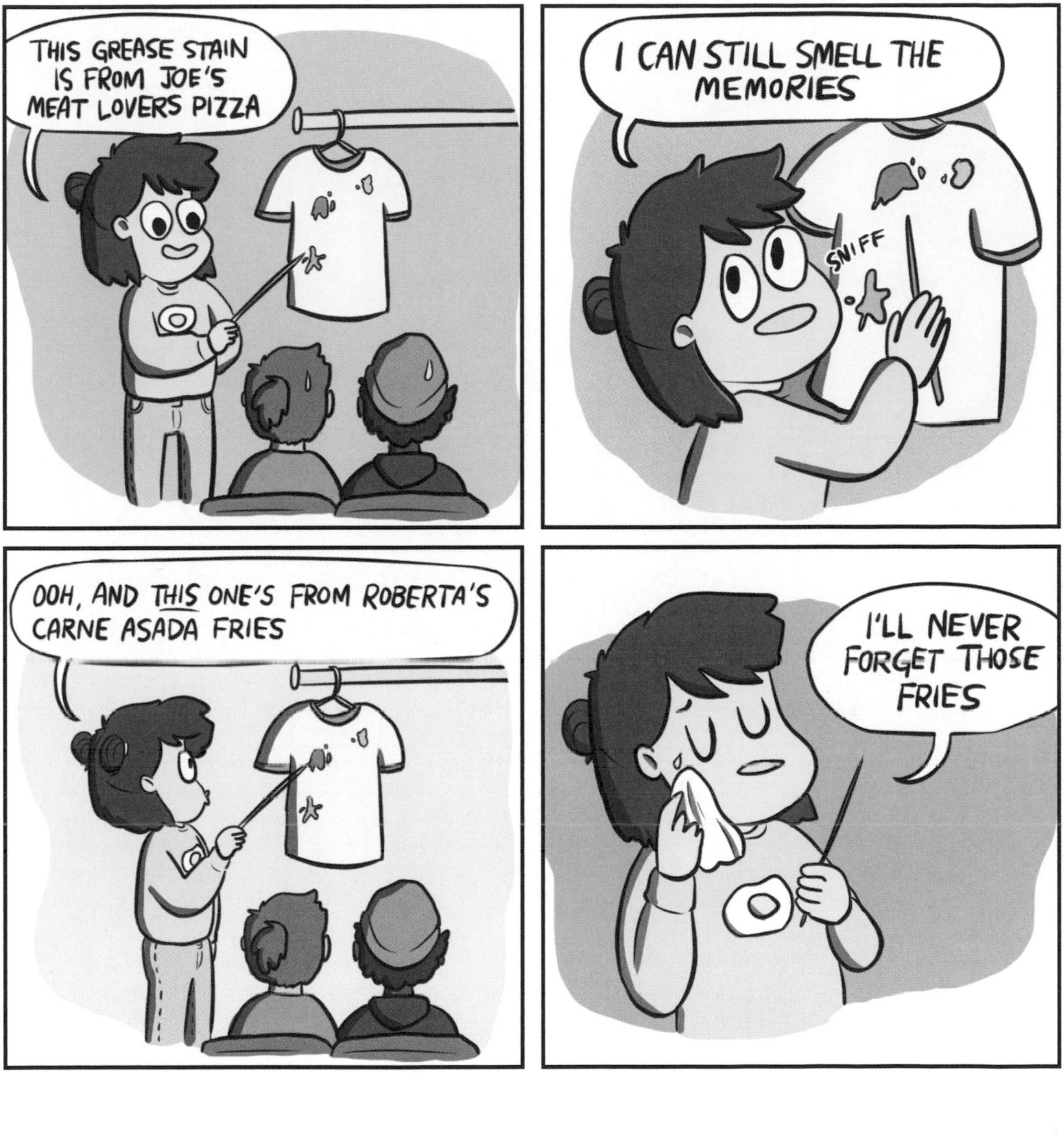
THIS GREASE STAIN IS FROM JOE'S MEAT LOVERS PIZZA
I CAN STILL SMELL THE MEMORIES
SNIFF
OOH, AND THIS ONE'S FROM ROBERTA'S CARNE ASADA FRIES
I'LL NEVER FORGET THOSE FRIES

FACETIME WITH MOM

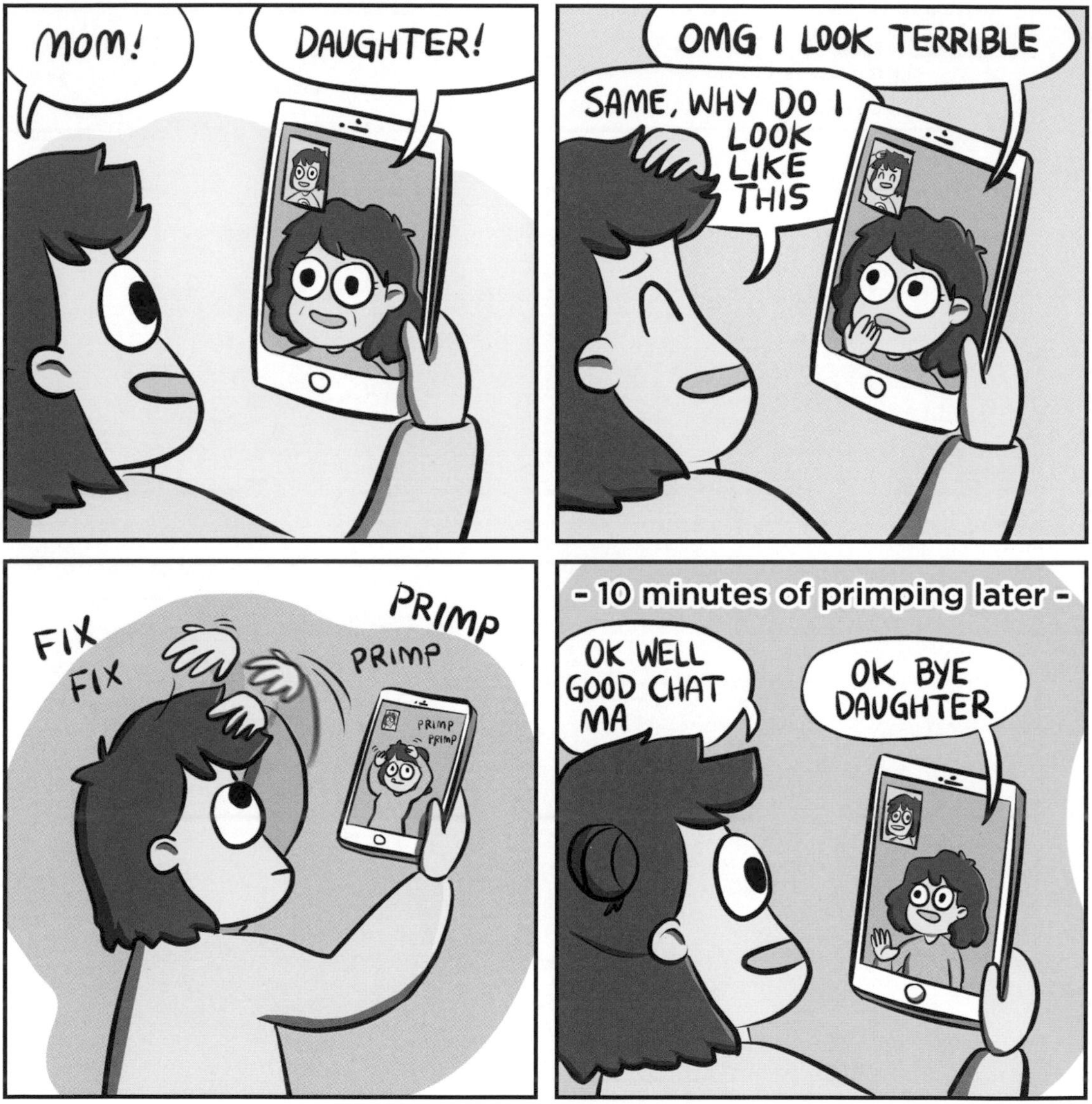
MOM!
DAUGHTER!
OMG I LOOK TERRIBLE
SAME, WHY DO I LOOK LIKE THIS
FIX
FIX
PRIMP
PRIMP
PRIMP PRIMP
- 10 minutes of primping later -
OK WELL GOOD CHAT MA
OK BYE DAUGHTER

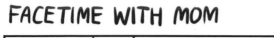

ZARA RETROGRADE

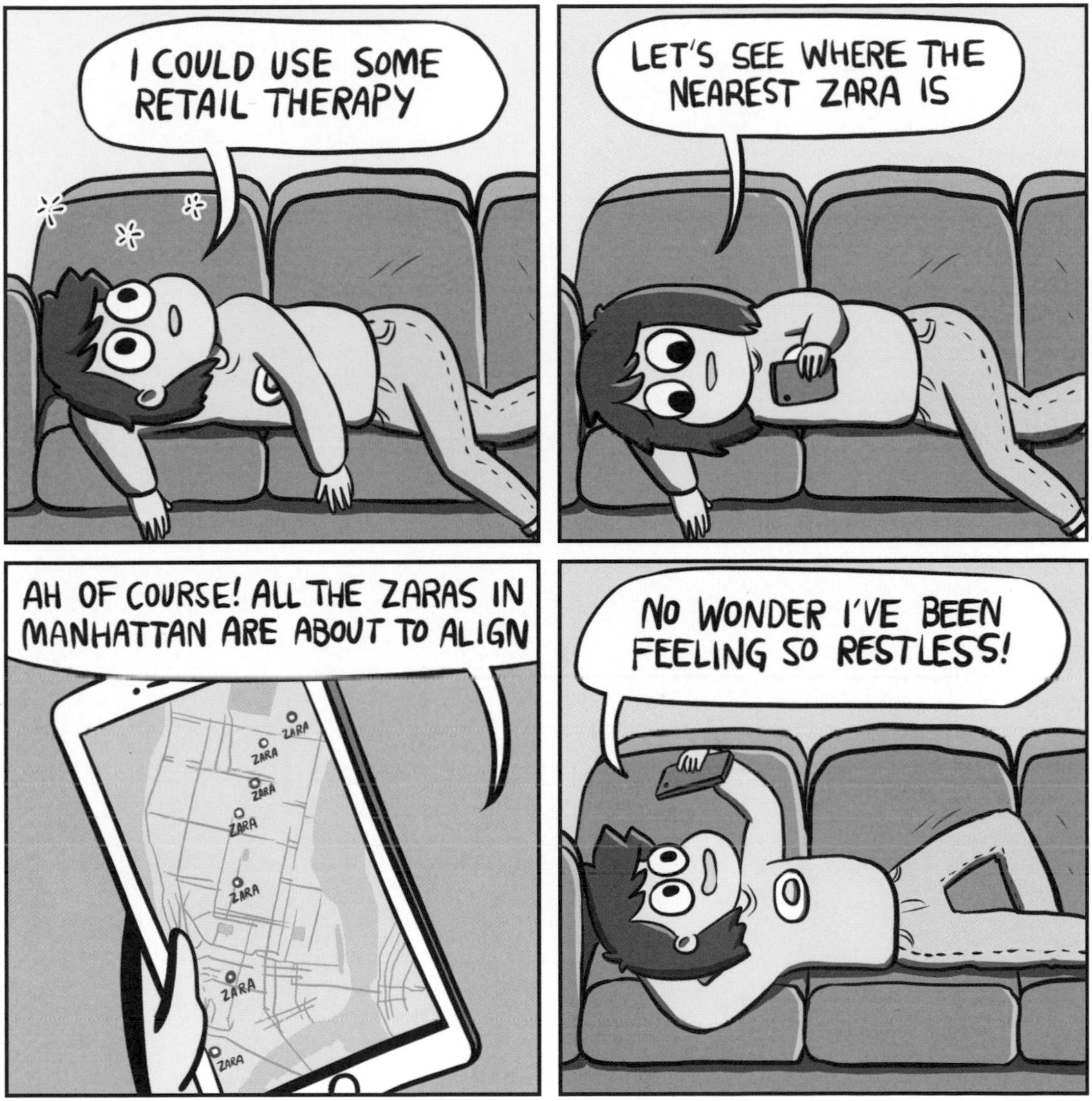
I COULD USE SOME RETAIL THERAPY
LET'S SEE WHERE THE NEAREST ZARA IS
AH OF COURSE! ALL THE ZARAS IN MANHATTAN ARE ABOUT TO ALIGN
ZARA
ZARA
ZARA
ZARA
ZARA
ZARA
ZARA
NO WONDER I'VE BEEN FEELING SO RESTLESS!

A MYSTERY

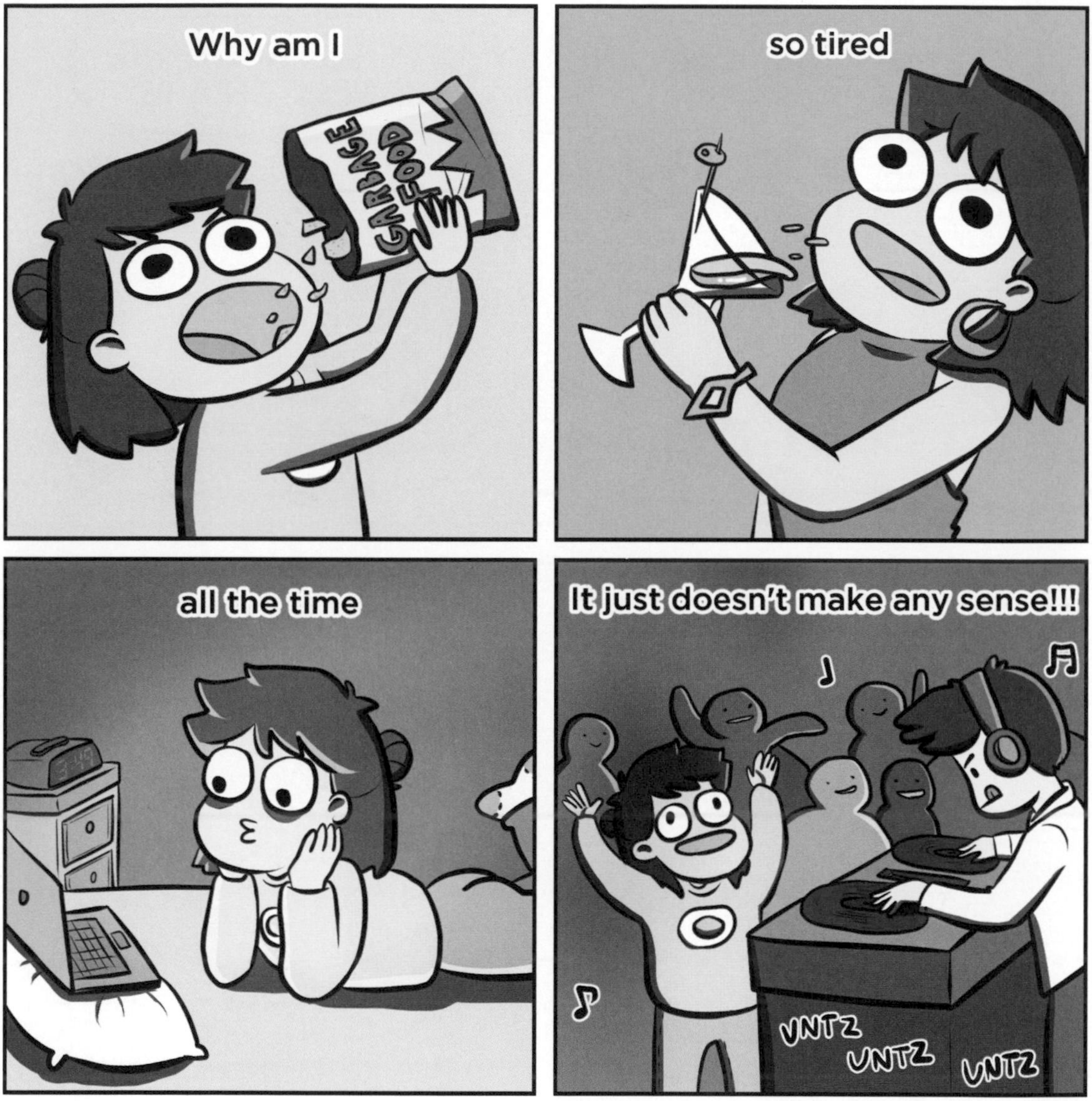
Why am I
GARBAGE FOOD
so tired
all the time
It just doesn't make any sense!!!
UNTZ
UNTZ
UNTZ

WHO PUT THOSE THERE

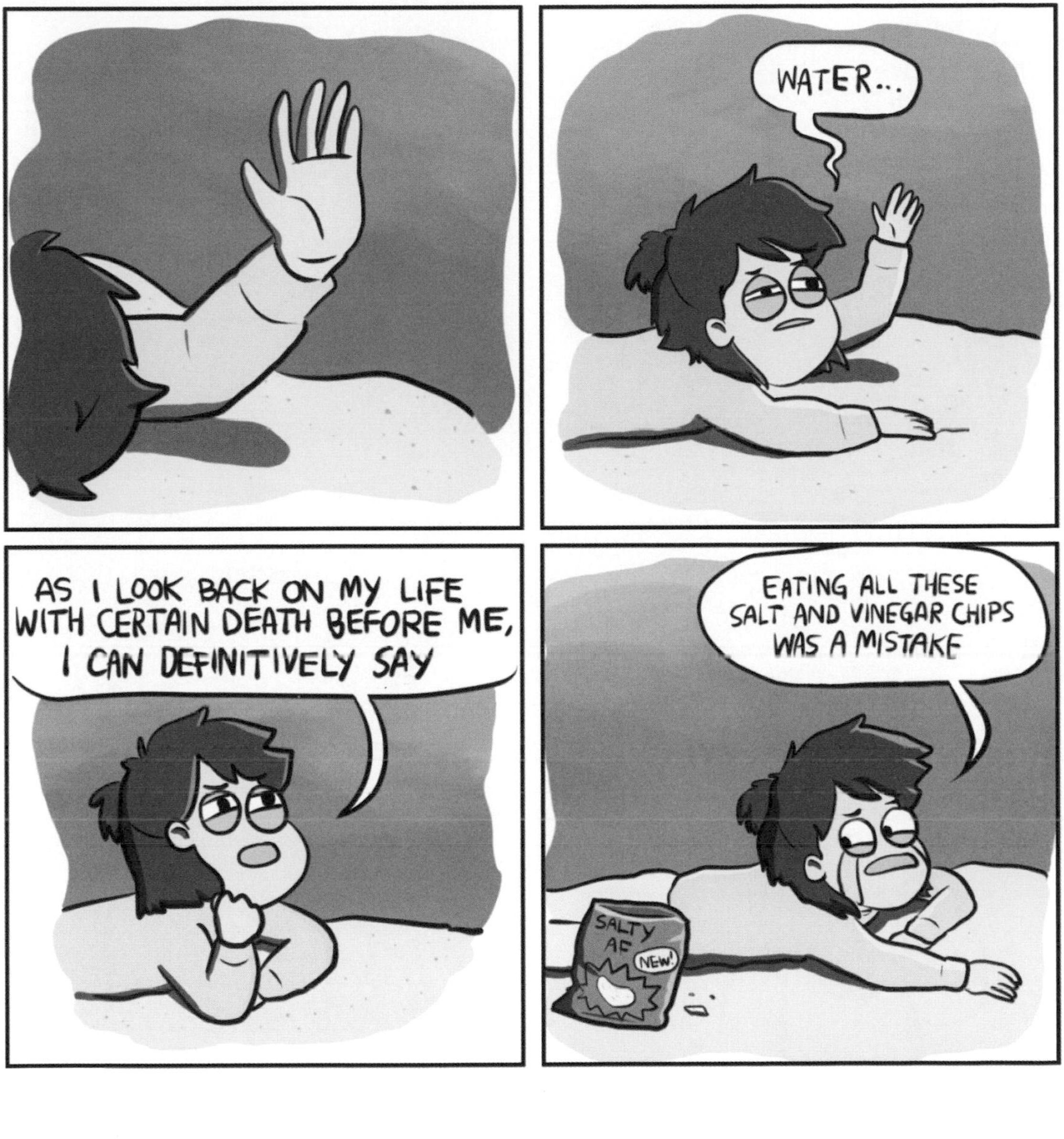
WATER...
AS I LOOK BACK ON MY LIFE WITH CERTAIN DEATH BEFORE ME, I CAN DEFINITIVELY SAY
EATING ALL THESE SALT AND VINEGAR CHIPS WAS A MISTAKE
SALTY AF
NEW!

APPETITE

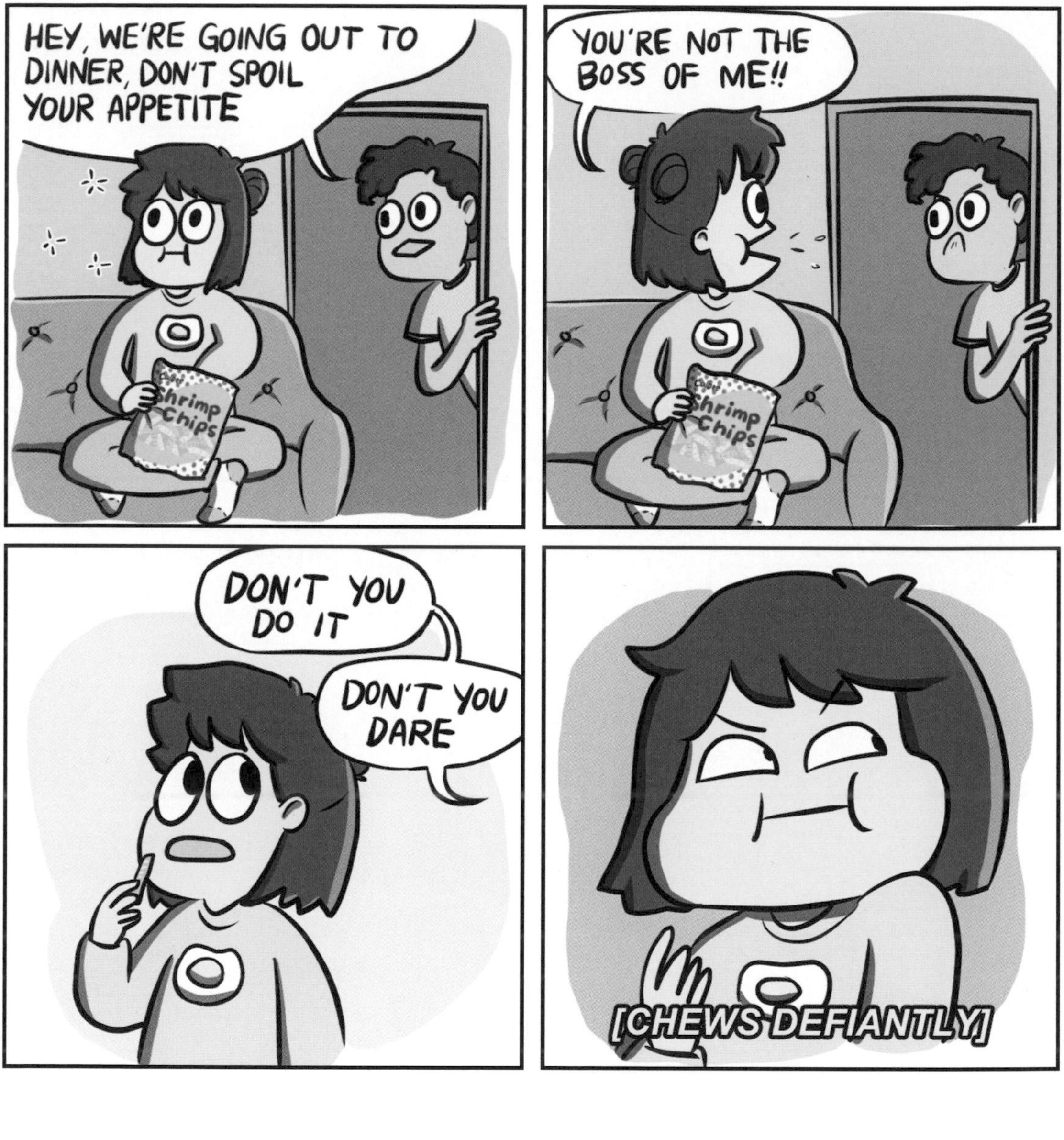

HEY, WE'RE GOING OUT TO DINNER, DON'T SPOIL YOUR APPETITE
Shrimp Chips
YOU'RE NOT THE BOSS OF ME!!
Shrimp Chips
DON'T YOU DO IT
DON'T YOU DARE
[CHEWS DEFIANTLY]

RESERVATIONS

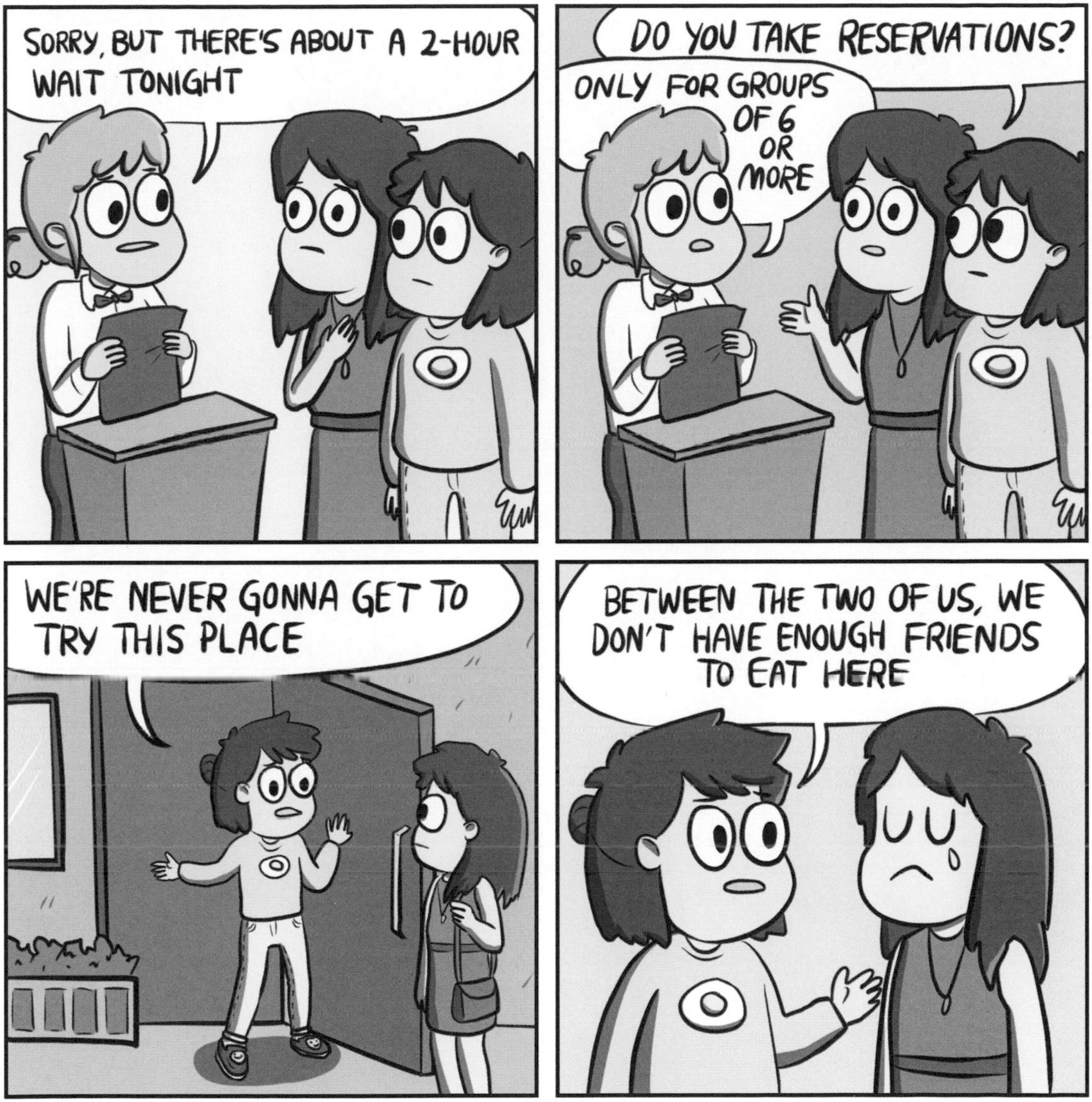
SORRY, BUT THERE'S ABOUT A 2-HOUR WAIT TONIGHT
DO YOU TAKE RESERVATIONS?
ONLY FOR GROUPS OF 6 OR MORE
WE'RE NEVER GONNA GET TO TRY THIS PLACE
BETWEEN THE TWO OF US, WE DON'T HAVE ENOUGH FRIENDS TO EAT HERE

HEALTHY EATING

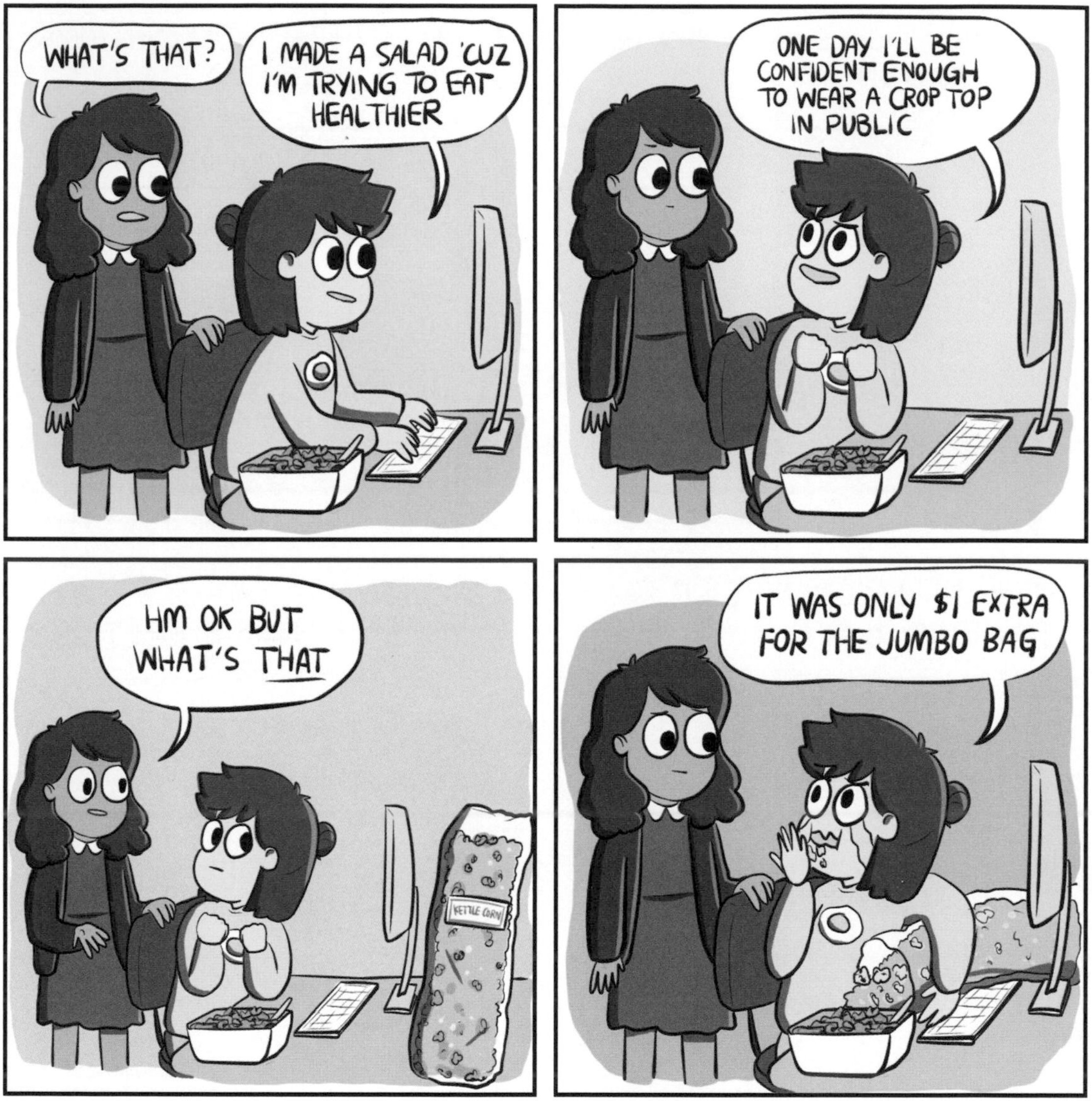
WHAT'S THAT?
I MADE A SALAD 'CUZ I'M TRYING TO EAT HEALTHIER
ONE DAY I'LL BE CONFIDENT ENOUGH TO WEAR A CROP TOP IN PUBLIC
HM OK BUT WHAT'S THAT
KETTLE CORN
IT WAS ONLY $1 EXTRA FOR THE JUMBO BAG

FOOD FRIENDS

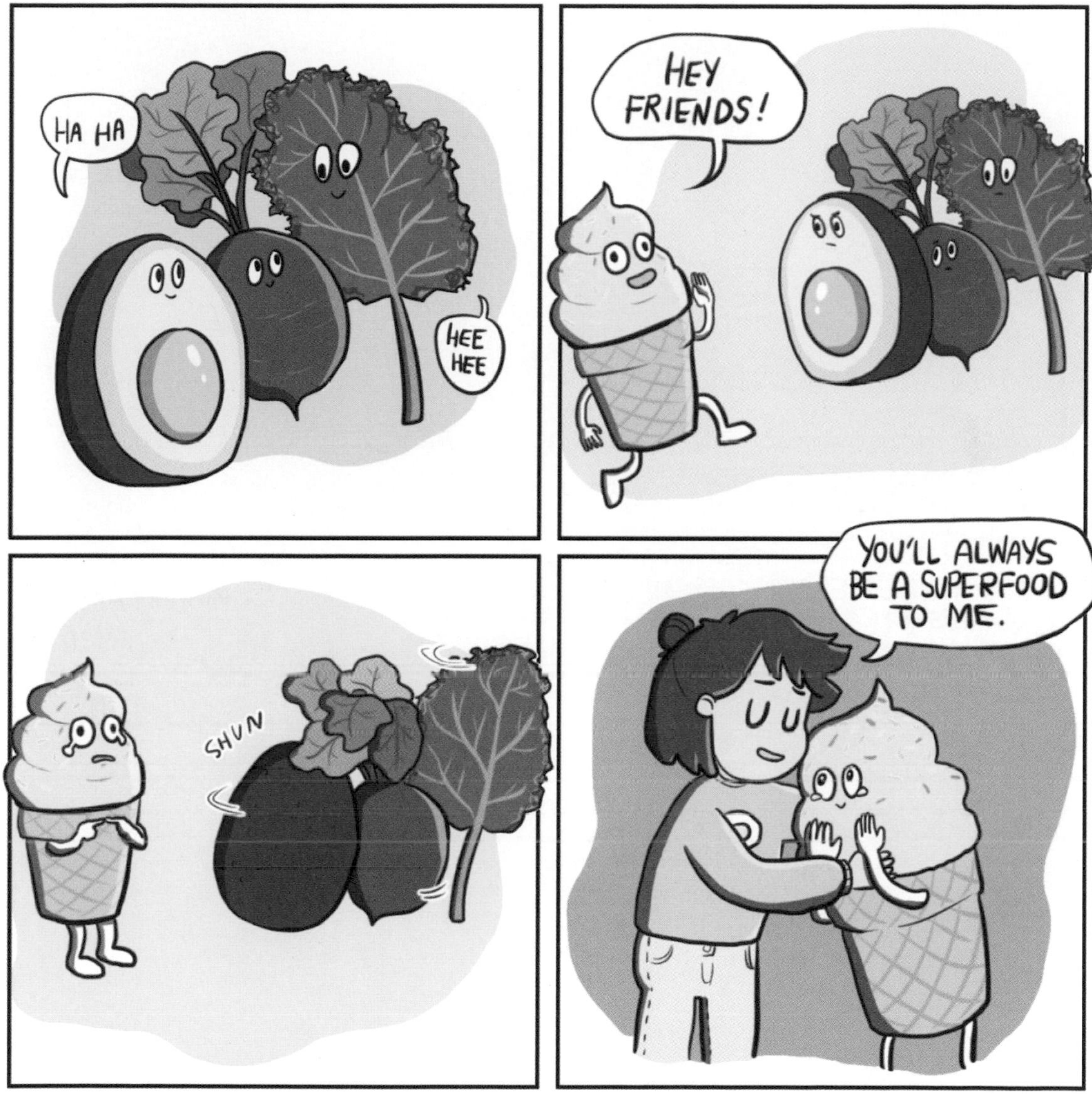
HA HA
HEE HEE
HEY FRIENDS!
SHUN
YOU'LL ALWAYS BE A SUPERFOOD TO ME.

GOLDFISH MEMORY PT. 2

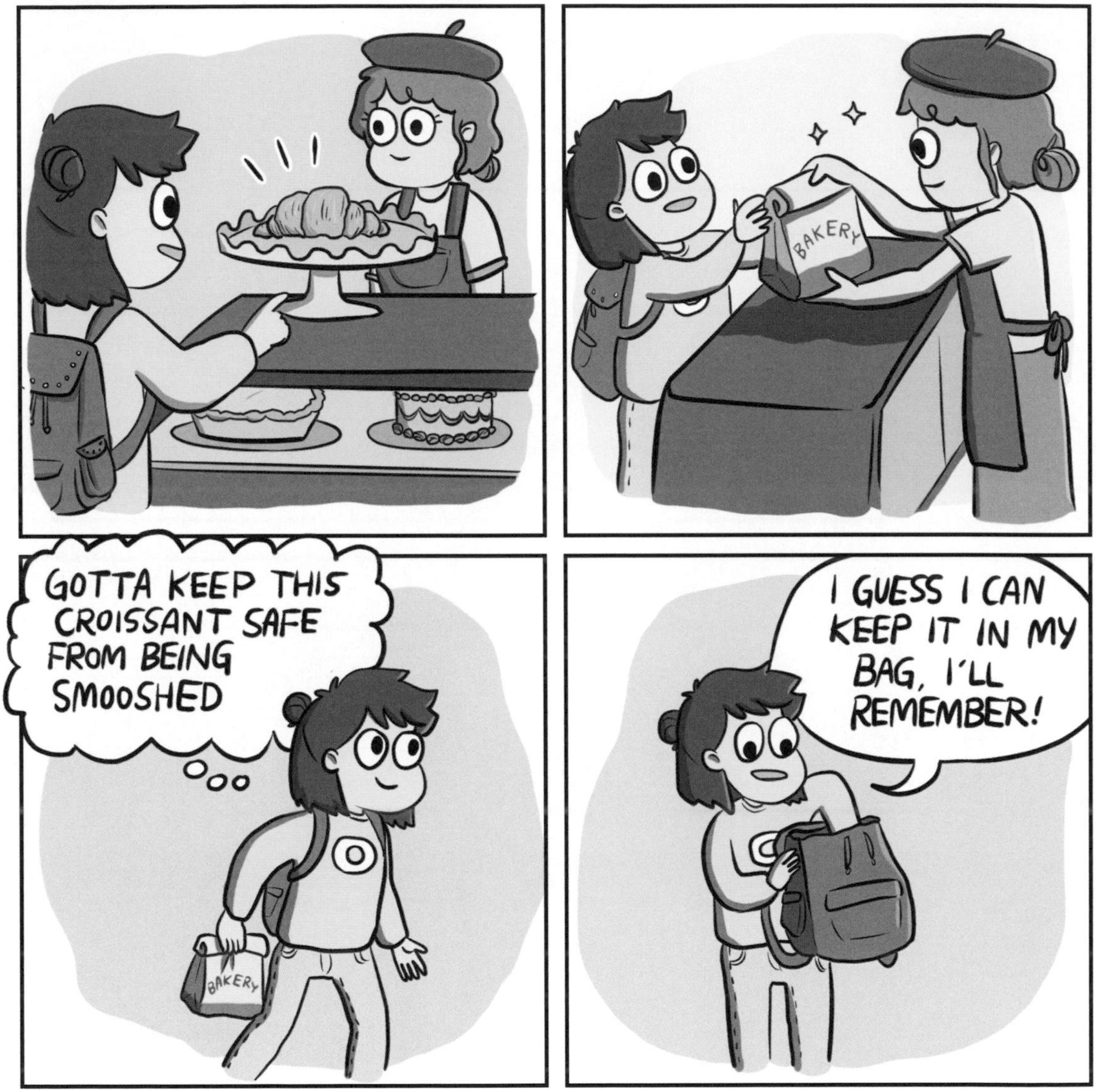
BAKERY
GOTTA KEEP THIS CROISSANT SAFE FROM BEING SMOOSHED
BAKERY
I GUESS I CAN KEEP IT IN MY BAG, I'LL REMEMBER!

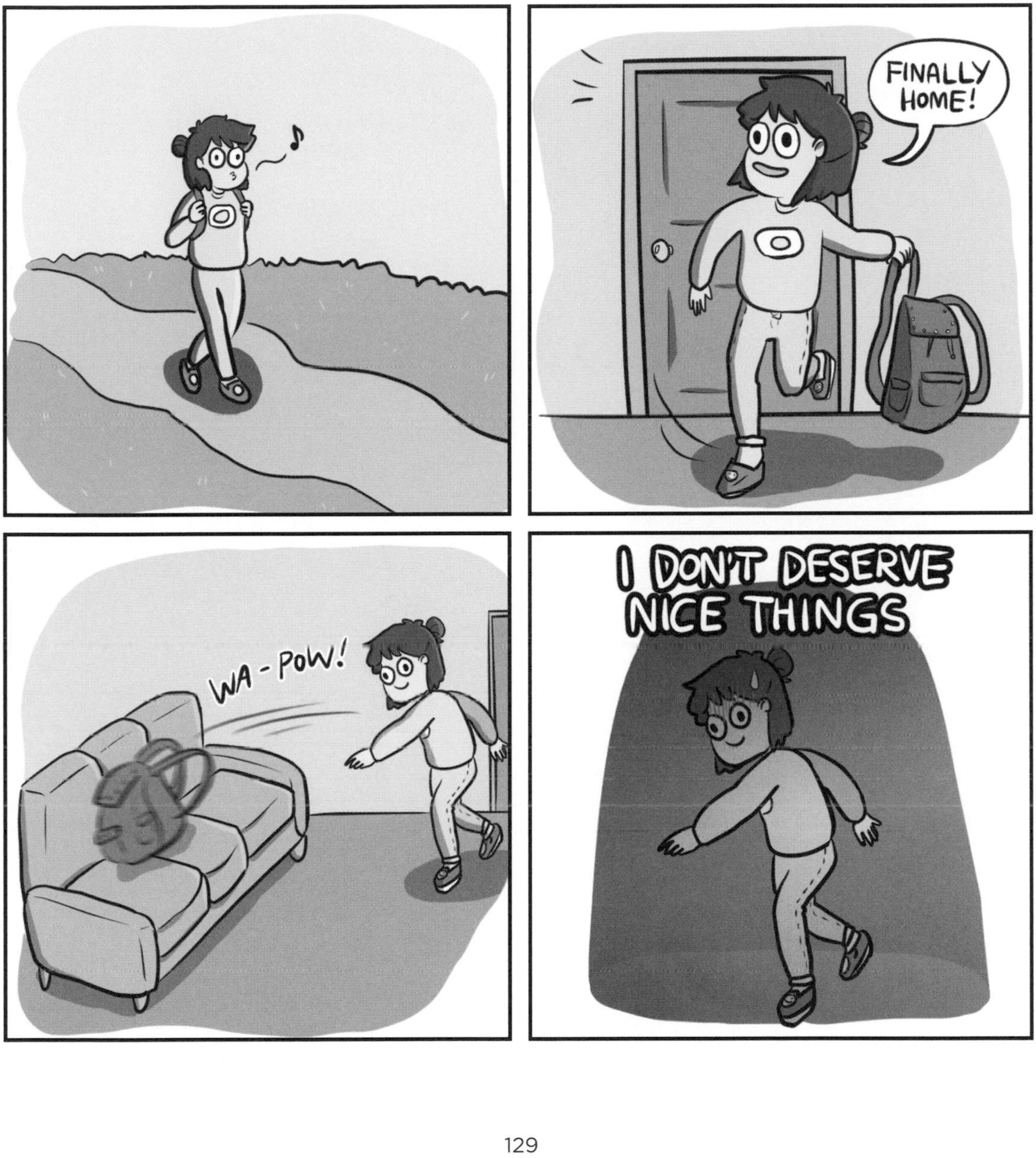
FINALLY HOME!
WA-POW!
I DON'T DESERVE NICE THINGS

ASSUMPTIONS

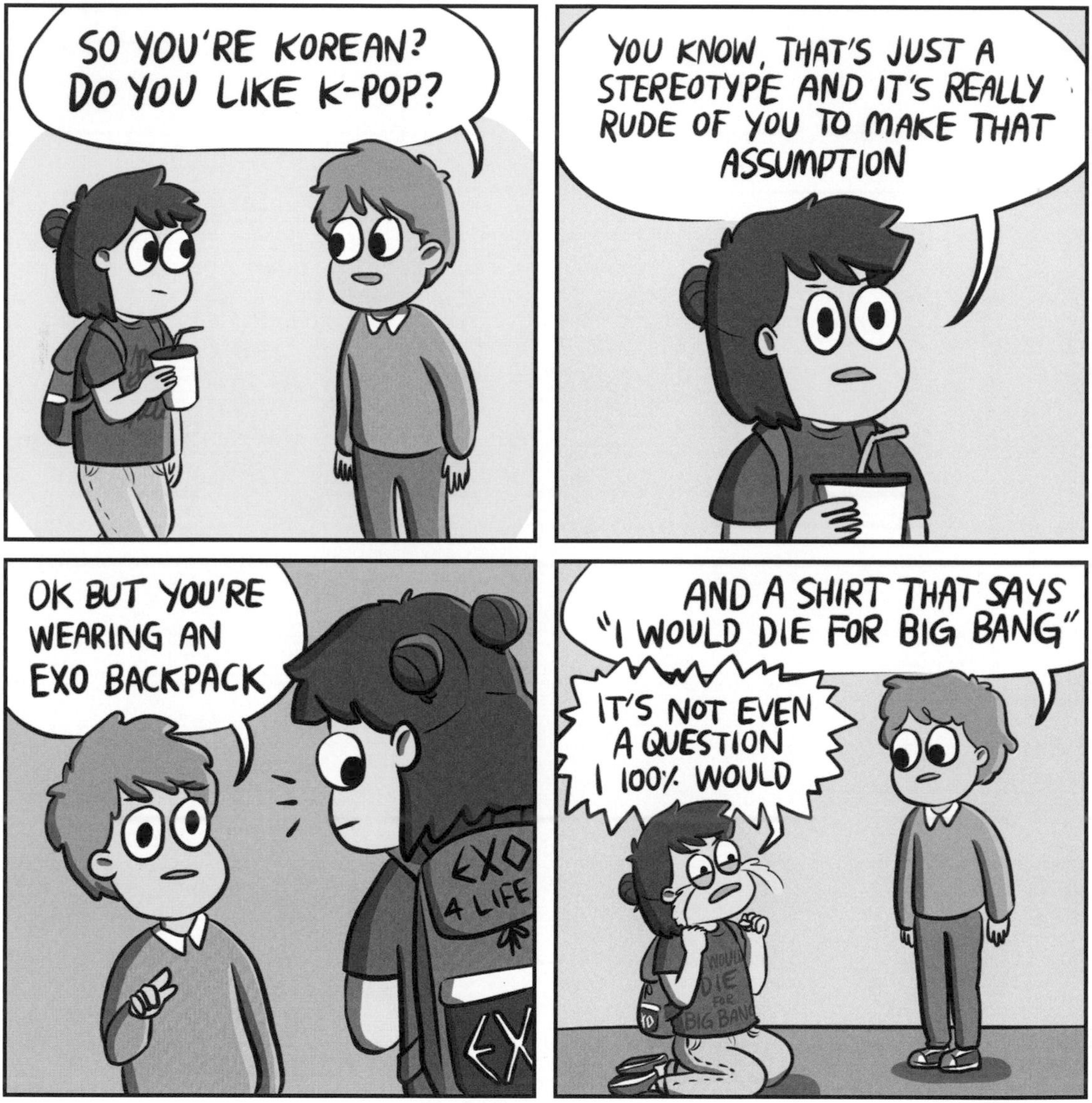
SO YOU'RE KOREAN? DO YOU LIKE K-POP?
YOU KNOW, THAT'S JUST A STEREOTYPE AND IT'S REALLY RUDE OF YOU TO MAKE THAT ASSUMPTION
OK BUT YOU'RE WEARING AN EXO BACKPACK
EXO 4 LIFE
AND A SHIRT THAT SAYS "I WOULD DIE FOR BIG BANG"
IT'S NOT EVEN A QUESTION I 100% WOULD

NAMING MY CHILDREN

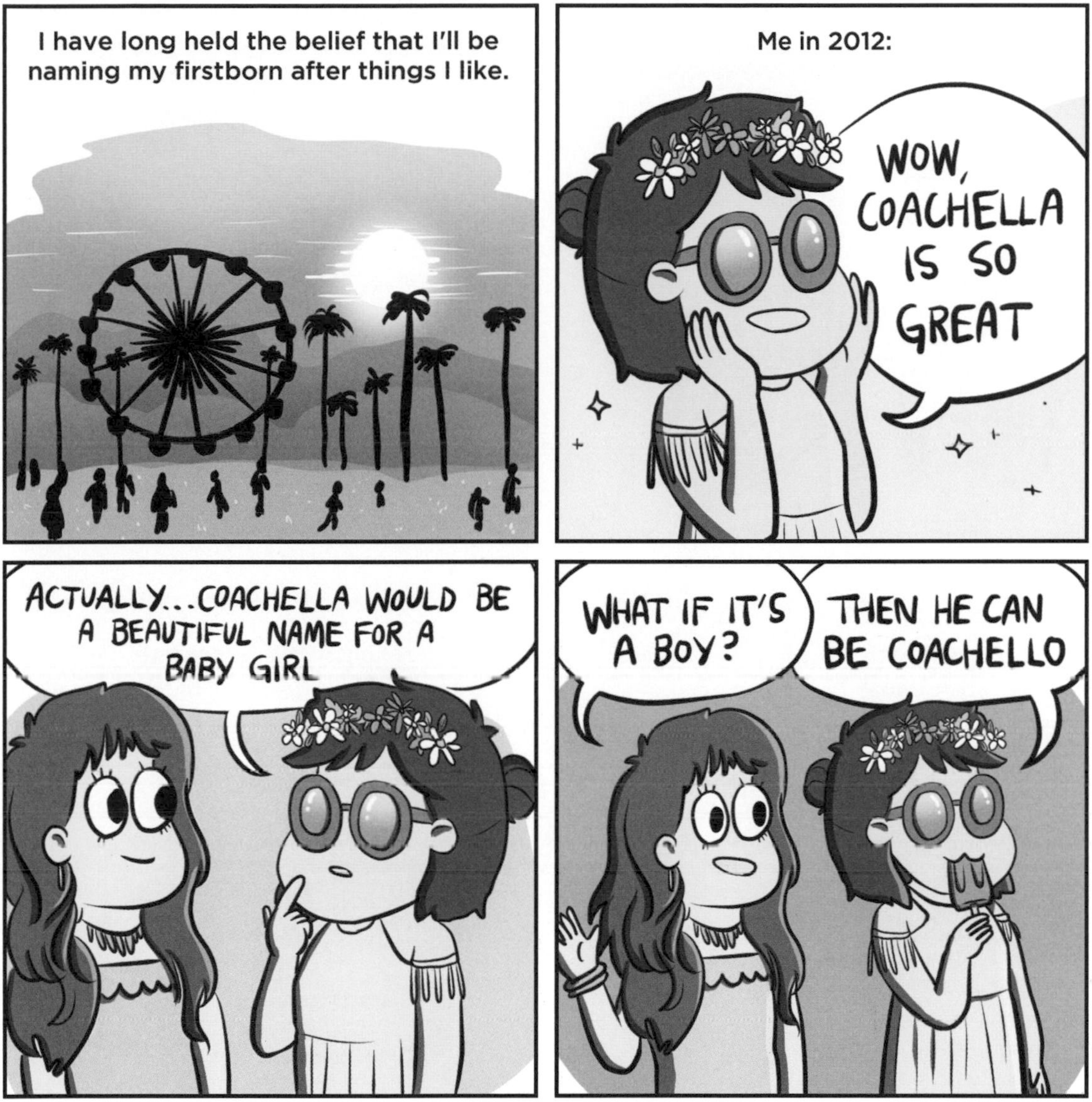
I have long held the belief that I'll be naming my firstborn after things I like.
Me in 2012:
WOW, COACHELLA IS SO GREAT
ACTUALLY...COACHELLA WOULD BE A BEAUTIFUL NAME FOR A BABY GIRL
WHAT IF IT'S A BOY?
THEN HE CAN BE COACHELLO

FUTURE MOM

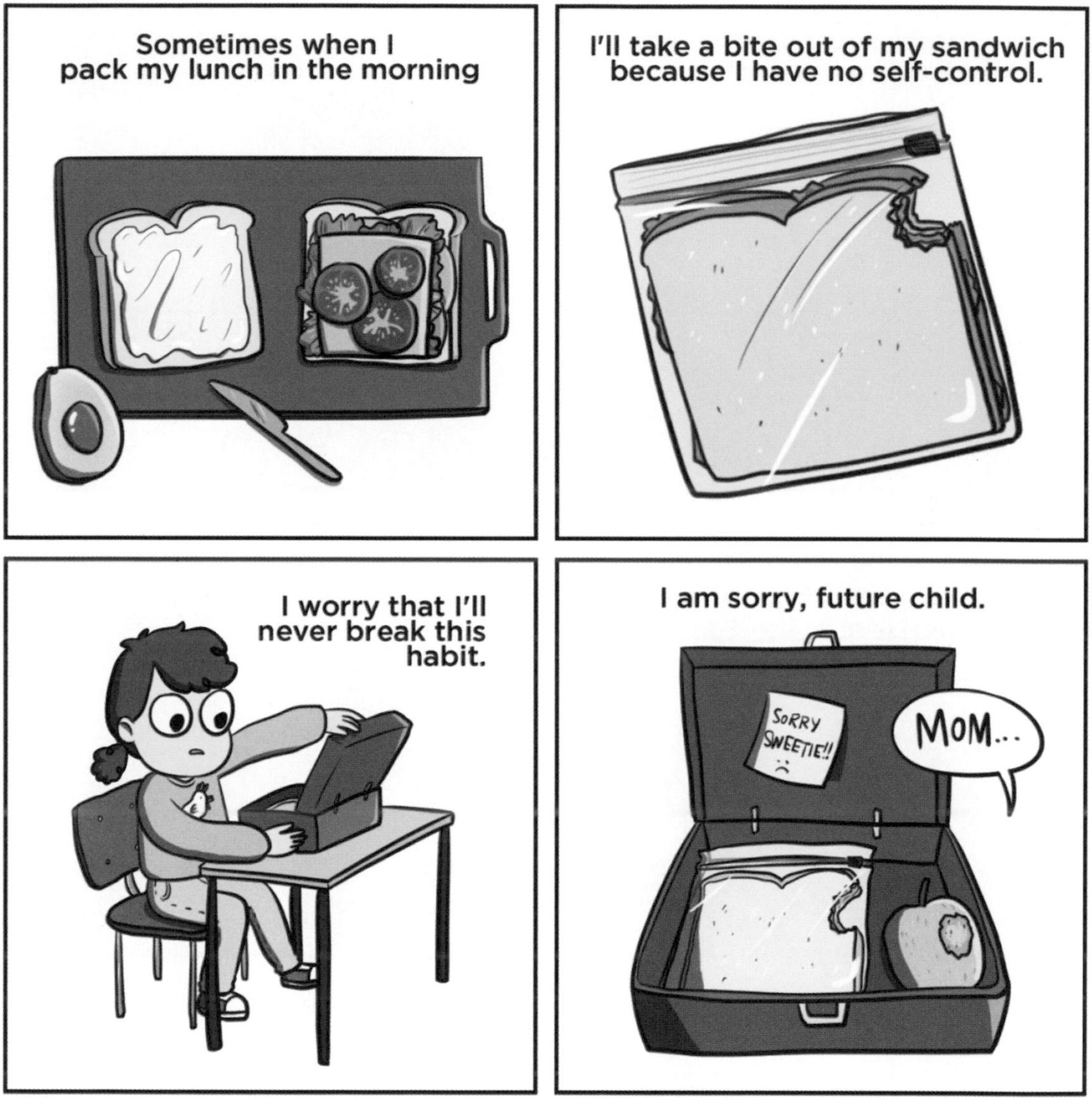
Sometimes when I pack my lunch in the morning
I'll take a bite out of my sandwich because I have no self-control.
I worry that I'll never break this habit.
I am sorry, future child.
SORRY SWEETIE!!
MOM...

MOMMY'S SPECIAL TIME

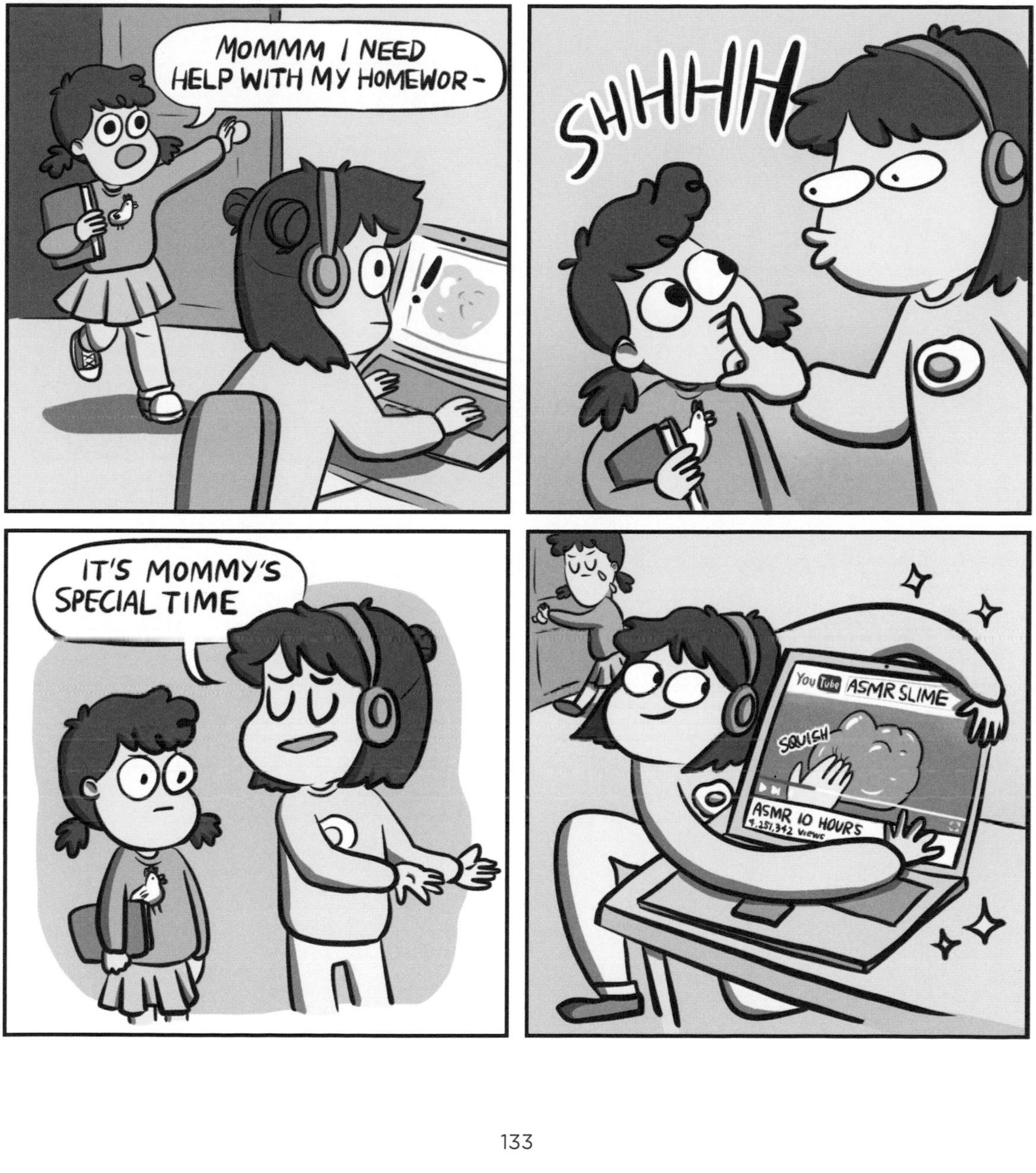
MOMMM I NEED HELP WITH MY HOMEWOR-
SHHHH
IT'S MOMMY'S SPECIAL TIME
YouTube ASMR SLIME
SQUISH
ASMR 10 HOURS
9,251,342 views

COMPETITION

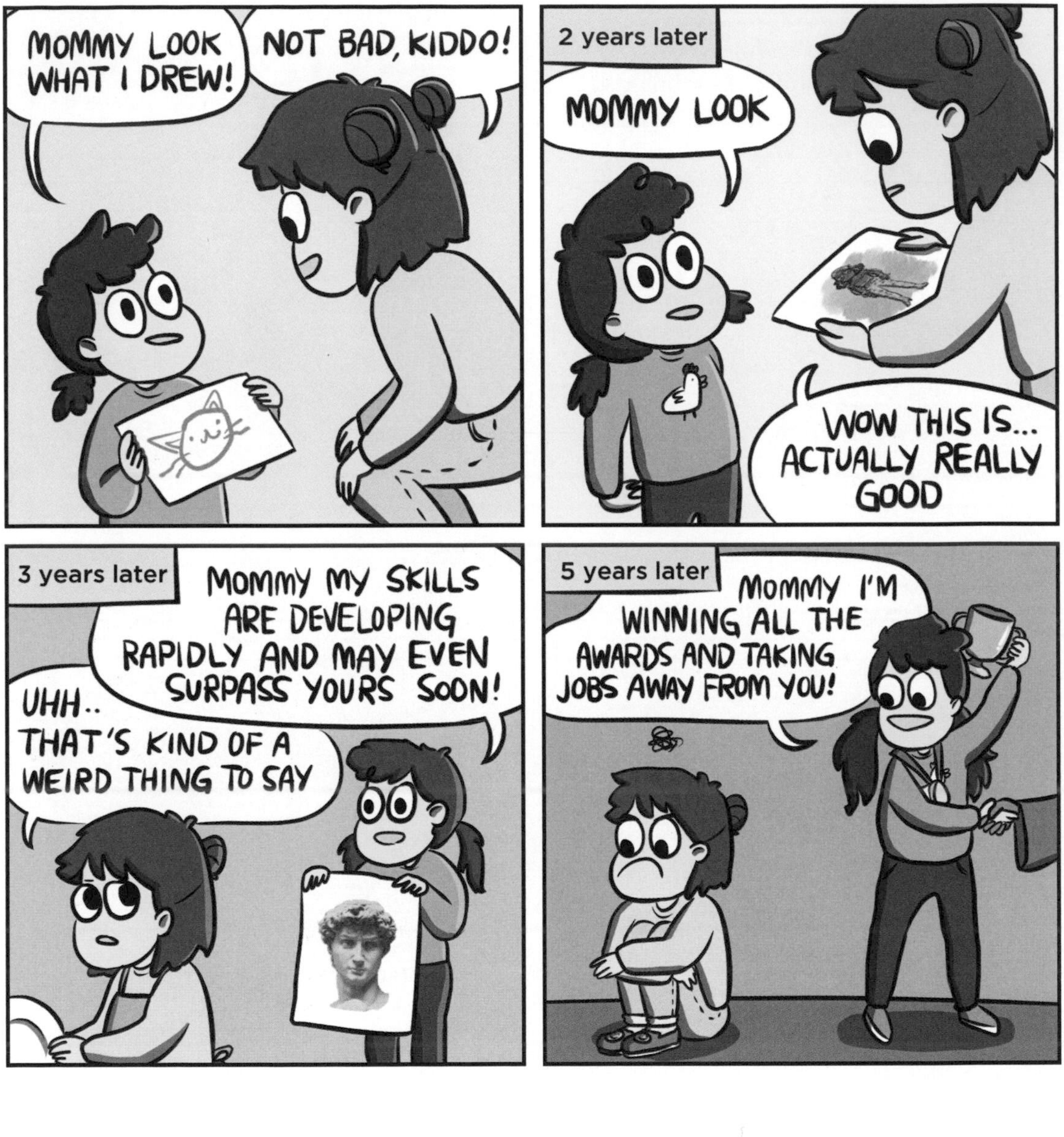
MOMMY LOOK WHAT I DREW!
NOT BAD, KIDDO!
2 years later
MOMMY LOOK
WOW THIS IS... ACTUALLY REALLY GOOD
3 years later
MOMMY MY SKILLS ARE DEVELOPING RAPIDLY AND MAY EVEN SURPASS YOURS SOON!
UHH.. THAT'S KIND OF A WEIRD THING TO SAY
5 years later
MOMMY I'M WINNING ALL THE AWARDS AND TAKING JOBS AWAY FROM YOU!

HONESTY

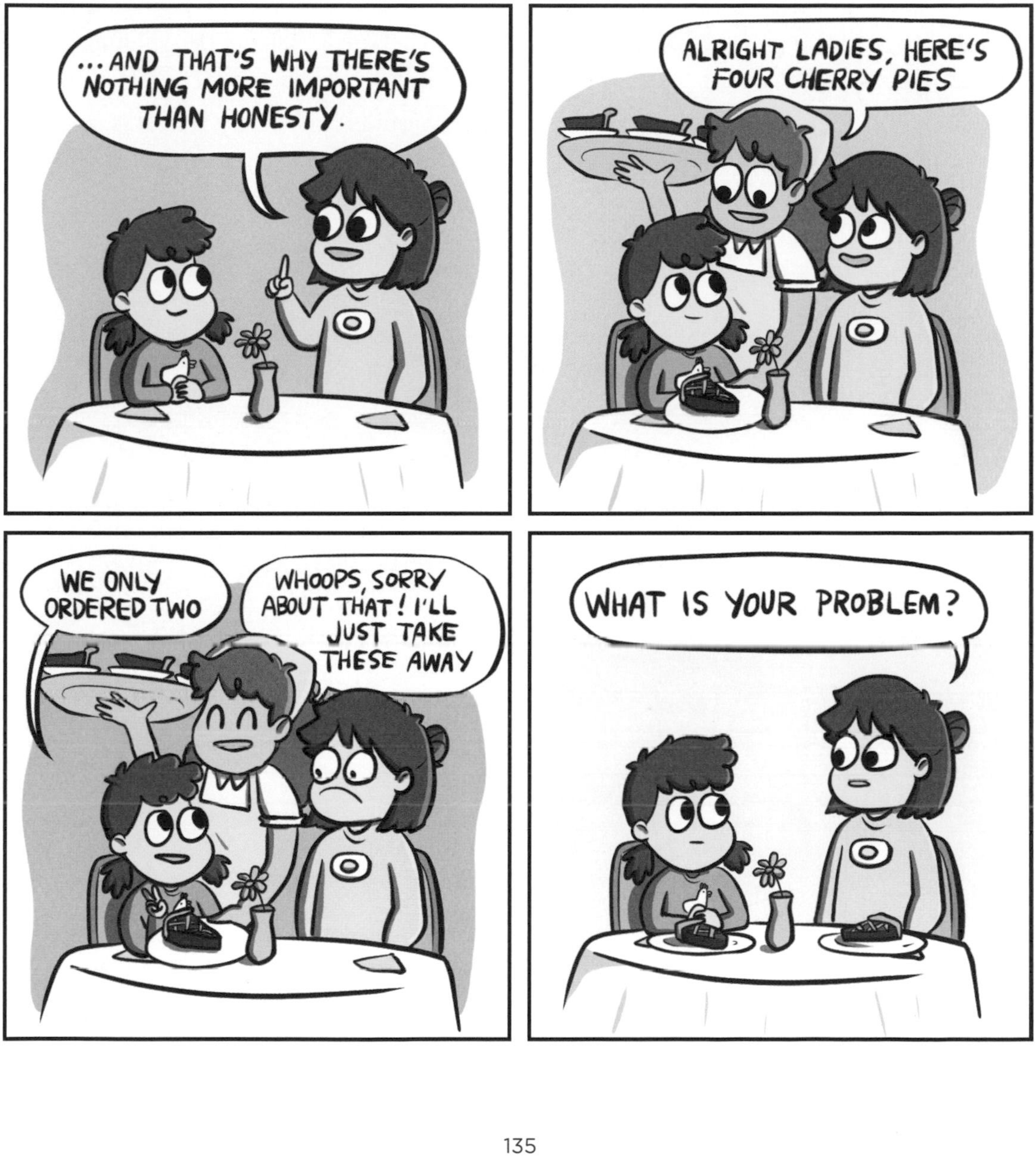
...AND THAT'S WHY THERE'S NOTHING MORE IMPORTANT THAN HONESTY.
ALRIGHT LADIES, HERE'S FOUR CHERRY PIES
WE ONLY ORDERED TWO
WHOOPS, SORRY ABOUT THAT! I'LL JUST TAKE THESE AWAY
WHAT IS YOUR PROBLEM?

HISTORY LESSON FOR TOMORROW'S YOUTH

HELICOPTER MOM

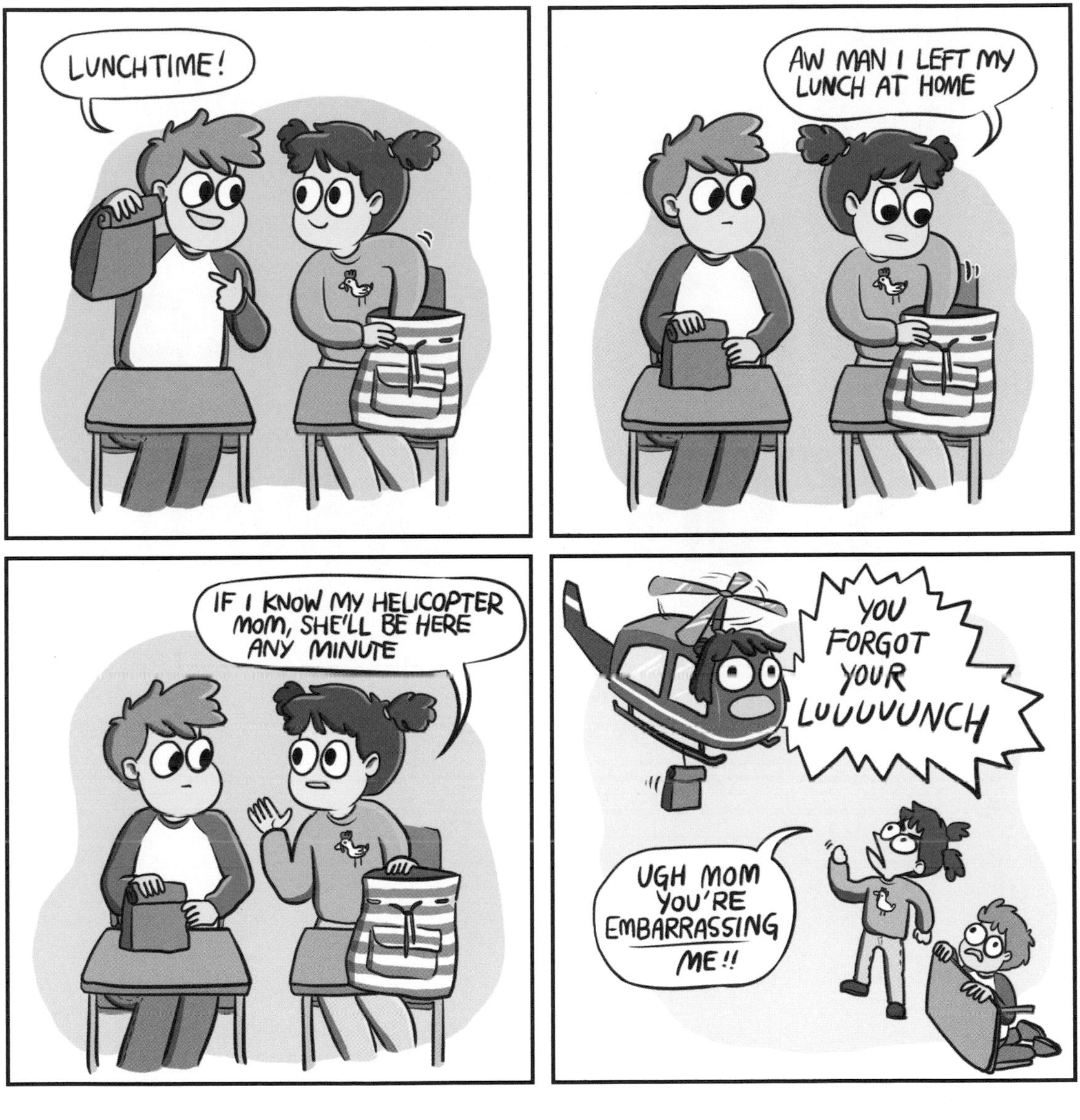
LUNCHTIME!
AW MAN I LEFT MY LUNCH AT HOME
IF I KNOW MY HELICOPTER MOM, SHE'LL BE HERE ANY MINUTE
YOU FORGOT YOUR LUUUVUNCH
UGH MOM YOU'RE EMBARRASSING ME!!

JUST LIKE, SOME REALLY POWERFUL LIFE LESSONS. DAMN.

People always ask why cartoon-me has an egg on her sweater. To me, eggs are a super inspiring example of versatility because they can be anything they set their minds to: scrambled, sunny-side up, poached, you name it!

An egg doesn't just decide to be these things on its own though; it needs a little guidance. And that's what this chapter is about: guidance to help you become the best egg you can possibly be.

As you take in these sweeping, classic wisdoms with no apparent downsides like "Never admit you're wrong" and "Snack like it's the last time you'll ever have nachos," remember that just reading this advice can only get you so far. You must experience failures on your own, and learn to stumble. You must sit on a wall, and you must have a great fall. It's okay if your shell cracks a little bit, because it's the inside that counts.

And if all else fails, don't sweat it too much. Honestly, the real reason for the egg sweater is that it's cute and easy to draw, so let's not overthink things.

GET SOME REST

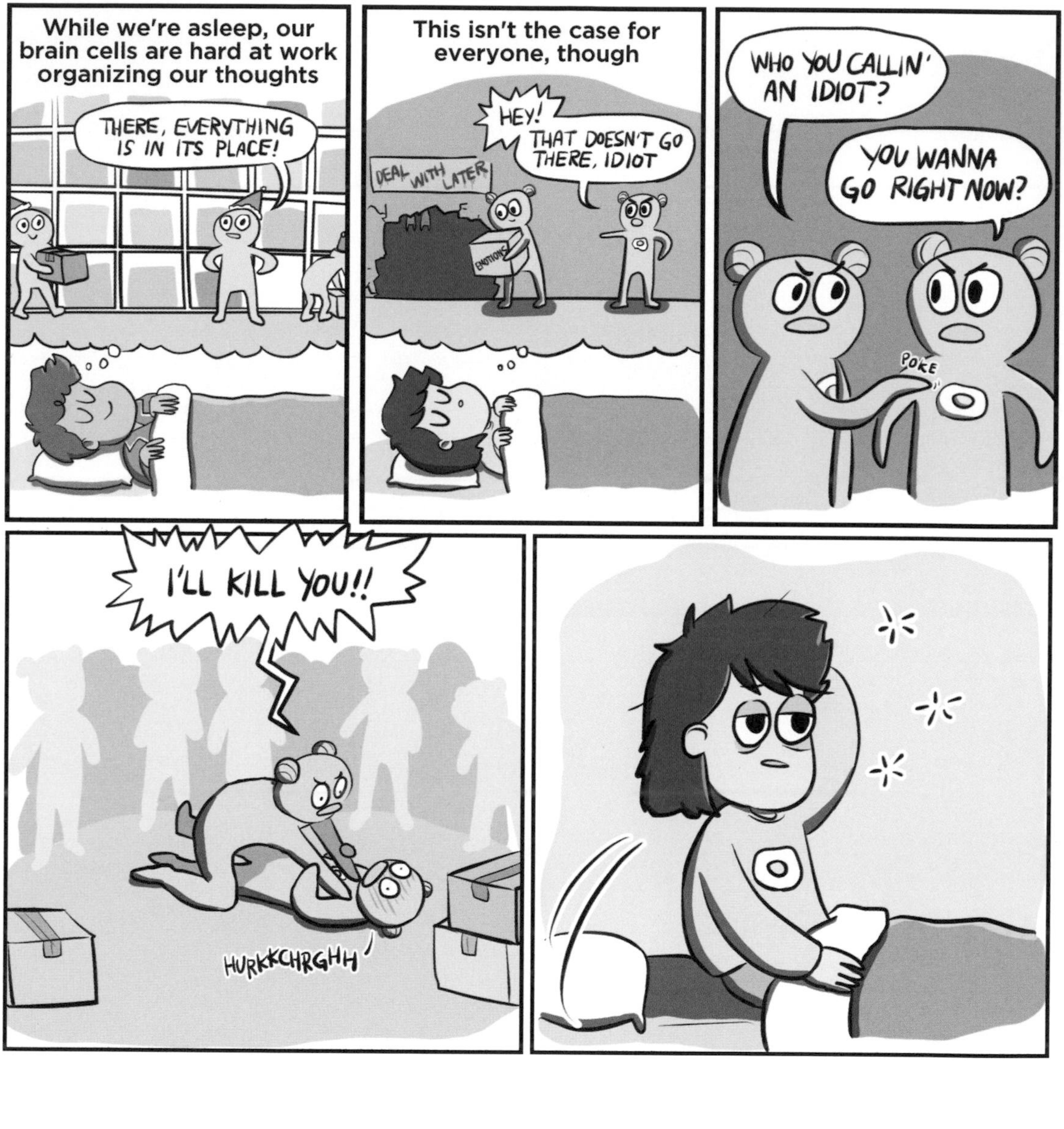
While we're asleep, our brain cells are hard at work organizing our thoughts
THERE, EVERYTHING IS IN ITS PLACE!
This isn't the case for everyone, though
DEAL WITH LATER
EMOTIONS
HEY!
THAT DOESN'T GO THERE, IDIOT
WHO YOU CALLIN' AN IDIOT?
YOU WANNA GO RIGHT NOW?
POKE
I'LL KILL YOU!!
HURKKCHRGHH

RECHARGE

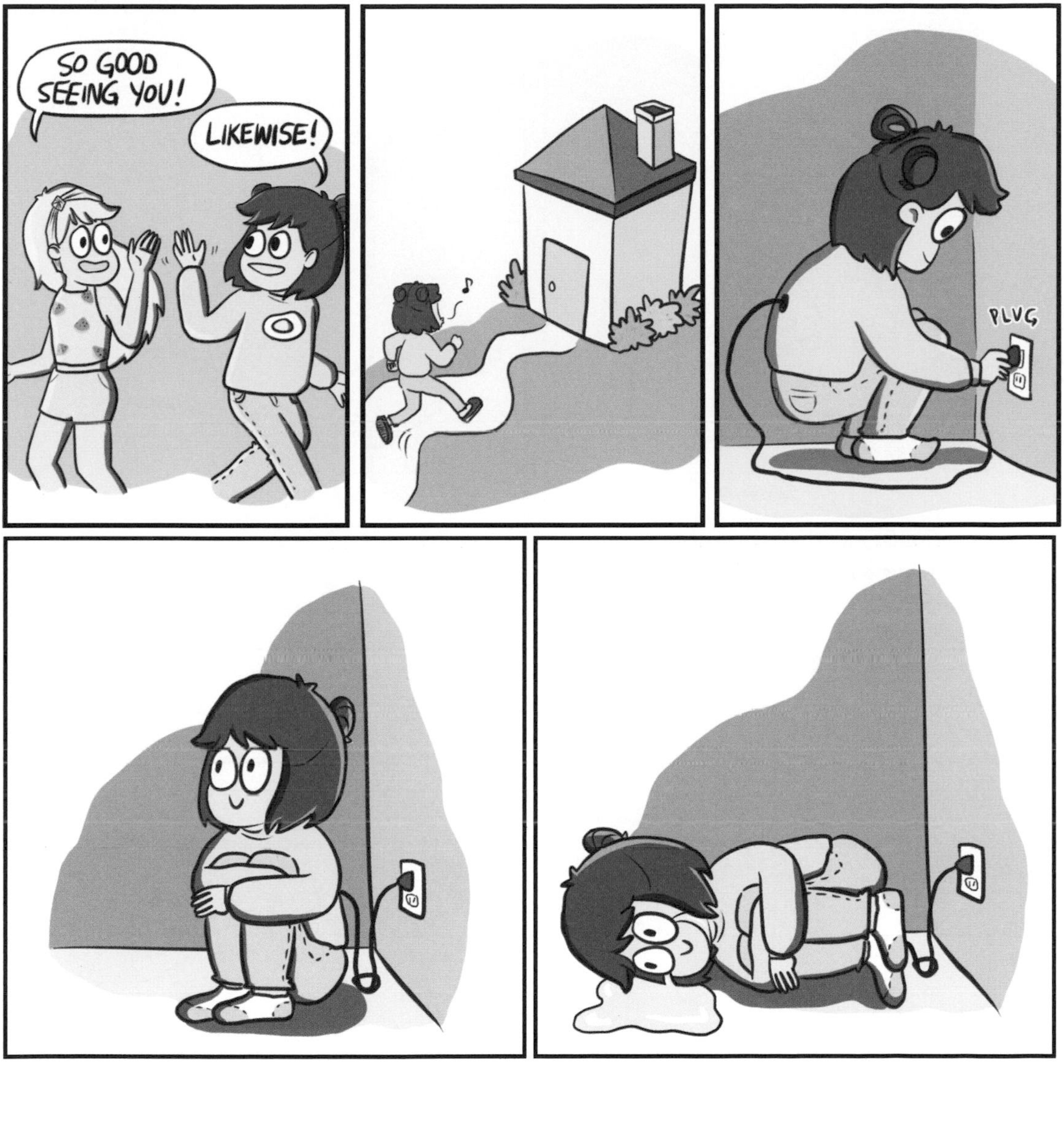
SO GOOD SEEING YOU!
LIKEWISE!
PLUG

IT'S OKAY TO BE ALONE

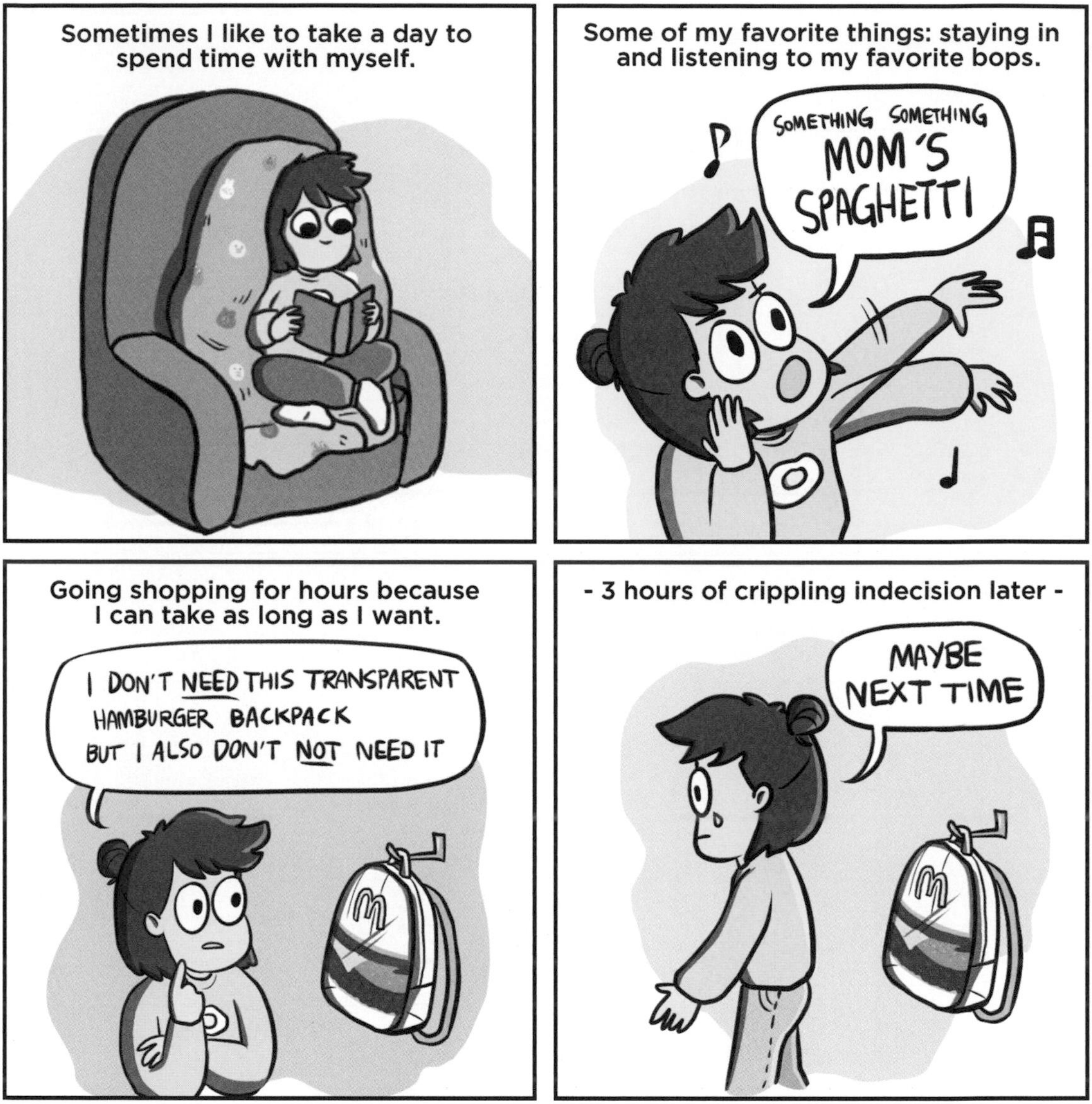
Sometimes I like to take a day to spend time with myself.
Some of my favorite things: staying in and listening to my favorite bops.
SOMETHING SOMETHING MOM'S SPAGHETTI
Going shopping for hours because I can take as long as I want.
I DON'T NEED THIS TRANSPARENT HAMBURGER BACKPACK BUT I ALSO DON'T NOT NEED IT
- 3 hours of crippling indecision later -
MAYBE NEXT TIME

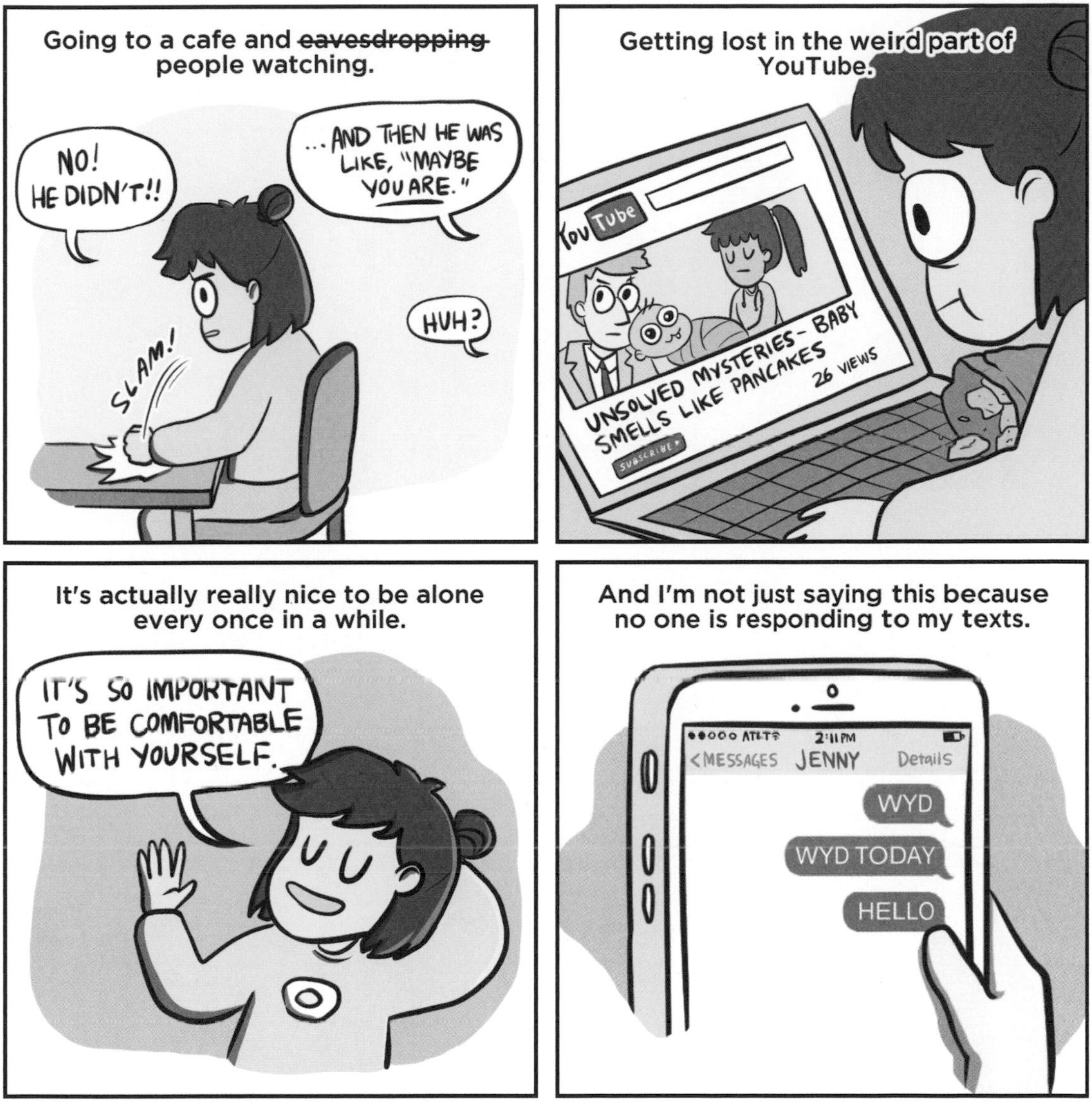
Going to a cafe and ~~eavesdropping~~ people watching.
NO! HE DIDN'T!!
...AND THEN HE WAS LIKE, "MAYBE YOU ARE."
HUH?
SLAM!
Getting lost in the weird part of YouTube.
YouTube
UNSOLVED MYSTERIES- BABY SMELLS LIKE PANCAKES
26 VIEWS
It's actually really nice to be alone every once in a while.
IT'S SO IMPORTANT TO BE COMFORTABLE WITH YOURSELF.
And I'm not just saying this because no one is responding to my texts.
2:11 PM
<MESSAGES JENNY Details
WYD
WYD TODAY
HELLO

REMEMBER TO STAY HYDRATED

DO EVERYTHING IN MODERATION

MAKE YOUR OWN FUN

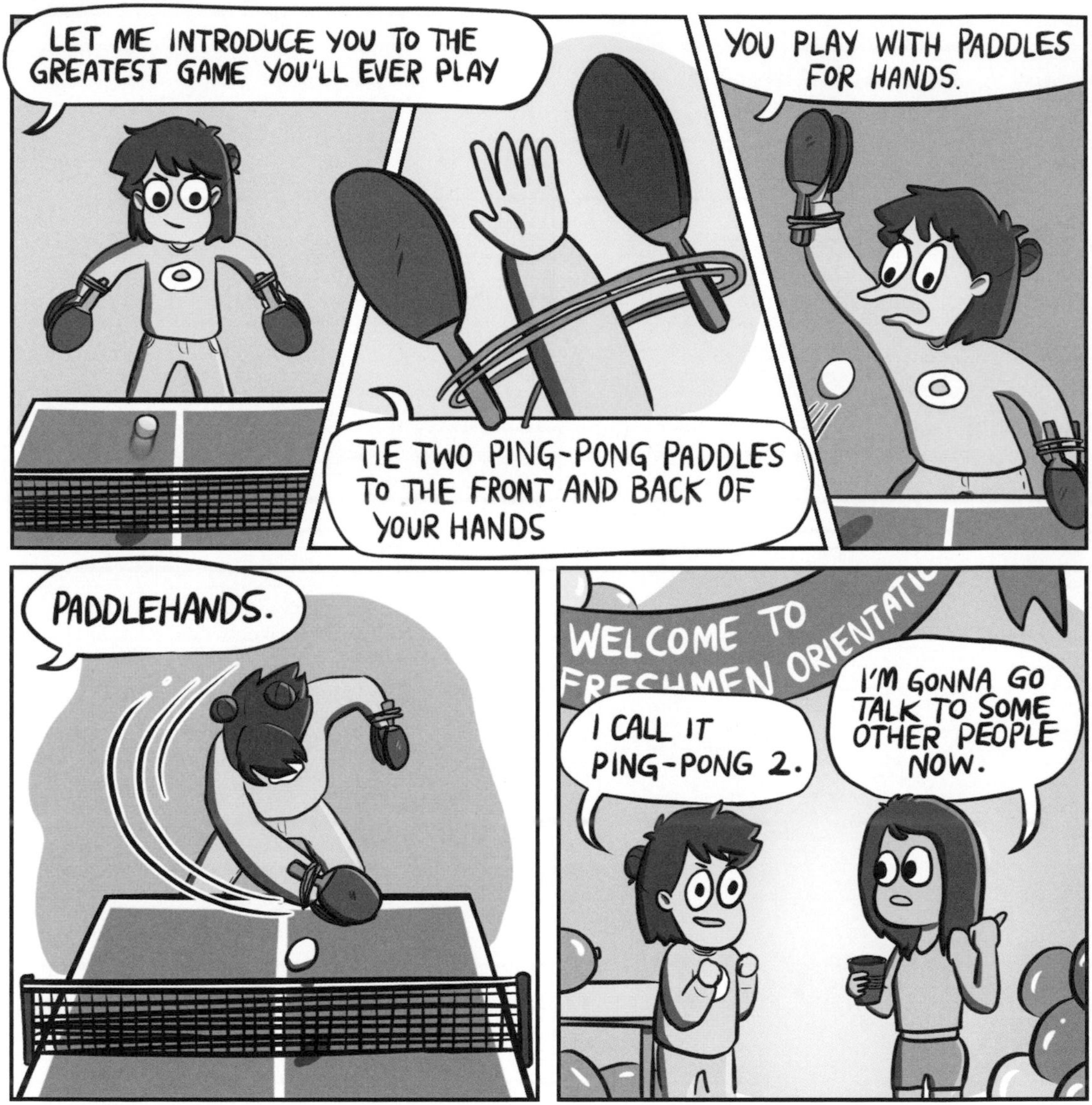
LET ME INTRODUCE YOU TO THE GREATEST GAME YOU'LL EVER PLAY
TIE TWO PING-PONG PADDLES TO THE FRONT AND BACK OF YOUR HANDS
YOU PLAY WITH PADDLES FOR HANDS.
PADDLEHANDS.
WELCOME TO FRESHMEN ORIENTATI
I CALL IT PING-PONG 2.
I'M GONNA GO TALK TO SOME OTHER PEOPLE NOW.

KEEP UP WITH CURRENT TRENDS

DON'T COMPARE YOURSELF TO OTHERS

MAKE MEANINGFUL FRIENDSHIPS

COUNT YOUR BLESSINGS

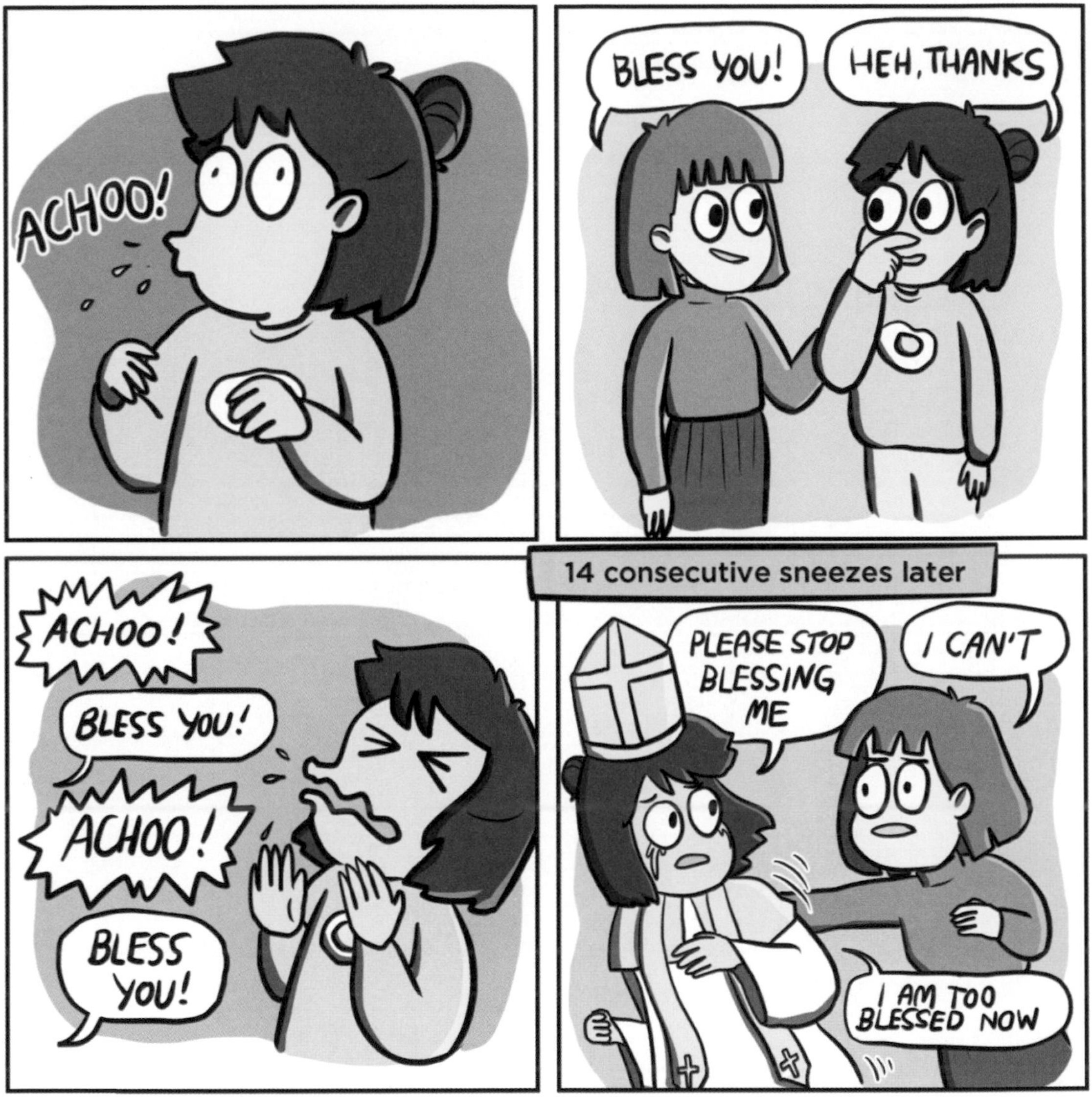
ACHOO!
BLESS YOU!
HEH, THANKS
ACHOO!
BLESS YOU!
ACHOO!
BLESS YOU!
14 consecutive sneezes later
PLEASE STOP BLESSING ME
I CAN'T
I AM TOO BLESSED NOW

YOU CAN DO ANYTHING YOU SET YOUR MIND TO

SNACK LIKE A CHAMPION

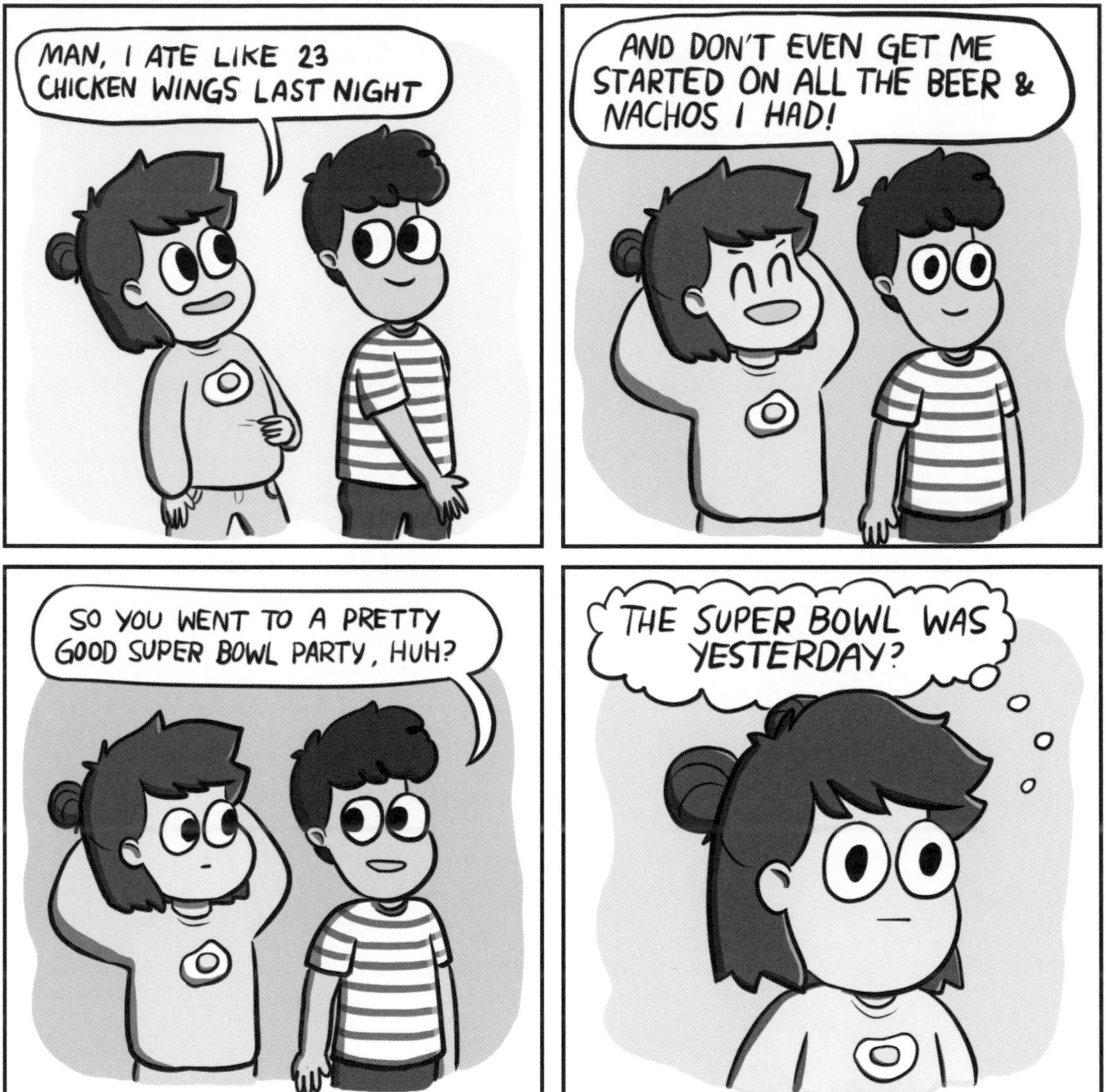
MAN, I ATE LIKE 23 CHICKEN WINGS LAST NIGHT
AND DON'T EVEN GET ME STARTED ON ALL THE BEER & NACHOS I HAD!
SO YOU WENT TO A PRETTY GOOD SUPER BOWL PARTY, HUH?
THE SUPER BOWL WAS YESTERDAY?

SEE SOMETHING, SAY SOMETHING

SPEND RESPONSIBLY

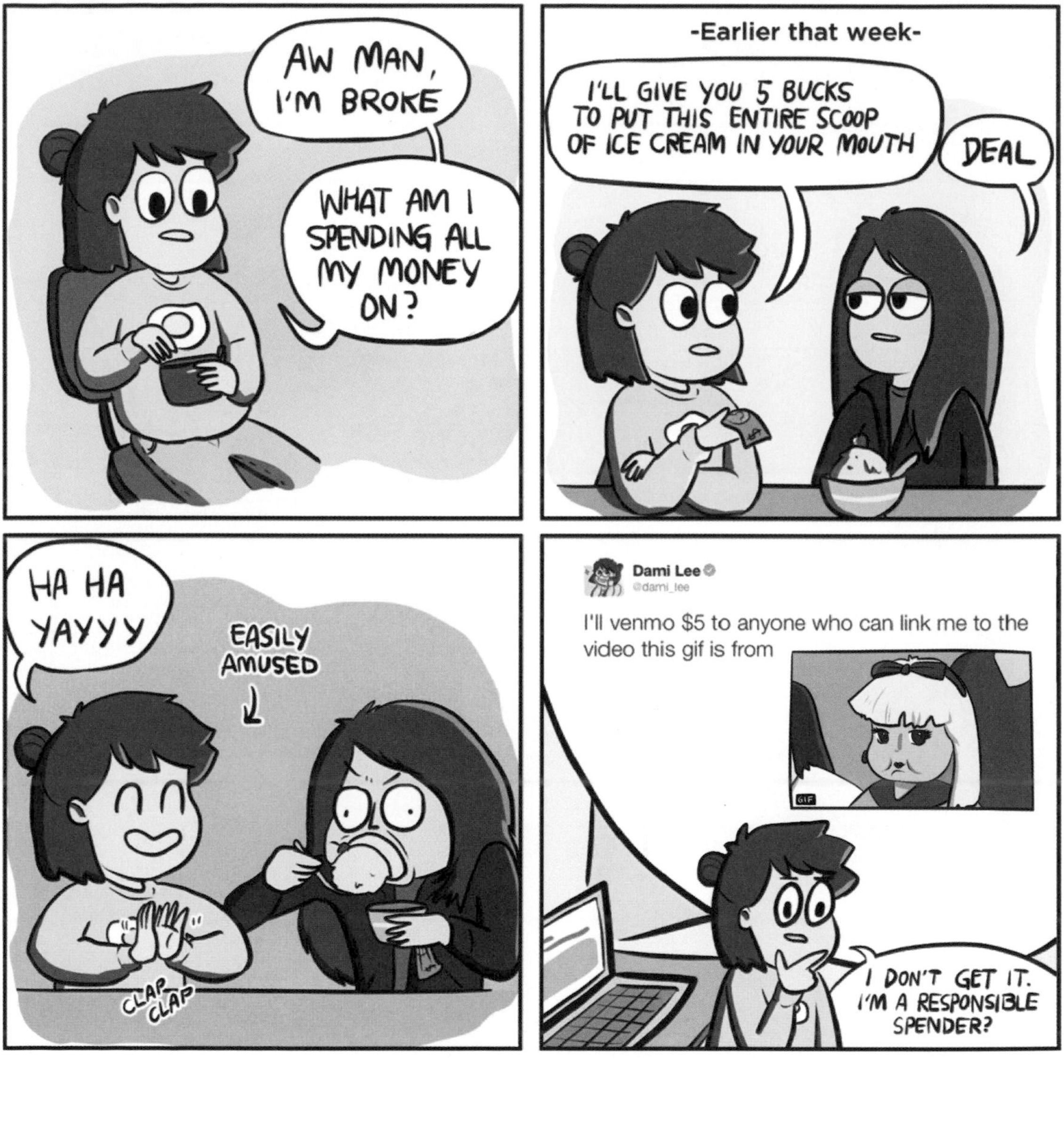
AW MAN, I'M BROKE
WHAT AM I SPENDING ALL MY MONEY ON?
-Earlier that week-
I'LL GIVE YOU 5 BUCKS TO PUT THIS ENTIRE SCOOP OF ICE CREAM IN YOUR MOUTH
DEAL
HA HA YAYYY
EASILY AMUSED
CLAP CLAP
Dami Lee
@dami_lee
I'll venmo $5 to anyone who can link me to the video this gif is from
GIF
I DON'T GET IT. I'M A RESPONSIBLE SPENDER?

NEVER BACK DOWN

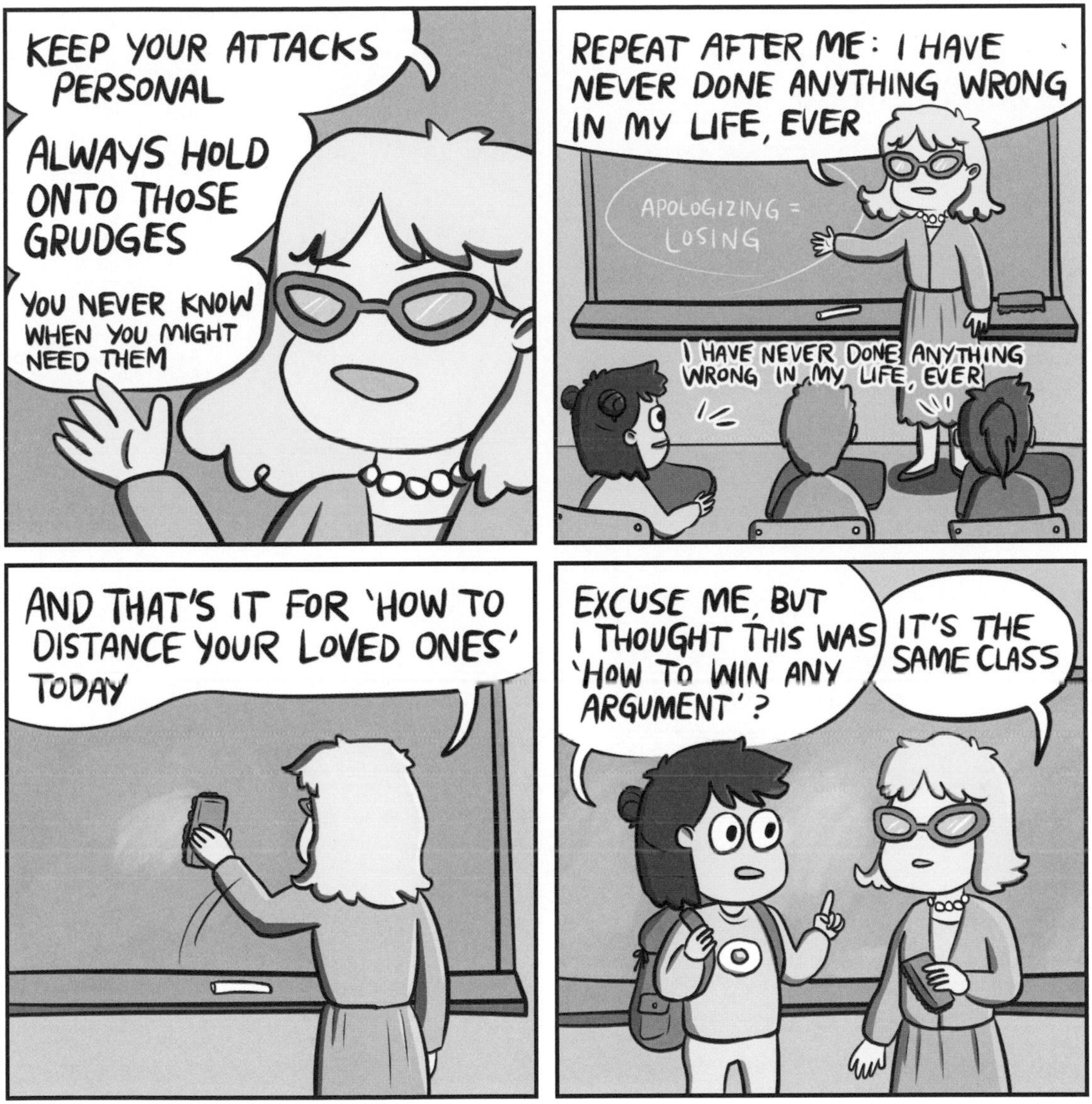
KEEP YOUR ATTACKS PERSONAL
ALWAYS HOLD ONTO THOSE GRUDGES
YOU NEVER KNOW WHEN YOU MIGHT NEED THEM
REPEAT AFTER ME: I HAVE NEVER DONE ANYTHING WRONG IN MY LIFE, EVER
APOLOGIZING = LOSING
I HAVE NEVER DONE ANYTHING WRONG IN MY LIFE, EVER
AND THAT'S IT FOR 'HOW TO DISTANCE YOUR LOVED ONES' TODAY
EXCUSE ME, BUT I THOUGHT THIS WAS 'HOW TO WIN ANY ARGUMENT'?
IT'S THE SAME CLASS

STAY ORGANIZED

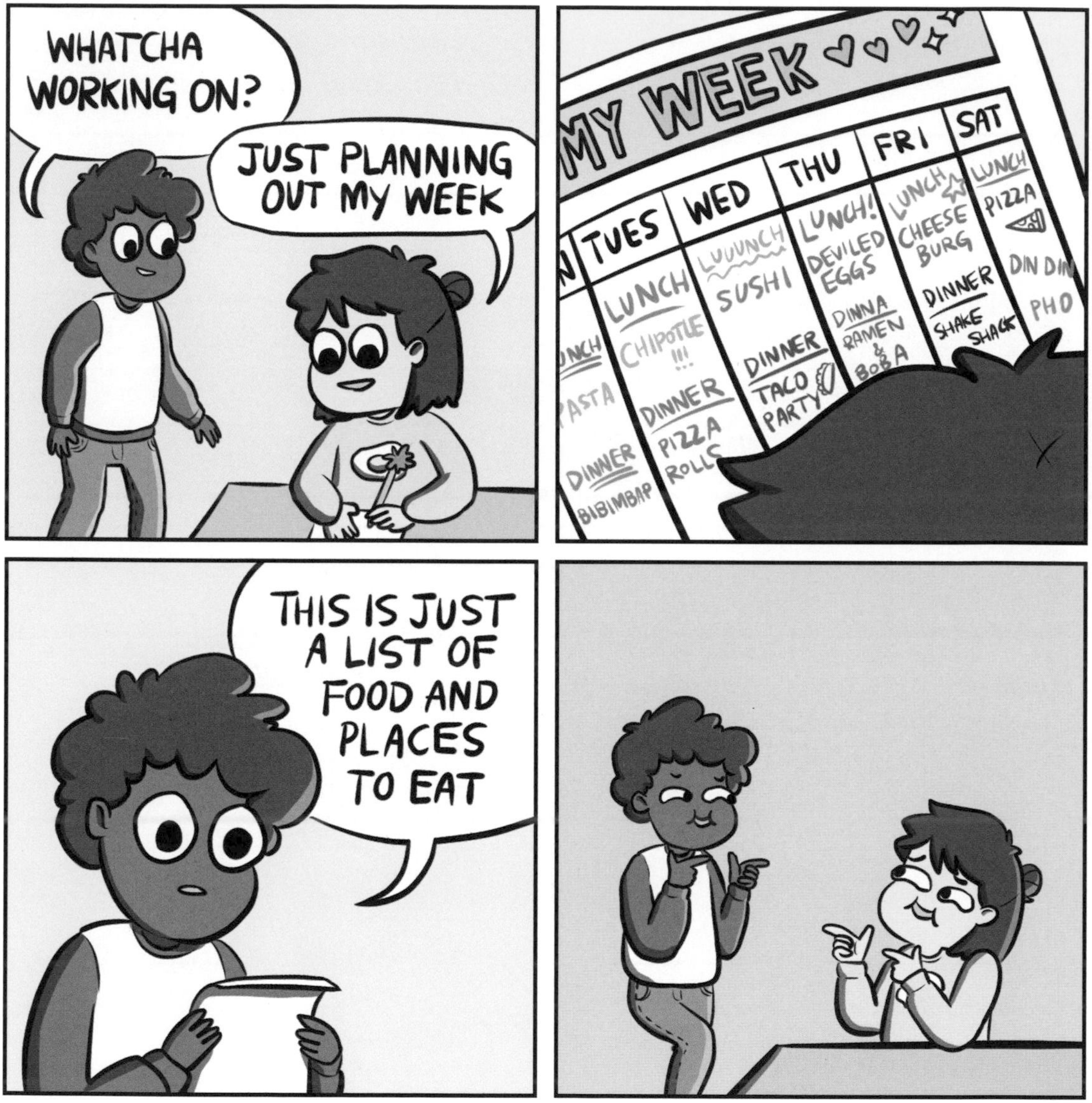
WHATCHA WORKING ON?
JUST PLANNING OUT MY WEEK
MY WEEK
TUES
WED
THU
FRI
SAT
LUNCH PASTA
DINNER BIBIMBAP
LUNCH CHIPOTLE !!!
DINNER PIZZA ROLLS
LUUUNCH SUSHI
DINNER TACO PARTY
LUNCH! DEVILED EGGS
DINNA RAMEN & BOBA
LUNCH CHEESE BURG
DINNER SHAKE SHACK
LUNCH PIZZA
DIN DIN PHO
THIS IS JUST A LIST OF FOOD AND PLACES TO EAT

PUT OTHERS FIRST

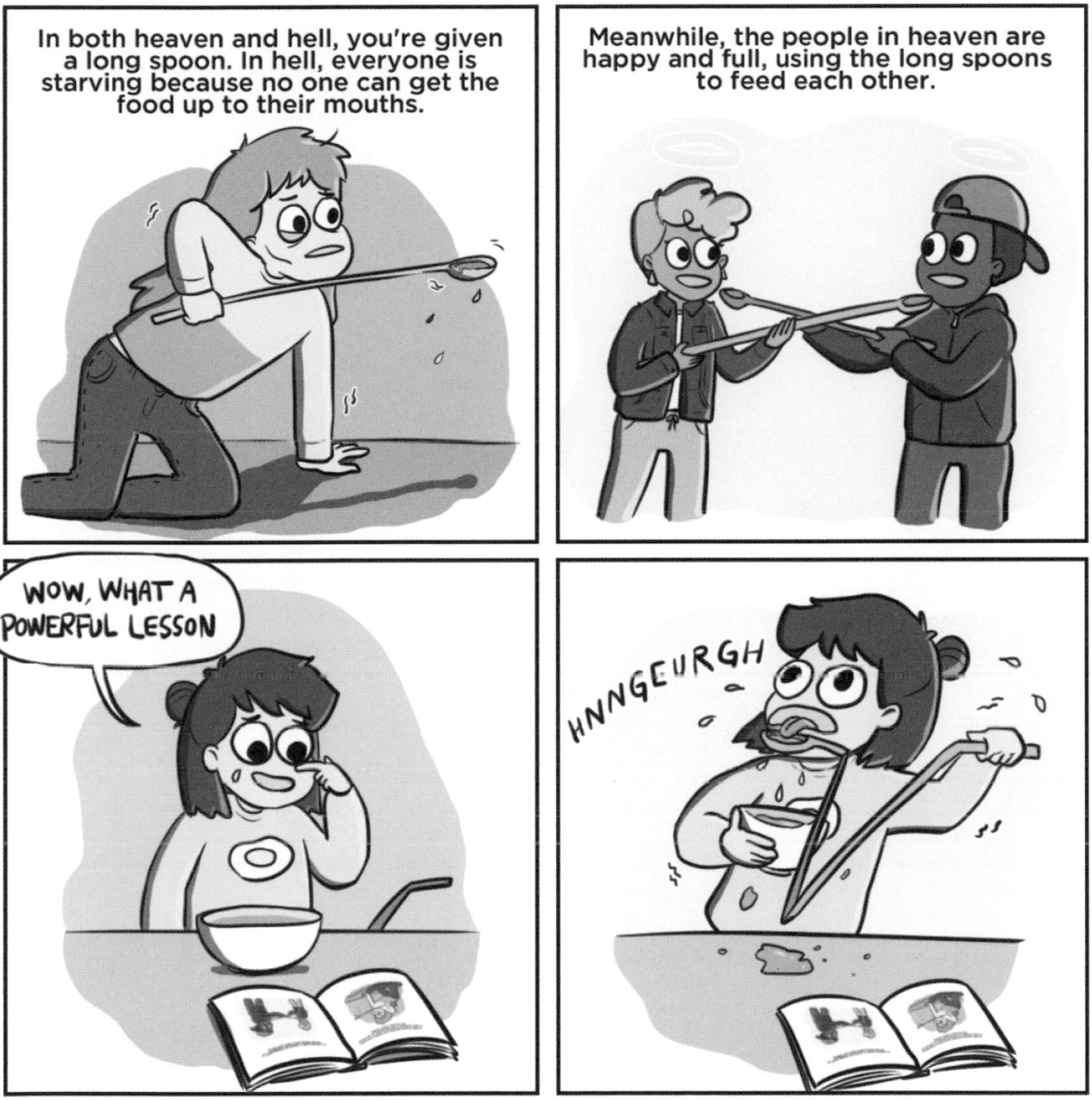
In both heaven and hell, you're given a long spoon. In hell, everyone is starving because no one can get the food up to their mouths.
Meanwhile, the people in heaven are happy and full, using the long spoons to feed each other.
WOW, WHAT A POWERFUL LESSON
HNNGEURGH

BE WHAT YOU LOVE

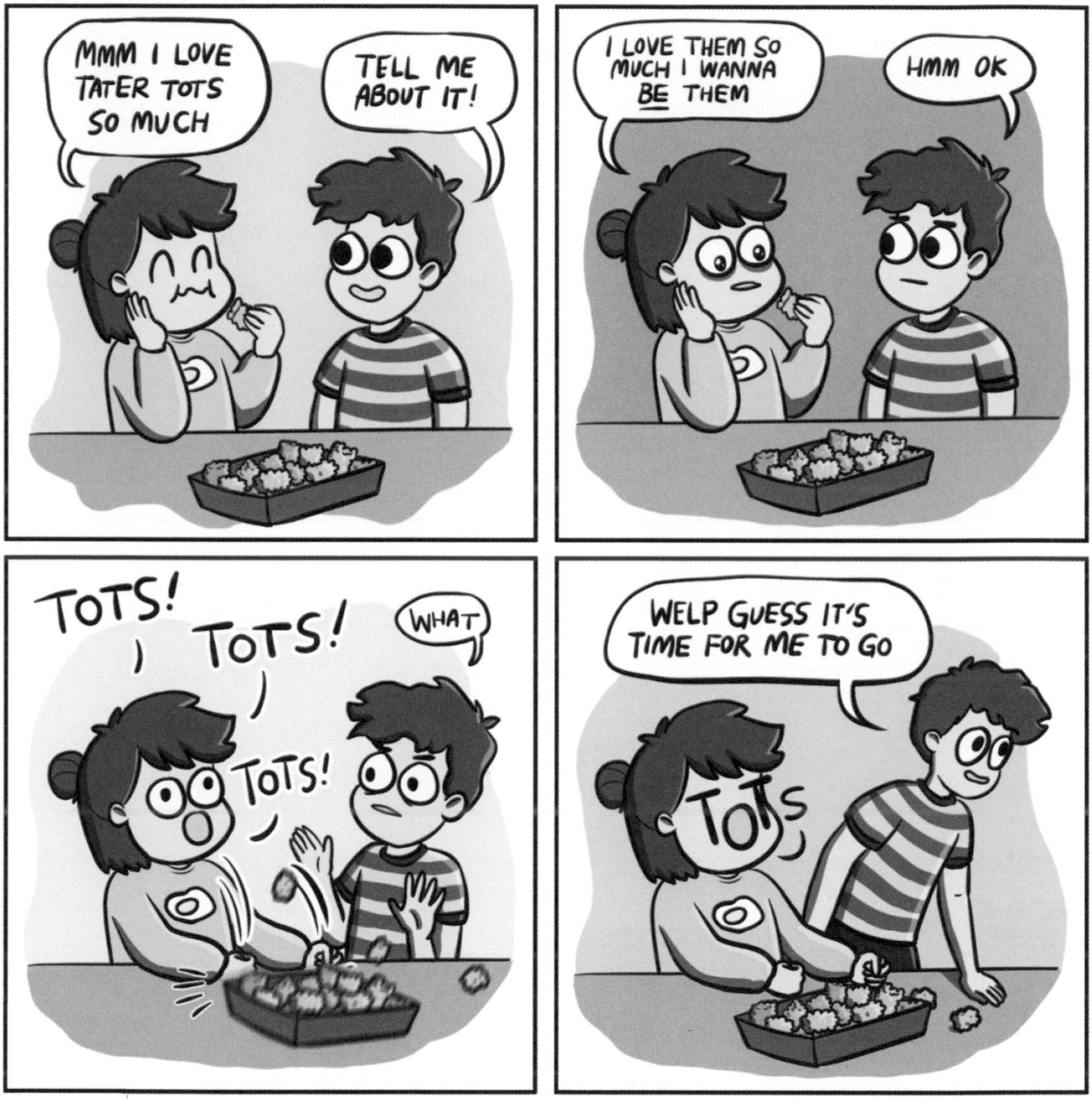
MMM I LOVE TATER TOTS SO MUCH
TELL ME ABOUT IT!
I LOVE THEM SO MUCH I WANNA BE THEM
HMM OK
TOTS!
TOTS!
WHAT
TOTS!
WELP GUESS IT'S TIME FOR ME TO GO
TOTS

USE MANTRAS

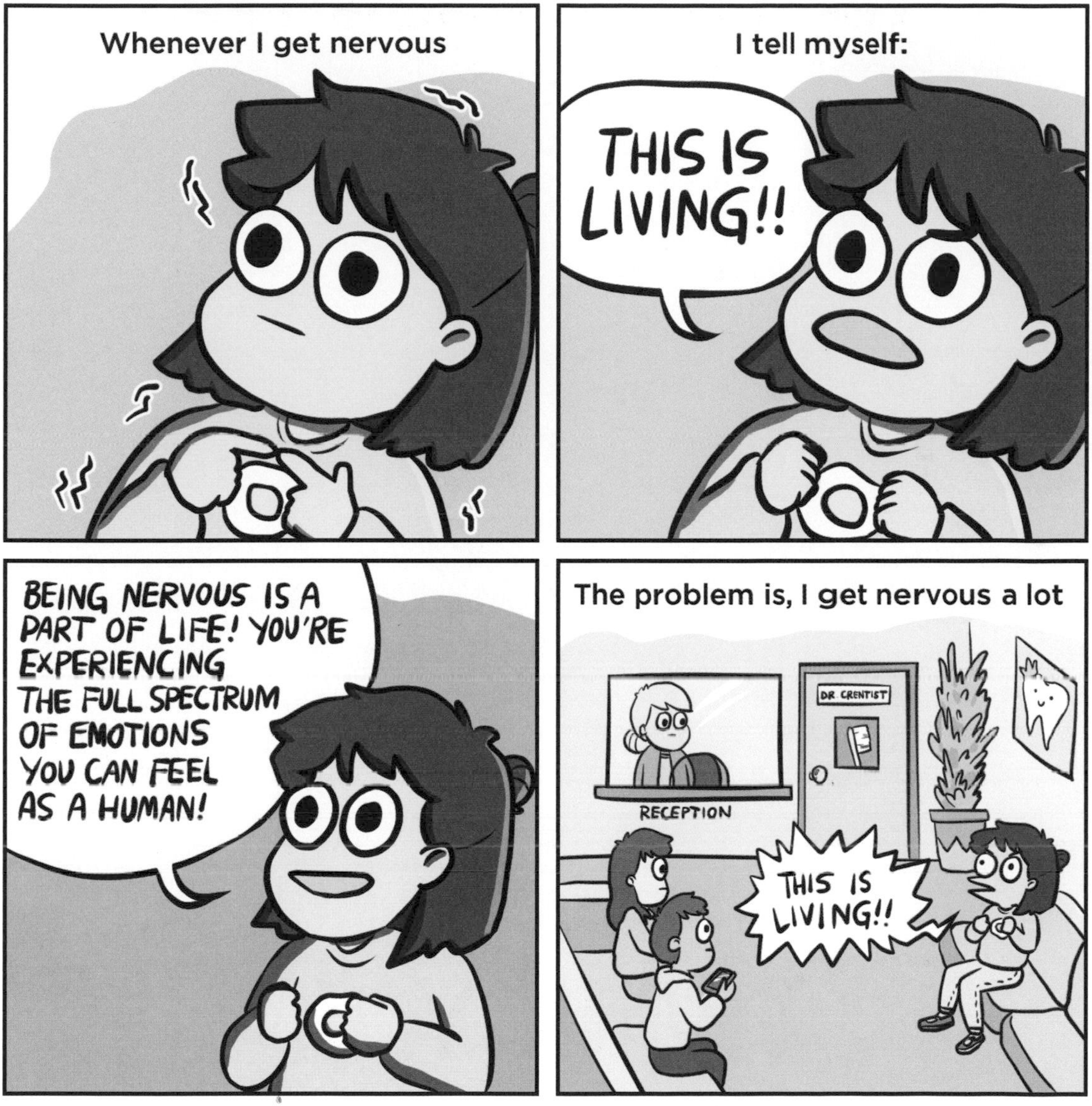
Whenever I get nervous
I tell myself:
THIS IS LIVING!!
BEING NERVOUS IS A PART OF LIFE! YOU'RE EXPERIENCING THE FULL SPECTRUM OF EMOTIONS YOU CAN FEEL AS A HUMAN!
The problem is, I get nervous a lot
RECEPTION
DR. CRENTIST
THIS IS LIVING!!

ACKNOWLEDGMENTS

Thank you to everyone who read my comics online and encouraged me to keep making them, you are the reason I'm able to do what I love. I'd also like to take the time to apologize to this same group of people who follow me online for comics, but sometimes get roped into looking at my selfies. This is a full-package deal, I hope you understand. I'm eternally grateful to Stephanie, my agent and actual angel, for turning my dream of making a book into a reality. Pippa and Julia, my wonderful editors who believed in my work and made me feel like the prettiest girl at the ball. Emily, Yooni, David, and everyone at Line Webtoon for being my comics cheerleaders. Summer, Jen, and Adam, for hiring me from across the world and being the most supportive eggs. Jenny, my sweet angel baby girl, for being with me on the best coast, in the best life. Robert Joe, for being awake at all hours to listen to me rant. Matthew, for being the inspiration for so many of these comics (all the good ones, I promise). And finally, thanks to my umma and appa for being the funniest people I know and the best parents in the world.

THANK YOU ☺